metal box:
stories from
john lydon's
public image
limited

First edition published in 2007 by
Helter Skelter Publishing
Southbank House, Black Prince Road,
London SE1 7SJ

www.helterskelterpublishing.com

Typesetting and layout by Graeme Milton

Cover design by Chris Wilson

Printed in Great Britain by Antony Rowe

A CIP record for this book is available from the British Library.

ISBN-10 1-900924-66-8
ISBN-13 978-1-900924-66-5

metal box:
stories from
john lydon's
public image
limited

by phil strongman

with additional research by justin lewis

Helter
Skelter
publishing

contents

foreword
by anthony h. wilson

It was around 3.30pm on a summery Monday afternoon in a darkened TV studio. Public Image Limited had done the final run-through of 'Death Disco' as I recall. They were on a small rostrum in front of the white cyc of Granada's Studio Two in Manchester.

Two was the least impressive space of the GTV dream Factory; it was the home of local programmes only – 200 yards up the corridor in Studio Eight they were busy recording that night's *Coronation Street* – but it was still the same white cyc against which The Stone Roses would perform and be photographed for their album sleeve ten years later. And only twenty yards from the beige news back-drop against which Iggy Pop had been photographed two years earlier for what became the cover of *Lust For Life*.

And there, on that grey carpeted rostrum, with his band Public Image Limited, was Iggy's bastard child, Rotten.

Only now it was PiL and it was Lydon.

And as the reverb died away and they prepared to do the take of what would be their first live TV, Superman growled at me from the rostrum:

'D'you still have that club of yours?'

'Yeah, why?' in a submissive tone (always had that problem with my heroes).

'Well since we've brought all this fucking gear all the way up to Manchester we might as well do a fucking gig. Sort it aht!'

I nodded but did nothing. This was madness. Late afternoon, a gig that same night? Bollocks.

When they'd finished the take – a good one, of course – they shuffled off towards the dressing room. I motioned to Keith Levene.

'Is he serious?'

'He's always serious'.

I ran straight to find a phone in the newsroom. No mobiles then, children, and called my partner Erasmus who was busy reclining on a deck chair in his Didsbury garden.

'Alan, PiL want to play the Russell tonight. Can we set it up and get the word out and get A Certain Ratio out of bed to support?'

Alan could do anything if he wanted to. And he wanted this one. Public Image in our club and supported by our Manc version of The Velvet Underground.

And it all happened. Impromptu. Important. Just like Public Image.

And what was that stuff they did that afternoon for the Granada cameras, and that evening for 250 grateful Mancunians connected to the grapevine?

I often think (and say) that Joy Division and U2 were the creators and owners of the thing we call post-punk. Propelled into the creative stratosphere by witnessing the Pistols they took the revolution forward, in Bernard Sumner's exquisite description, by taking the pure power, simplicity and anger of punk and allowing it to express more complex *emotions*.

So what about PiL? In their case I think they did something even more difficult but less noticeable – and less saleable. They took the purity and simplicity that had resurrected the wonder that Robert Johnson had sold his soul for; they took the power of music as encapsulated in the Pistols' explosive music and performances and in their case allowed it to express more complex *music*.

Unthinkable. John and Music.

But it's true.

And that was what thrilled about PiL. You couldn't change the emotional content from the sublimity of punk. John's oedipal snarl was a given. But the music now swirled and roared around the brain, rather than beating and battering it. Forgive me for being a hippy, and I never though it at the time, but there was an improvisational spirit to PiL's music, almost like Hendrix moving through landscapes of noise.

But it never lost one iota of the purity of the world that Lydon had created way back in '76.

While Devoto got carried away in keyboard based symphonics (pace, Howard) and the Clash became the fucking rock and roll band they always threatened to dissolve into – and the Ramones went Republican and prepared the world for Busted – it was only Lydon who progressed, who moved forward while holding on to the truth he had found in his disdain for a shitty boring world.

All praise.

Forget Grundy and Malcolm's grandiose claims.

John came again.

In different clothes.

That were just as beautiful.

introduction

Public Image Limited were the first real alternative group, the first group as concept, the first successful 'industrial' group, the first group as limited company, the first to break big without a manager, the first to self-consciously sweep all before it – for many they were the true Year Zero that the Sex Pistols had been too chord-driven to deliver.

To the mainstream press they were merely a bizarre extension of the notorious Pistols, the punk heroes that had been led to anti-social super-stardom by John 'Rotten' Lydon – Jubilee's 'Public Enemy Number One.'

But to a growing army of dedicated fans, Public Image were much more than a post-punk phoenix rising from punk's ashes. To the PiL kids their group were the ultimate cult band, as groundbreaking, and as uncontrollable, as the Pistols without the latter's rock'n'roll conventions and 'classical' rock line-up.

An illegitimate New Wave love child – born of Lydon, punk face John 'Jah Wobble' Wardle and ex-Clash guitar hero and speed freak, Keith Levene – Public Image recruited Canadian jazz drummer Jim Walker and exploded on the British music scene in 1978. They did so with a post-punk impact that still reverberates today on both sides of the Atlantic. Their first three albums – *First Edition*, *Metal Box* and *Flowers of Romance* – were as original as any ever issued and the group's corporate styling and innovatory sound were unique – dub-sonic bass overlaid with shimmering guitars and Lydon's banshee-type wailing, a meeting-point somewhere between indie, punk and dance.

Yet Public Image's headline-making tours of Europe, the US and Japan invariably ended in tear gas, riots, sackings and recriminations and the original line-up lasted barely ten months. Despite the additions of, amongst others, master percussionist Martin Atkins and Acme Attractions' beauty Jeannette Lee, by the early eighties PiL were falling apart in a welter of money squabbles, 'stolen' master tapes, drugs and bitterness as their founder toured the world playing 'Anarchy In The UK' with a pub band. Ultimately, after Lydon's various solo projects and the Pistols' reunions, Public Image, the ultimate revolutionary band, soon began to exist as merely a legal entity.

Wobble, Levene and Walker from the original line-up, as well as Atkins, all have stories to tell. So do the likes of Dennis Morris, Don Letts, Dave Goodman, Anthony H. Wilson and Alan McGee. Despite continuing sales for Public Image albums, there has been no real outlet for such stories – no major PiL book – for over a decade and a half.

The following then is my own attempt to redress this, to cast some light on the music, myths, madness and methodology of Public Image Ltd – the group one ex-member called 'the most dangerous band on the planet', and the group that, in Lydon's own words, 'let all the angry horses run wild…'

prologue
15 may, 1981: white riot

History does not matter!
John Lydon, 1980

Rock and roll is dead!
Keith Levene, 1980

The crowd of New Yorkers have waited outside for over an hour in the pouring rain to see their heroes' first gig in a year. And now they can't even see them. A white screen, 13 metres wide, covers the entire stage. Despite the deafening volume and the tiny side-lights, only vague silhouettes of the band can be seen. That and fleeting video images of the band in a helicopter – plus the 'event' happening behind the screen.

Amongst the performers: Sam Ulano, a 60-year-old bebop drummer recruited only 18 hours ago who is playing his first and last gig with the group, teenage visual technician Ed Caraballo, and Jeannette Lee, former shop assistant turned ideas-woman... plus one former Sex Pistol...

For a few minutes the crowd buys it – the silhouettes, the drums, the general racket that promises to be the greatest gig build-up ever. But, eventually, patience begins to run out and there are angry mutterings. Where is the song? Where are the band? Why can't we see them...?

Within minutes the muttering becomes a chorus of catcalls, boos and demands that the club – or the band – should 'Raise the screen!' Bottles have been flying in ones and twos even during the jive-ass MC intro of cable TV starlet Lisa Yapp. Now they come in dozens, perhaps because of the singer's sarcastic taunts: 'Silly fucking audience! You ain't throwing enough!' When the crowd don't respond with sufficient fury Lydon turns it into a seven syllable Cockney chant – 'Sill-Lee-Fack-Ing-Au-Dee-Ence! Sill-Lee-Fack-Ing-Au-Dee-Ence!' Soon bottles and glasses are shattering against the edge of the stage and the metal pole that lays upon it. The shards of glass fly into the packed punters crammed against the stage as the angry shouts from the back are now joined by screams from the front. 'New York, New York's a helluva town!' croons the former Pistol Lydon. Behind him Ms Lee shakes a tambourine to Ulano's off-beats.

A desperate club management finally overrules Caraballo and inches the white projection screen up a couple of feet, but the blindingly bright silhouette lights only infuriate the crowd further. They start to tug at the mats which underpin both group and PA. Wires snap and spark, and all the half-hearted attempts at music stop. Ulano clutches fearfully as his kit starts to waddle away from him and some bouncers try to push back the throng. But the security staff is outnumbered – they can only get to the edges.

From above, a large chair is pulled from its moorings and heaved out of the balcony. It crashes down onto the stage thirty feet below, splintering the boards as it rips through the screen. A raging Keith Levene appears through the rip a nanosecond later, looking like an insanely dissolute rock'n'roll angel. He'd earlier threatened 'If you destroy that screen then we will destroy you!' and the veins in his temples are now throbbing visibly. Despite his skinny frame – and despite being outnumbered a thousand to one – he seems ready to kill them all.

But after a couple of bottles have bounced off him, a half-full one smacking his forehead hard, it seems that it is the twentysomething guitarist who will be killed. As the crowd surges towards the now unsteady Levene, a forest of arms reach out to pull him offstage, a bouncer appears from nowhere, bodily lifting him and throwing him back behind the slashed screen. The club security man has sacrificed Levene's dignity but he has also perhaps, at that moment, saved his life.

After less than 25 minutes the gig is abandoned completely – a fully-fledged riot now rocks New York's Ritz Club. As bouncers argue – and sometimes fight – with clubbers, the cops arrive outside. Inside the dressing room Levene, Jeannette and a laughing John Lydon share beers with the one and apparently only punter who has been badly cut. The latter is thrilled to be having a beer with the group and, rather than threaten lawsuits, he even smiles for the cameras. Lee puts down the tambourine she'd been half-heartedly shaking during the performance and hands the bleeding fan an ice-pack.

Apart from the clubbers who have been ejected or arrested, the only real losers are the club's owners. The song title 'Putting On The Ritz' has taken on a whole new meaning tonight, something the club's frantic management does not appreciate.

In little over two years, the group themselves have already lost a founding member, their best bassist and their founding drummer. Some argue they have also lost their raison d'etre. For these skeptics, the group has little more to lose. PiL's first gig for over a year, the following night's performance at the same venue will be cancelled, and they would not play live again for another year. A video event, music as outrage, new wave 'art', visual industrial, deadly serious – and somehow darkly comic too.

When the media runs the story big the next day, to most Americans it will be their introduction to the wonderful, wacky world of Public Image Limited. A 'brave new beginning' that is, in truth, the beginning of the end.

01
public image:
got what you wanted

Born on the last day of January 1956, John Joseph Lydon was the eldest of four sons of first-generation Irish immigrants. Father John, a crane-driver, hailed from Galway, while mother Eileen Barry was from Cork, and they had settled in London. Benwell Mansions was a Victorian tenement on the fringes of an industrial estate in Finsbury Park, and the Lydons' family home was a two-room flat with no bathroom.

Having begun to attend school at Eden Grove Primary, John suffered a traumatic attack of spinal meningitis at the age of eight, and was isolated in hospital for the best part of a year. The illness caused most of his early memories to be erased and it affected his eyesight, causing a fixed stare that would accidentally become a trademark of notoriety in the years to come.

Although a bright child, the illness caused him to be moved back a year in class, and he became a challenge to authority, even in lessons that interested him. Add to that the dogmatic, unquestioning approach of a Catholic secondary school – namely William of York School near Pentonville – and the seeds were sown early for Lydon's characteristic mixture of irreverence, fury and scorn.

By the age of fifteen, after a period where the family had moved around the south-east because of Lydon senior's job, John Lydon had had enough of scholarly suppression. He had become firm friends with classmate John Gray, and they were regulars at Arsenal FC's Highbury ground, and rock venues like The Roundhouse. Now with long hair, John found an unlikely ally for his burgeoning and increasingly outré musical taste: mother Eileen was entranced by the Hawkwind, Captain Beefheart and Can LPs that appeared in the Lydon household. An early attempt at singing in a strait-laced music class at school already marked Lydon out as an unforgettable vocalist – in Lydon's 1994 autobiography, Gray remembered him sounding 'like a yodeling cat being strangled'. However, Lydon would later claim that he also learnt how to read music on a late-night course 'down the Liverpool Road' during his teens.

Having been thrown out of William of York, Lydon began attending Hackney and Stoke Newington Technical College of Further Education, eventually achieving six O levels and two A levels. According to a 1986 interview with Jack Barron of *Sounds*, his attempt to pass a third A level – in Art – was thwarted by the examiners, primarily because of his interpretation with an idea called 'Enveloping Forms': 'I painted an envelope and the examiners weren't amused. But that's exactly what an enveloping form is – a bloody envelope. On top of that, the picture started with a mother and child, and I carried it through to something really gross and vile; the mother eating her child in vivid, bright colours'.

It was while at Hackney and Stoke Newington that Lydon met photography student John Beverly, soon to be awarded the moniker of 'Sid Vicious' after Lydon's pet hamster. Then, in 1974, and now at Kingsway College, he encountered 16-year-old John Joseph Wardle, soon to be known as 'Jah Wobble', a nickname that a drunken Vicious happened upon. Like Lydon, Wobble came from a tough working class Catholic background though his 'manor' was the East End rather than Lydon's Finsbury Park. At primary school, Wardle had been taught by the Sisters of Mercy: 'They were humourless, not warm. What amazes me when I look back is that there wasn't even one of them with a bloody smile. It was neurotic and dark and really not healthy.'

Wobble rejected the formality of his religion at '13, 14. The idea of God that was peddled to us by the nuns and priests was very much the Old Testament model; a fearful, wrathful, judgemental and jealous God. I don't disbelieve in the strength of the religion, but I think a lot of the mystery went out of it when they changed the Latin mass to English. The Latin mass gave people a release... bringing it down to a chat on the doorstep wasn't so clever.' Instead of the church, Wobble took to cramming on Hindu mysticism in the local library. Appropriately, the origins of the universe in Hinduism 'began not with light but with a sound, "om".'

'I'm out of Stepney and it's a bit monochrome,' Wobble now says of his background, 'very multi-racial but not really cosmopolitan. It's all council flats. So I started to gravitate more towards Hackney, it was more of a buzz, you had more Jamaicans about, more streetlife kinda thing. Musically, I was into the stuff they called bluebeat, Prince Buster. If you say that to people now they go, "Wow, you were really into it, weren't you?" like it was all so strange and obscure. Well a lot of it wasn't. In fact, actually, that was some of the most popular music of its day.' In 1994, he told *Melody Maker*, 'The Trojan compilations were the first things that really did the trick for me. It was the pure bottom end that attracted me. It was obvious then that the bass was the only instrument for me.'

By late 1974, John Lydon – a big Alice Cooper and Lou Reed fan – had been obliged to leave the family home, supposedly because of his new green hair, but most likely as an aggressive form of encouragement from his father for the 18-year-old to stand on his own two feet. Lydon and Vicious (a Bowie and T. Rex fan) lived in squats and took dead-end jobs together. Vicious soon drifted down to the cutting edge 'couture' clothes shop known as SEX, whose co-owners were Malcolm McLaren and his partner Vivienne Westwood. Vicious later 'discovered' the shop and eagerly reported his find back to Lydon and Wobble.

Wobble, by this point, had also dropped out of college. 'I'd picked up two O' Levels [but I had] left halfway through the second year, never stuck with it. And my old man said, "If you're not gonna go to college then you either bring in 20 quid a week or you fuck right off." Which is quite reasonable, in a way... so I started doing the various squats with John. I had a cheap bedsit for a while too. In those days most places wouldn't take DHSS [Welfare], it was the days of horrible landladies. "Are you married to your young lady-friend or not? This is a respectable household, young man, not a knocking shop, you know..." Oh, man, it was horrible, horrible.'

Jah Wobble also remembers a period of living with Lydon and another friend Ronnie Britton in a haunted house in Edmonton, North London: 'Ronnie was gonna marry some bird and it all fell through. So the Edmonton place turned into a kind of bachelor pad despite the fact that there was some real heavy duty poltergeist activity there. I moved in with John and the first night going back there with him there were weird things going on. Doors and windows flying open and all the rest.'

Meanwhile, over in north-west London, a brilliant young guitarist called Julian Keith Levene Jr – whose father owned a clothing factory – had started to emerge from a lower middle-class Jewish household. Although Levene, born on 18th July 1957, and who chose to prioritise his middle name over his forename, himself today laughs at the oft-repeated story that he was classically trained – 'That's just one of the stories me and Wobble would make up to wind-up journalists' – others insist that he did receive some expert tuition. Rumour has it that Steve Howe of prog-rockers Yes gave the young hopeful informal instrumental lessons, partly in exchange for some guitar roadie work. Indeed, he won a few more six-string tutorials after one eventful night in Glasgow, when Howe and his cohorts were confronted by a gang of street toughs that the ever-watchful young Keith had warned them about. Classically trained or not, Levene had soon become tuned-in enough to be a front-row regular on the 1974-75 pub rock scene. 'I used to go to Dingwalls and see all those bands, the Kilburns, The Stranglers and Kokomo and so on. Those bands did kind of set the scene for punk rock, for the Pistols.'

It was in early 1976, in a Warwick Street squat that Levene first encountered Jah Wobble. 'Levene seemed likeable,' asserts Wobble, 'he had his own kinda charm. He genuinely loved music – which was one of the things I liked about him – and he was a real guitarist. He was also a serious speed freak. I mean, I did a lot of speed myself back then but he did even more – plus he did a little smack on top, as I recall. He wasn't innocent but he had a child-like quality – a bit like Sid. He had a gentle side too, though he tended to hedge his bets, to sit on the fence in arguments and watch which way the wind was blowing.'

Wobble had also attended the occasional pub rock gig, with Lydon in tow. John Gray had recommended Dr Feelgood. 'Me and [Lydon] went to see them out in Essex a couple of times. Nice, great performers, though it was very sixties style. But the rest of the groups were... well, it was that whole era of Emerson, Lake and Palmer and being a mock virtuoso and shit like that. It was either that or the inner city working class thing of listening to records – soul, reggae and all that.'

By 1975, Wobble was also a regular listener to Tommy Vance's weekly reggae show on London's Capital Radio. Here he heard a dub version of Burning Spear's 'Marcus Garvey': 'One of the very first dub versions I ever heard. I used to listen to that show religiously.' Wobble was also developing a love of the Philadelphia soul scene: 'I used to get all me records from this light-fitting shop near Petticoat Lane, near the junction with Middlesex Street. That's where you got the real pukka imports. I can still remember some of the records I liked then – Jimmy Castor Bunch doing "Potential", The Ohio Players' song "Fire", The Isley Brothers' "Fight The Power" and The O'Jays and all that stuff.'

Lydon, Grey, Wobble and Vicious – 'the four Johns' – had become regulars at soul clubs around the capital, partly because they attracted a genuinely interesting mix of 'outsiders' from different backgrounds, but also because of the music policy which favoured extended mixes of disco cuts, where no single instrument dominated the sound for too long. A favourite haunt was Lacey Lady's in Ilford. Nearly twenty years later, Lydon explained: 'I like to see huge varieties of people supposedly not capable of getting on with each other and being perfectly fine together.'

In late August 1975, John Gray talked Lydon into attending an impromptu audition at SEX. The audition was for the position of lead singer for a new teenage band called the Sex Pistols. Lydon attempted a version of Alice Cooper's 'Eighteen,' singing along to the single on the store's jukebox. He couldn't hold a note for too long and his 'stage moves' were bizarre in the extreme – but his manic energy and acerbic wit were without parallel.

The band – bassist Glen Matlock, guitarist Steve Jones and his friend, drummer Paul Cook – gave Lydon a reluctant welcoming and Malcolm McLaren, who'd briefly managed the New York Dolls, eventually nominated himself manager. Wobble, for one, was astounded by the revelation that Lydon was now a frontman for a group: 'It's like me now saying to you, "I'm about to become a doctor, mate. Yeah, I've been working at Guy's Hospital, final degree tomorrow."' On checking out the Pistols, Wobble was surprised a second time, this time at 'how great they really were. It's funny, 'cos someone asked me recently, "Do you think it would have been better if you'd been the bass player in the Pistols?" And, no, it wouldn't have been. Because it needed that kinda British rock bass playing that Glen Matlock did really well. I thought he was the best musician in it – he was already something.'

The Pistols' first gig took place at St Martin's College of Art on Friday 7th November 1975, supporting Bazooka Joe, whose lead singer was future pop star Adam Ant. The gig had been organised by Glen Matlock, then a student at the college. Various gigs around London followed over the next few months, usually at colleges, and then in the spring and summer of 1976, dates further afield were arranged. A growing number of Pistols fanatics in London, the North of England and Wales were making the band figureheads of the new punk rock movement. Previously bored products of suburban England were attracted into the fold, some of whom would even become stars in their own right, like Bromley's Susan Dallion (soon to become 'Siouxsie Sioux') and William Broad ('Billy Idol'). The watchword was 'individuality'. Twenty years later, when the Pistols reformed, John Lydon remained proud of the group's early incarnation and its diverse audiences – everyone from 'John Travolta types' to 'little teenyboppers', and 'boot-boys mixing it up with bikers'.

Having been signed to the EMI label in October 1976, The Sex Pistols' first – and, as it turned out, only – single release for the label, 'Anarchy In The UK', was unleashed on Friday 26th November. Reviews were decidedly mixed: Cliff White in the *New Musical Express* remarked that it wasn't quite bad enough to be memorable, while even those who had been following the burgeoning punk rock movement were not unconditional in their praise. Alan Lewis in *Sounds* commented that 'They may want to push the old farts aside but they've borrowed a lot from 'em', not least from The Who. Even BBC Radio 1's John Peel, happy enough to play the record, was surprised at its length, well over a minute longer than, say, The Damned's 'New Rose' or almost anything off the Ramones' LP.

Two days after the single's release, *The London Weekend Show*, Janet Street-Porter's regional youth magazine for LWT, transmitted a special film report on punk rock, in which Rotten would scornfully attack 'complacent' hippies. The programme captured the complexity and individuality of punk extremely effectively, but on Wednesday 1st December, the Pistols made a live TV appearance which was to simultaneously make and break them.

EMI act Queen, scheduled to be interviewed on Thames Television's nightly topical magazine *Today*, were unable to appear, and so were replaced, just 90 minutes before transmission, by the Sex Pistols. Sneered at by veteran interviewer Bill Grundy, they were invited to 'say something outrageous', and, as a thousand nostalgic clip shows have since reminded us, duly complied. Self-righteous lorry drivers kicked their sets in, tabloid front-pages virtually wrote themselves, Grundy was suspended from his job, and unfortunately for the band itself, councils around Britain forbade them to play most of their upcoming tour.

With it becoming increasingly difficult to see the band live, or hear them on the radio, the 'Anarchy In The UK' single was at least still in the shops, and inched as far as number 38 in the charts. But on 6th

January 1977, EMI announced that they were terminating their contract with the group, a decision that inspired the blisteringly sarcastic ode 'EMI (Unlimited Supply)'. The demo was cut, along with several others, later that month at Gooseberry, a 16-track basement studio on Gerrard Street in London's Chinatown. At the helm was the Pistols' first serious producer, Dave Goodman, and Mark Lusardi was the in-house studio engineer. Lusardi was later to work with PiL and a solo Jah Wobble, although his first impressions of John Lydon were a little less than impressive:

'We were all surprised that Johnny Rotten wasn't some huge tough guy but was, instead, this seven stone weakling. And basically, he couldn't go to the pub unless three or four of us went with him – mainly because he stood a good chance of being attacked by skinheads, boot boys, football yobs, whoever. The Pistols were already pretty notorious by then.'

News of the group had now become international; a crew from NBC-TV turned up to film footage from the Gooseberry sessions, after reading 'Punks', Mick Brown's piece for *Rolling Stone*, published in the 27th January 1977 issue. And someone else who read the very same article was Canadian drummer Jim Walker, born in Edmonton in the mid-Western province of Alberta, and by now based in Vancouver.

Walker's musical background had leaned further towards jazz than rock: 'Rock was dead, at that time, especially where I was from in "Redneckville", which is like the West. People over in England then were listening to David Bowie and Sweet. And to me that was just a load of shit. I was mainly into jazz-rock 'cos it was electric. Back then you had the Mahavishnu Orchestra and Earth Wind & Fire and Return To Forever were still good and it looked like there was a future in it. It really looked like jazz was gonna mutate with rock 'cos of Miles [Davis] and Weather Report. [So] I went for a term to Berkeley College, the big music college in Boston, a jazz school. It's bullshit really but you get to meet some cool people. It was the first time I was away from a hick town and it was an unbelievable experience – I saw Miles Davis, The Band, they were literally at the next table. And I met Coltrane's drummer Elvin Jones who sat at my table and chatted for half an hour. There was all of that.'

Eventually, though, Walker became disillusioned with his musical direction, and left Berkeley, heading back west to Vancouver. By January 1977, he had decided to return to Boston: '... And I was gonna practice eight hours a day, just build up my chops 'cos I was pretty talented and I really wanted to get my technique up. I was always a fanatical kind of musician. And then I saw this *Rolling Stone* magazine in Vancouver and there was this little tiny article on the Pistols. There was this picture of Johnny Rotten, this nasty little face and I just thought, "This is fantastic! I've gotta be with that guy! This looks like a really cool thing. He looks like the kinda guy that I could relate to." Because I didn't relate to people, as a kid I was nuts – I mean really nuts, you know? So I thought, "Punk's kinda interesting".'

Meantime, Keith Levene's habit of 'hanging around Portobello Road market' had led to him meeting future Clash guitarist Mick Jones. 'One day, after the market was over, we went to some squat and talked for hours about music, what was happening, what wasn't happening. And there was obviously a gap for another group to do something. Afterwards we went up to Hampstead to this squat where John [Lydon] was for a time and I got to know him – at least on a shallow, social level I got to know him.'

On 4th July 1976, Levene and Lydon met again, this time on the same bill in a Sheffield pub called The Black Swan. The Pistols were the headlining band, with a very early line-up of The Clash featuring Keith Levene as one of two guitarists, supporting. Levene had recruited Joe Strummer from The 101'ers: 'They were a wild rock'n'roll band. Joe used to wear zoot suits and just go fucking mad all over the place.' Levene says now: 'I got on quite well with them and [manager] Bernie Rhodes, I only did a few gigs – the rehearsal gigs, the showcases, and a couple of out of town things – and then I left.' In December 1989, he told the *NME*'s Jane Garcia, 'There's a lot of me in The Clash. I was contributing to the velocity of how the songs were played, making things go much faster... I knew Mick well enough to know that what he wanted to do was just play really nice love songs. Really, The Clash would have sounded like Squeeze if Mick had had his way...' Levene left The Clash in September 1976 and joined The Quick Spurts, but two months earlier in that Sheffield pub, Lydon and Levene had recognised kindred spirits, and vowed to collaborate at a later date.

Levene now expresses no disappointment that the subsequent line-up of The Clash became so successful: 'When people say to me, "It must have been so gutting to leave The Clash then see them go on to become so big," I always say, "No, not at all, I always knew they'd be big." And I did, I knew they would be massive, right from the start. It was obvious to me. So what? It was what was gonna happen... so it wasn't that big a deal for me after I'd left and they got signed up. There was such a strong vibe back then, anyway, you felt loads of different things could happen.'

Although Levene will say little about his extensive drug-taking of the time beyond commenting 'There was a lot of stuff flying around back then', his addiction to amphetamine sulphate or speed was said to have been considerable. The cost to Levene was physical and emotional, but there was financial strife too; when he had left The Clash, their parting gift to him, a vintage Gibson, had been hawked within 72 hours, mainly to pay for more speed. It was one of many mistakes that hard drugs were to lead him into.

Levene's next band was the Flowers of Romance, who by October 1976, was rehearsing around London. They were named after the Sex Pistols' opening live number – an unmelodic, wordless racket that the Pistols used to scare those spectators who were seeing the band for the first time. In cultural terms, it was the first hint at how 'dangerous' the Pistols – or any Lydon-led band – could be.

'The Flowers of Romance line-up was with Viv Albertine, Palm Olive and Sid Vicious, whom I did teach bass to,' Levene confirms now. 'Because Sid could play bass – punk bass, at least. Obviously Glen [Matlock] could wipe the floor with Sid when it came to a bit of fancy bass work but if you're talking about some punky bass, just chugging along with the odd change or two then Sid was in there, he could do it, in time, no problem. He could play bass – no question.

'We'd stay awake practising for hours and hours, day after day, and I'd teach him certain things. Mick [Jones] did the same thing for Paul [Simonon] before that, at the very beginning of The Clash, showing him this and that and helping him tune up and things. I did the same thing with Wobble later, when we were starting Public Image, showed him how to do the odd change, a middle eight type thing or whatever.'

Vicious was also the frontman for the group, but by early 1977, when Glen Matlock was fired from the Sex Pistols, Vicious was in the unlikely position of being headhunted by Malcolm McLaren to replace him. As Levene remembers, 'There were discussions before it happened – Sid really did not wanna give up his own thing, his own group. But I think Malcolm could clearly see that Sid had already become Mister Punk incarnate, someone a lot of people were talking about... and any band he was in was going to make waves, were gonna get a lot of attention. I dropped out of the Flowers myself for a time when Sid was in the band – I was out, I was in, Viv Albertine was out-in, it kept changing. [But] I did say to Sid at that time, "Well you've gotta go for it"... being in the Pistols, being in a band with John Lydon, a band that was getting so famous, so fast. It was a great opportunity, because I never really thought then that I'd ever get that chance.'

It was a chance that Jah Wobble wasn't expecting either as he drifted from job to job: 'There were still plenty of jobs paying cash around then. The unemployment situation didn't get bad until late '77 and it didn't get really bad 'til Thatcher got in.' One of the better jobs was a part-time messenger job in the City, 'which I really liked. I got £45 a week if I put in the overtime – good money back then. Got the sack for going to BP's London head office in combat trousers without a tie. I had me army trousers pressed but that wasn't good enough.'

Another job Wobble undertook was to find him in the vicinity of a future major pop star. In March 1977, Ronnie Britton, managing a British tour by Johnny Thunders & The Heartbreakers, offered Wobble a few weeks work as a roadie for one of the tour's supporting acts, an early incarnation of Sting and The Police.

'They hadn't formulated their own sound yet and were just pumping out this second-rate heavy metal. Their [original] guitarist [Henri Padovani] was a little bit full of himself but Sting was alright. And I think, as well, Sting liked the music me and Ronnie used to play backstage, that really heavy reggae, the dubby bassy stuff that I always had with me then. Which maybe influenced them a bit. Sting listened a lot, I know that.

'But Ronnie and me weren't the best tour people for that gig – we were supposed to go to Eric's, in Liverpool, but by mistake we went through the Wallasey tunnel and into North Wales. Funnily enough, the three group members that were in the bus did not seem to be concerned in the slightest at this detour; we were the most useless road crew in the world. At one point Ronnie got fed up with Stewart Copeland and so he put his foot through the snare drum. On another occasion he threw Heartbreakers drummer Jerry Nolan to the floor, injuring his back which meant that the performance scheduled for that night was cancelled.

'To be honest, I saw things around that group [The Heartbreakers] that I didn't like, especially the prolific use of heroin, and I advised Ronnie not to stick in that situation for too long. I said to him: "Ronnie, they're cunts. Rob them and fuck off."'

It was while sharing a squat with Sid Vicious that Wobble felt an instinctive passion for Vicious's bass: 'I'd borrowed [it] and I kinda knew what to do with it, somehow. To me, playing bass was relief of pain, it was like healing.' After some early attempts at practice with

Vicious's instrument, Wobble was forced to accept the proceeds of crime: 'Ronnie Britton nicked me a bass guitar and amp a couple of weeks later. It was a crappy little Music-Man bass, actually, very high action... I said, "Hang on, Ron, I need a lead as well, where's the lead?," and he said "Don't worry, son, I'll nick you one!" And he shot off and came back half an hour later with a lead. I sold the amp for beer money, early doors, so I then had to lean the neck against the headboard of the bed to get a vibration, to get a sound. Which was great actually, because when I got a good bass it was like going from an old Cortina with a high slippy clutch to a reconditioned Ford Zephyr that's really well tuned. It's like doing martial arts training with big brass rings on your wrists, take 'em off and, yeah, you can really move now.'

Just becoming a competent bass player wasn't enough for Wobble, though. Soon he was busy conceptualising about music, thinking of all the possible directions something new could go. '"Hmmmm... what if you had a heavy bass going with this kinda keyboard?" I was actually getting into electronic music, getting pretty far out. It was very simple thinking in a way – "I like bass and maybe with this kinda drum." I always remember thinking, "If you had a Donna Summer-type drum" – but I knew they'd got some kind of sequencer – "with a heavy bass then that'd be nice. Then what about with some short-wave static, some texture over it?" I was getting into drones as well, drone sounds. So I was getting into this weird fantasy world of music. Doing me own soundscapes and trying things out on this crappy bass, get things done then get 'em down on cassette. Try a few mad things. But, of course, there was no outlet for it, no outlet at all.'

It was a situation that was about to change – drastically.

02
holidays in the sun

By the mid-summer of 1977, the Sex Pistols had become the most controversial group in Britain. Having been signed for £75,000 then dumped by A&M Records in March after threatening *Old Grey Whistle Test* presenter Bob Harris (a friend of A&M UK's managing director Derek Green), the group's recording career was only rescued when Richard Branson's Virgin label signed them in May. Next came a second single 'God Save The Queen', which despite a complete ban by radio and television, and with several record shop chains refusing to stock it, only missed a number one placing by a whisker in Jubilee week, and sold over 250,000 copies, enough to earn it a silver disc.

The song, assumed to be a direct insult to Queen Elizabeth herself, was far more a critique of the complacency which the Queen's 1977 Silver Jubilee festivities celebrated – idolatry of the past, and indifference to the present and future state of Britain. But this was a complex argument that the mass media would never acknowledge, nor wish to. It was much easier to gibber about the record calling Her Majesty 'a moron' than to untangle the strands that had made Britain and its attitude to the monarchy so entrenched and inflexible.

On Tuesday 7th June, two days before the Queen's own river progress through London, McLaren and Virgin Records pre-empted it with a publicity stunt on the Thames – a boat trip during which the Pistols would perform a live gig. As the boat docked, the police moved in, exacerbating an already tense situation, and arrested eleven participants (although none of the Pistols themselves). Producer Dave Goodman remembers Jah Wobble from that night: 'The boat got pulled over by police launches and there were dozens of coppers waiting on the quayside. As the boat pulled in, Wobble was throwing loads of beer cans at the cops. When they stormed on the boat he disappeared into a crowd, then came out the other side and sat down next to me saying, "Pretend we're having a conversation, like I've been here all the time. Chat, chat, chat, talk, talk, talk." It wasn't too bad an idea and it seemed to work because I think he got away with it. I don't remember him being arrested that night.'

But the other effect of the 'God Save The Queen' controversy was that the protagonists were in danger of being attacked on the streets – designer Jamie Reid, drummer Paul Cook, and Johnny Rotten himself. 'John was left high and dry at this point, McLaren rejected him at the worst possible time,' claims Jah Wobble. 'At that time he was under pressure the whole time – Public Enemy Number One.' Finally, on Sunday 19th June, Rotten was cornered and slashed by a gang in London but fortuitously Jah Wobble's pal Vince Bracken and another man known only as Joseph happened to be passing and chased the assailants off. Lydon claimed that the leather trousers he was wearing helped save him: 'If it wasn't for those trousers I'd be a one-legged hoppity'.

Rush-released as a third single on July 1st, 'Pretty Vacant' – an experiment to see if radio would play a relatively harmless Pistols track – also leapt into the top ten and resulted in gaining them a slot on *Top of the Pops*. But the damage regarding the public property of the band had been done, and Rotten in particular was tiring of punk's 'formula' – recording sessions with Chris Thomas were dominated by creating a wall of sound for Steve Jones's guitar work, with Rotten's lead vocal almost considered an afterthought.

Besides, Rotten had no particular love for the clichés of rock'n'roll which, to some extent, punk rock had been obliged to emulate. His musical tastes were much more varied and eclectic than almost anyone at the time would have given him credit for, and to Malcolm McLaren's disgust, on Saturday 16th July, Capital Radio in London broadcast 'A Punk and His Music,' a 90-minute pre-recorded programme with Rotten in conversation with Tommy Vance, interspersed with some of Rotten's favourite tracks. The interview itself was memorable enough, contextualising his early interest in music ('I remember *Ready Steady Go* when I was small and that was great fun') and his boredom with the punk movement: 'A lot of it is real rubbish. A lot of bands are ruining it. They're either getting too much into the star trip, or they're going the exact opposite way'.

The musical interludes, however, were a revelation, belying the popular view of the Pistols' frontman as 'nihilistic'. 'The Blimp' from Captain Beefheart's 1969 album *Trout Mask Replica* was a favourite, as were two tracks from lapsed Catholics Kevin Coyne ('Eastbourne Ladies') and Peter Hammill ('The Institute of Mental Health is Burning'). Albums from the likes of Lou Reed, Tim Buckley and Neil Young were plundered, Bobby Byrd's 'Back from the Dead' was a cherished example of soul-funk and a few selections (David Bowie's 'Rebel Rebel' and Gary Glitter's 'Doing Alright With The Boys') even seemed to highlight a fascination with showmanship.

But it was reggae and dub that marked perhaps the most surprising departure from the populist view of Johnny Rotten, genres that opened up almost endless possibilities for using texture and space on the canvas of recorded sound. Excited by a dub version of Culture's 'I'm Not Ashamed', he commented, 'They love sound, any sound... music is only sound, innit?' Fred Locks, The Gladiators and Aswad were all championed, and one recently-issued track, 'Born for a Purpose' by Dr Alimantado was cited as having powerful resonance during this particularly frightening time: 'When I'd been beaten up, I came home and played this.'

If McLaren was aghast at this public display of Rotten's 'taste', Jah Wobble was heartily impressed. Later he told Neil Spencer of the *NME*, 'To me that was more important than the Pistols getting the front page of the *Daily Mirror.*'

Apart from a few music press descriptions of 'A Punk And His Music,' there was little chance that Rotten's public image would be altered by one interview on local radio, no matter how much it challenged that persona. Rotten had insisted elsewhere, '"Anarchy In The UK" is not political, it's self-rule, if you think you're right then you must do what you believe in... I'm talking about cultural anarchy, not political anarchy. People should be free to play a guitar as badly as they like – or as well as they like...'

But this was far too complicated for the tabloids which, with their mass circulation, were prepared to compress complex statements into inflammatory headlines. 'Our Songs Are Anti-God, Anti-Monarchist, I Am A Revolutionary, An Anarchist!' roared one *Daily Mirror* front-page in August 1977.

By the time the Capital interview was broadcast, the Sex Pistols had left Britain for a hastily-arranged tour of Scandinavia. On their return, the SPOTS tour (Sex Pistols On Tour Secretly) was a necessity, simply to enable the shows to go ahead at all. The tour began at Lafayette Club in Wolverhampton on 19th August. At their Outlook Club date in Doncaster, the group were known as 'The Tax Exiles', while in Scarborough they were billed as 'Special Guest', in Middlesbrough as 'Acne Ramble', and Plymouth as 'The Hamsters'. The tour ended in Cornwall on 1st September – this time with the band advertised under the name 'A Mystery Band of International Repute' where an old friend of Rotten's became part of the entourage.

'At Penzance Jah Wobble turned up and was hanging out with John,' recalls Pistols' photographer Dennis Morris. 'I figured there was something happening there, you know? Like it was the start of something.'

'I just went there to have a good drink and a laugh really,' claims Wobble now. 'I thought the gig was alright. Afterwards Sid didn't seem to be around and Steve and Paul seemed a bit wary of me – I dunno why, it wasn't like I was gonna attack 'em or anything. Maybe they were fed up with losing Glen and getting Sid, and just couldn't stand the sight of another of John's nutty mates turning up. I certainly wasn't thinking about me and John being in a band together, honestly, and I'm not sure that John was thinking along those lines at that time. I mean, the Pistols were still topping the charts, you know? The talk of the town.'

Over in North America, meanwhile, Jim Walker had finally been able to gain some experience in a punk band. 'In April '77 The Furies asked me to join them. Some little ratty punk band, one of the first punk groups out West, on the Pacific West Coast. We were a good little band; we'd definitely have been signed if we'd come over here to the UK. I'm the only one who has any tapes, they're in a mountain in Colorado, buried. We were kinda like a combination of The Heart-breakers and... a very New Yorky sorta influenced sound 'cos our guitar-player writer was into The Stooges and The [New York] Dolls and all that. I just came along and said, "Plug me in". I arranged some of the stuff 'cos I can arrange a bit. We were just together for the summer of '77 and it was good fun 'cos I'd just thought, "Fuck jazz rock, I'm young and I wanna have fun."'

On 11th September 1977, The Furies split up. Walker's response was to get drunk for a month ''cos I basically thought my life was over, as you do.' But then his thirst for British punk rock got the better of him: 'I thought, "It's either LA, New York or London as they're the punk places". And I thought, "Well, LA can wait until I'm really old, like 25 or something, or I could go to New York". But I'd been in Boston and it was like that movie *Taxi Driver*, very crime-ridden, infested with dirt and cockroaches and rats in the wall. It was quite nasty and the music was boring. [So] I borrowed some money and flew to London with £675, a drum kit and a return ticket.

'London was just so wild, so interesting, I thought. There was good and bad – it was like the War had just been fought here on one level. Bomb-sites everywhere, everything in black and white, pubs shutting early, all the guys wore suits. But I loved the Kings Road though, because it was still so magical, to come from where I came from and to see chicks who were 30 years old and still gorgeous, y'know, the sixties' babes? And the guys had real good self-respect and they weren't just all broken lumps.

''Cos American society's really weird, you're basically brought up to breed and that's it and as soon as you've reached that age you're just meant to fall apart. So on October 13th 1977 I arrived here, fell in love with the dump and determined to get a record out with a name band before the next October 13th came round.'

With almost surreal speed the chance to work with one of the big new bands fell straight into Walker's lap – via the traditional method of scanning the small ads in the weekly *Melody Maker*. 'I read through and saw that Rat Scabies had just left The Damned. Now I loved their first album, I played it over and over again that summer so I knew their music inside out. So I auditioned for them in Lillie Road, Fulham, some ratty little studio. And they had the same Hi-Watt amps all lined up like they did on the back of their first album and I thought, "This is really cool". That's what it's like when you're from over there, it's like icon worship or something. We did "Neat Neat Neat". I hadn't really played it before but I had listened to it over and over so I did it blindingly well, 'cos it was probably the only song by them that I could do really well 'cos it had a normal beat. We're totally opposite drummers, Rat and I, 'cos I'm off beat and jazz-trained and I swing. But it was Rat's band, it was like The Who leaving Keith Moon.'

Initially, Walker seemed to have got the gig since there was talk of tours and union membership for TV and radio appearances. 'During the last week of October I went back for another session with them at Shepperton Studios and I just saw all these really weird things going on. I was shitting myself really 'cos they made me wait eight hours to audition for them. They said, "Show up at 12" – they showed up at seven and then we went to eat. My nerves were so shattered, waiting there for seven hours, eight hours, with roadies in a big soundstage like an aeroplane hangar. My nerves were shot and I played like shit.

My hanging out with The Damned lasted four or five days – there'd been talk of me doing a live TV show but I wasn't in the Musicians Union – so they got Jon Moss, later to be the Culture Club drummer, instead. I didn't like The Damned anymore anyway 'cos I didn't particularly care for the new guitar-player [Lu Edmonds]. It wasn't The Damned that I knew, not with this new second guitarist...so I starved that winter, my money ran out, I was homeless, just shuffling around for a couple of months, drum kit stuck in some rehearsal place. It was almost like that *Midnight Cowboy* film, it was really rough.'

Sex Pistols play Brunel University, 1977
© Suburban Kid Archive

Then, on 16th December, Walker attended one of the final British gigs by the Sex Pistols. The venue was Brunel University, in Uxbridge, on the fringes of West London. Word had leaked out early and hundreds came, some looking for drunken trouble as cider bottles and chairs flew back and forth.

'That was really interesting,' says Walker, 'because it was 60 per cent the greatest band I'd ever seen in my life – or ever will – and 40 per cent was crap. But that 60 per cent was so good, they really were a great band, even with Sid – I mean, he looked great. I'd heard the soundcheck and him and Paul Cook were doing super-slow rhythms – so Sid could hit the right notes basically. They sounded great, though, they were a really great band. Cook was great, Steve was a great guitar player and Rotten was just fantastic.'

Walker's perception was heightened by his recent arrival in the UK. 'When you're young and alone in a foreign place it's like being in the jungle, it's very instinctive. And I just knew immediately that the Pistols ruled London or England. They had these huge, full-colour posters that were glossy, big artwork – and all the other bands had these shitty little black and white A4-sized things. That kinda confirmed it. There was just something in the Pistols' vibe, you just knew. I thought "These guys are the best, nobody touches them". I never much liked The Clash, and The Damned without Rat were nothing much and that Damned tour I missed flopped anyway so what the hell...'

Dave Goodman, who had produced some of the Pistols' earliest recordings, was by now presiding over records by roots reggae rockers The Tribesman. He remembers that by late 1977, two of the their number were desperate to move on: 'I remember [Lydon] and Sid Vicious later coming round to the headquarters of The Label [Goodman's own indie label] in Dawes Road, Fulham – in late 1977 – and asking me a lot of questions about our set-up. John and Sid were thinking of forming a band outside of the Pistols and maybe they wanted me to help them but they couldn't seem to agree on what kind of structure they wanted.'

On the face of it, The Sex Pistols' career was going from strength to strength. 'Holidays in the Sun' had given them another top ten hit in October, and an album provocatively titled *Never Mind The Bollocks Here's The Sex Pistols* had raced to the number one spot in Britain heading a top ten dominated by 'easy listening artists' and greatest hits collections. Nevertheless, as Jon Savage subsequently noted in his book *England's Dreaming*, the record was 'a tombstone' and 'airless', with no room for the songs to breathe. Underneath it all, they were desperately short of new songs, and the intense scrutiny placed on the group remained.

Occasionally, a Pistols gig was enjoyable and worthwhile. A Christmas Day concert at Ivanhoe's Club in Huddersfield was preceded by an afternoon show for the children of striking firemen, laid-off workers and one-parent families. But a brutal tour of the United States in January 1978 showed the Pistols' unity disintegrating – while Cook and Jones joined McLaren on flights, Vicious and Rotten chose to travel by road. Rotten grew fond of America, but the prospect of the Pistols becoming The Rolling Stones filled him with dread and horror, and after a show at Winterland, San Francisco on 14th January (in front of a crowd of nearly five thousand people), he had decided enough was enough.

After deriding Vicious, now a blood-spattered junkie as 'a living circus', Rotten was heard to announce from the stage, 'Ever had the feeling you've been cheated?' He later claimed that the words were as much directed at himself as the audience.

But, either way, by the end of the month the Pistols were a memory though McLaren and the others clung onto the name as a disillusioned Lydon exited. 'I'm carrying on and the rest are quitting,' Lydon told British journalists but no one was sure, at first, if it wasn't yet another Pistols' publicity stunt. But as the fur flew between the opposing McLaren-Westwood and Lydon camps it soon became obvious that Malcolm and John had worked together for the very last time.

McLaren's style of management – avoiding gigs, misinforming the group, paying the Pistols £50 a week despite scoring six figure record deals, diverting some of the group's royalties into film projects – had turned Lydon into a bitter enemy. An enemy who had to fight to keep his own nickname – Johnny Rotten – which, like the name Sex Pistols, McLaren was claiming for his own.

Legend has it that John and former Roxy Club DJ Don Letts then took a 'busman's holiday' in Jamaica in February '78, ostensibly to sign reggae bands for Richard Branson's Virgin label.

But, as photographer Dennis Morris recalls, Lydon and Letts were actually the last people to join the trip: 'Richard Branson was going to Jamaica to sign a few reggae acts and David Bailey had been approached to do the pictures of the trip [and] make a big splash of it. But Jamaica was very volatile then and Bailey demanded extra danger money for covering the visit. And so Richard asked me to do it instead.' Morris had already taken pictures for Virgin before – capturing various reggae performers including the classic album cover shots of Bob Marley that had first attracted Lydon and led to Morris' work with the Pistols.

The entourage that journeyed to Jamaica grew when, according to Morris, 'Richard realised that he really needed someone to A&R the trip, someone with a big knowledge of reggae and so he invited John Lydon along. We were staying in a big hotel. Me and John were in one suite and Richard [Branson] had an adjoining suite.'

If Lydon was unsure about the extent of his fame, he was soon put right as he stepped onto an island then considered almost as violent as war-torn Beirut; The Rolling Stones had just been more or less driven out of Kingston, its capital, amid a flurry of security concerns.

'The minute we stepped off the plane in Kingston,' Morris remembers, 'there were lots of armed police and then, a few moments later, there were these three heavy-looking dreads staring at us. John didn't know what to expect but they suddenly started going, "Hey, Johnny Rotten, Sex Pistol man, God Save the Queen – cool". And it was all smiles, they loved him and that was it – he's got a cool spirit and that's important in Jamaica, that's more important than the colour of your skin. You can be black and they'll knock you back if your vibe's all wrong. But John fitted in, smokin' chalices all day, meeting U-Roy, Big Youth, Prince Far-I.'

Lydon got on well with some of his reggae heroes – in as much as Lydon ever allowed himself to have heroes. He even recorded some songs with Lee 'Scratch' Perry, at least one of which got near completion. 'But,' Morris says, 'I never heard it again. I dunno what happened to those tapes... Don Letts turned up [in Jamaica] a few days later, out of the blue, he wasn't really expected or anything. But he was welcomed in.'

According to Letts it was John Lydon who'd invited him over – and Lydon who made sure Virgin picked up the tab for the flight and the accommodation. 'I'll always be forever in John's debt for that – he was the first man to take me to Jamaica. When the Pistols broke up he wanted to escape that paparazzi nonsense – and he was going there to advise Richard Branson. John asked me to go along 'cos he figured, I'm black, I'm Jamaican, it'll kinda ease the pain a bit. I'd never been to Jamaica before. The closest I'd been was seeing that *The Harder They Come* movie in Brixton. We stayed for about a month, at the Sheraton Hotel, [and] Richard had taken the whole of the first floor.'

With a punk star and a rich white label owner in town it didn't take long for, in Letts' words, the 'jungle drums to send out a message across the island. Quite literally, there was an exodus of every reggae artist – apart from Bob [Marley], Burning Spear, Bunny Wailer and Peter Tosh – me and John were sitting round the pool and they were all there, Tapper Zukie, I-Roy, U-Roy and loads of others.

'And everyone seemed to respect John – if someone heavy looked at him, he'd stare straight back at them, look 'em in the eye, he never mumbled and looked at the floor, he met everyone head on. Anyway, most of the big reggae stars were there every day – if they didn't get a deal they'd make sure they got a meal, and if they didn't get a meal they made damn sure they got copious amounts of Red Stripe.'

There was a genuine bit of new work flying around for them too – though not all of it was of the highest quality as Letts recalls.

'Some bright spark at Virgin thought it would be a really good idea to do reggae versions of the Pistols' most outrageous songs, "Belsen Was A Gas" and "Holidays In The Sun." I heard them being recorded, mixed and finished and they sounded a bit cheesy to be honest, the brothers were just trying to make a bit of money, you know? So it was more Bread at The Controls than Dread at The Controls.'

A routine of sorts was swiftly established. 'Everyday,' says Letts, 'we'd have breakfast at U-Roy's, and breakfast there was a big ganja pipe loaded with an ounce of weed. And I'd be struggling to keep up with John. Went round to Joni Mitchell's hotel suite with John and there's this music playing. And I said to Joni, "What's this fucking music? It's shit, can't you take it off?" And she said, somewhat predictably, "It's my latest album" [*Don Juan's Reckless Daughter*]. That was the only time I saw John Lydon go red.'

Letts also remembers a minor stalking problem for John Lydon: 'The girlfriend of Dirty Harry, the top horn player, developed an obsession with John that caused us plenty of consternation. She'd be sipping champagne with us and Dirty Harry would be glowering from the corner or whatever. And the island was pretty wild then; at night, there'd be horsemen with guns chasing people as they legged it past the hotel.'

As Morris later confirmed, 'I think it was all a bit of a culture shock for Don – he'd never been to Jamaica before.'

To Lydon's chagrin, also on the island was Glitterbest employee John 'Boogie' Tiberi, under express orders from Malcolm McLaren to film John's response to the question, 'Who killed Bambi?' Lydon's reaction could then be inserted into the Pistols' feature film *The Great Rock'n'Roll Swindle*. (The *Swindle*'s unfilmed predecessor, 'Who Killed Bambi?' concerned the music industry's assassination of youthful innocence, as symbolised by the much-loved Disney cartoon deer Bambi). For all Boogie's troubles – he spent hours hiding in undergrowth – all he got was a fully-dressed bath as he was 'captured' by his prey and thrown in the hotel swimming pool. For most of those present it was all very amusing but for Lydon it showed that, even over two thousand miles from home, there was no escape from the pressure, the harassment.

It was also an early indicator that problems, and attitudes, from Lydon's recent past were not going to fade away gracefully.

03
john's children:
this ain't no romance

It's hard to recall today the ambivalent cultural mood circa 1978. Although much has been made of punk rock's domination of the singles charts in 1977, the Sex Pistols (and to a lesser extent The Stranglers) had been its only band to truly enjoy major hits and high sales. Furthermore, the sales power of the more established pre-punk acts was intact – Paul McCartney & Wings had spent two months at number one with 'Mull of Kintyre', Abba continued to score number one hits, and Elton John, Genesis and Rod Stewart were as popular as ever. If anything, it was disco that had invaded the singles charts – Donna Summer, Chic and The Bee Gees' soundtrack to *Saturday Night Fever*. And perhaps the most unlikely hit of early 1978 was the cult reggae single 'Uptown Top Ranking' by Jamaican female duo Althia & Donna, which had graduated from John Peel airplay to a huge-selling number one hit.

The interest in what ex-Pistol Johnny Rotten would do next, meanwhile, was intense to the point of claustrophobia. The February trip to Jamaica and the camaraderie there with Dennis Morris and Don Letts had inadvertently convinced Johnny that there were several key criteria for any musical venture he would be involved in. Trust was, perhaps, the key issue. After the outrageous machinations of McLaren, the bulk of any John Lydon-led band would be composed of Lydon friends or friends of friends. Those Who Could Really Be Trusted.

To prevent the above alliance being disrupted there would be no manager. Ever. As Lydon was to tell music author Mike Nicholls the very next year, 'You can't trust anyone in this business, not anyone – they're all crooks.' Nor would there be any of the managers' sound studio equivalent – the big name producer – hanging around the new band.

Another criterion that would be easier to achieve without any mixing desk maestros was innovation – the group's structure and sound would be like nothing else before. The rapier slash of modern rock guitars somehow mixed with the bass rumble of reggae. But that was just one notion – there could also be rants, poems, movie score parodies, ironic ballads, free-form arrangements and even some bitter jokes. Lou Reed meets Prince Far-I, Captain Sensible meets Captain Beefheart. In fact, anything at all. In Lydon's own words, 'No uniforms, no labels, no tags, no tours, no set ideas. If it ain't danceable, don't do it. Music's all bullshit anyway, it's all just the heartbeat, so why not make the bullshit enjoyable?'

PiL were not going to put out mere records but objects. Morris could supply the photos and visual ideas. John Gray was another ideas man with a huge and diverse music collection who could also chuck in some original clothes. The latter could also come from Kenny Mac-Donald, the co-owner and chief designer of the fashion stall Marx in Chelsea's Great Common Gear Market. Keith Levene, if he could be found, could bring his considerable guitar skills to the party. Don Letts and his girlfriend Jeannette Lee could help with any promo videos that might be needed. Drums remained, and would always remain, a major problem for Lydon's next group. And there was the matter of the bass...

'I remembered Wobble,' Lydon said later, 'I thought, "A-ha, he can play bass a bit – vaguely!" Let's give him a call.'

In March 1978, Jah Wobble, now back at his parents' house for nearly three months after falling out with a friend in a Borough squat, received the all-important phone call from his former flatmate. 'I certainly wasn't expecting a call from him. I'd had two years of being a waster at a young age 'cos I couldn't find my niche in life. And you know what that working class thing is like – no one ever says, "Oh, you're really good at that" – but maybe John had seen I was pretty good on the bass front. Me parents were soon looking to tell me to fuck off again – and they were probably right – because I just wasn't working at all.'

Wobble's arrival, with a hat-full of attitude and bass ideas, was not initially welcomed by Dennis Morris who at one point was even short-listed to share bass guitar duties with him. 'We almost had a big fight over that,' the lensman recalls, 'after Wobble turned up, over who was gonna be the bass-man, but Wobble was much more passionate about it and he was right – the best bassist won that particular argument and got the gig. And so I stuck to me cameras.'

As well as contributing plenty of what would now be called 'marketing ideas', Morris had already started capturing the Public Image experience on 35mm stills film. 'John is very image-conscious,' he said decades later, 'you could never tell him where to stand or what to wear. Much more so than the others. I knew they were important. And that's reportage to me – you go looking for a story that's interesting and maybe important and you get into it. I shot dozens of rolls of film of those guys then, only about two per cent has ever been seen. I just kept shooting, and thought I'd maybe worry about selling the pictures later.'

John Lydon could have been in front of more than stills cameras if things had gone the way he wanted. As Wobble recalls, 'John was short-listed for one of the main roles – maybe the main role – in that *Quadrophenia* movie. I was quite intrigued 'cos The Who's album was the soundtrack of my adolescence. So John went along to several auditions and seemed to be close to getting something big out of it.' Lydon's audition was unsuccessful – Phil Daniels and Sting landed the two starring roles – but in Wobble's opinion, it was a lucky escape: 'I'm glad John didn't get the part, really, because the film was pretty bad in my opinion, it's well overrated, especially when compared with the album...'

For the role of lead guitarist in his new project, Lydon remembered the disillusioned Clash guitarist in the Sheffield pub over 18 months earlier: 'I'd been up in Mill Hill, away from the centre of town,' says Keith Levene, 'doing various things including an album with Ken Lockie. He was someone who could play piano and keyboards and who could sing quite well. I'd never really worked with anyone like him before so that was interesting. Anyway, one day in the spring I'm in Soho and a couple of people approached me – I think one of them was Paul Young, one of John's friends from way back. And they said, "Where have you been all this time? John Rotten's been looking for you". And that was the start of it. Wobble I'd already met before and we both knew John so we just got on with it.'

According to Wobble, 'Keith was the best musician on that scene by a country mile. He had a wonderful harmonic sensibility. I'm pretty sure that he was classically trained. I mean his real name is Julian and that goes hand in hand with piano lessons in leafy North London suburbs, but it would of course be a complete anathema to a bloke like that to admit their bourgeois background. Most of those people around those squats were like that, nice boys and girls from the home counties, temporarily slumming it. Most of them were pretty well educated. That's one of the reasons that I quite like Strummer, he was smart enough not to try and hide that.

'Anyway Julian, sorry Keith, certainly wasn't a musician to 'initiate' things in regards to getting new songs written. He always needed somebody else, such as me, to start proceedings. Where his help was invaluable to me was in the more general areas; how do you work a PA, how you get a good sound in the rehearsal room, and most importantly, how do you play and tune a drum kit. He was far more sensible and articulate about that stuff than most drummers are. His example led to me having a regular bash on the drums at quite an early stage in proceedings. Understanding drums really helped my bass playing.

'When I first met him he was helpful to me in regards to bass playing, "This is how it's tuned, like this", and, "I'll show you a couple of bass-lines that I've learned". But I'd always be like, "No give it to me now - I wanna do my own lines." I was never interested in learning other people's bass parts. I never heard Keith or any of those other musicians around that squat scene come up with a proper bass line. I just kinda knew how to play the bloody thing. It (the bass) felt "right" in my hands. I had a feel for the correct combination of open strings and octaves and fourths - I never called them fourths back then - in essence my feel is a very "old feel" very mediaeval and back to the origins of music, it is in essence really quite primitive.

'Plato would have liked it, actually - I dunno if you know Plato's *The Republic* but he was gonna bar certain kinds of music while keeping others that he liked. And the modes he's referring to, in regards to liking, are the modes that I tend to play. Very determined, ethereal, transcendental but not sickly sweet kinda modes. Not pop or rock. Plato would've fucked the New York Dolls right off. He would've shown them the doors of the city right away, "Thank you very much, now fuck right off!"'

The final piece of the new band's jigsaw was the drummer. In the classified section of *Melody Maker*'s 6th May 1978 issue, Virgin Records placed an advert which read 'Drummer wanted to play on/off beat for modern band with fashionable outlook and rather well-known singer'. Jim Walker, who saw the ad, had actually applied for the job nearly two months earlier. 'I'm a bit of a hunter,' he said later, 'and once I really want something, I'll stalk it. When the Pistols broke up I thought, "Rotten's got to be in another band soon and I'm gonna be in that band as well". So I wrote a letter to him straight away, soon as I heard about the Pistols' split, and then posted it to Virgin. He ended up getting it eventually but he later told me he just threw it in the bin saying, "Fuck this Yank!"'

'I just knew it was Rotten,' Walker says now. 'A mate of mine phoned up Virgin. Steve Someone answered, shitting himself, saying, "Anything could happen! Anything!" because of his somewhat tense relationship with Rotten, the whole Rotten thing. So I was ready for abuse – specially after being kept waiting for over eight hours by The Damned.'

Walker's first feeling at the audition was consequently one of disappointment. 'Well, I'm ready for anything, you know? Like fuck! I don't care either. "They can do what they like but I'm not gonna get pissed on – I'm gonna have my pride intact," that's how I went in. The rehearsal place was just off Tooley Street [near London Bridge], which looked all black and is like 500 years old. And I went down and the band had not turned up, not one of them's actually there.

'It was just me and this other would-be drummer – the guy just looked like an accountant or bank clerk or something. He was definitely never gonna be hired and that really wound me up because he was gonna be first in to play – 'cos it's all very competitive, this game. I was kind of tense but I just sat there, all quiet and composed like a boxer ready for the fight. And then they come in one by one. It's like, "Oh yeah, that's Rotten, I remember him".'

Mark Sanders was the 'bank clerk type', a teenager who seemed to be more than a little overwhelmed by the presence of Lydon, Levene and a surprisingly quiet Jah Wobble. After nervously playing for five minutes he hung around long enough to see Walker's try-out.

'Anyway,' says Walker, 'I had to put up with this other guy doing his stuff... And then I thought, "I've gotta get something out of this", so I said to Rotten, "You got a cigarette?" He just kinda stares at me so I said again, "You got a cigarette, please?" And he's, "Yeah, yeah, alright". And I take one thinking, "Good, I got something – no matter what happens, at least I got something, I got a cigarette off Johnny Rotten". Public Image didn't have that name back then – they didn't have any name as far as I can recall – so, of course, didn't have any songs either. So my audition song was [the Pistols'] "Belsen Was A

Gas". It went well. I was pretty explosive. I hit the drums so hard I was breaking them – I was so keyed up – and they loved that, of course. We played for about ten minutes and they were just like, "We want you!" Levene screamed out loud, "He's the one! He's The One!"

'And Lydon actually said to me, "I don't wanna let you out of my sight!" The weekend was coming up and he was worried that something would happen to me before Monday morning. Rotten just clung to me 'cos he knew I was valuable. I was like a sweeper in a football team, I could hold everything together. I wasn't that great a drummer but in punk terms I was a bit more than advanced. I knew what I was doing and he knew that. I told Rotten that I ripped off Paul Cook and that was real funny, 'cos when I saw the Pistols, I just watched Cook like a hawk. He's great, but he does one fucking beat, right? And I watched that beat all night, so it went into my DNA or whatever. He's a great drummer, basically, but I could do that thing a bit better.'

Many years later, Mark Sanders would collaborate with Jah Wobble on albums like *Passage to Hades* and the live recording *Largely Live in Hartlepool and Manchester*. But Walker was obviously the man for the, as yet unnamed, Public Image band, information that Lydon swiftly took to heart. Lydon himself told *Sounds'* Caroline Coon that most of those who answered the ad were 'terrible – denim-clad heavy metal fans' and described Walker as 'the only person I liked from the audition. He's amazing. He sounds like Can's drummer. All double beats.'

Jim Walker: 'Rotten then gave me the Lydon charm offensive... That's his technique, you know, when it starts off he's really charming, really nice. And you think, "Hey, what a nice guy, he's really nothing like you hear." I thought then, when I first met him, "I'd do anything for him, this guy's so cool, this is gonna be so great."'

Not that Walker was completely happy with the first musical line-up he saw – two guitarists, one of whom was Levene, the other being 'some kid with blonde hair: It's punk rock, for fuck's sake! It's bad enough having one guitar!' By the next rehearsal, the second guitarist was gone.

'Keith was the musical director of the band,' Walker continues. 'He's the greatest musician I've ever worked with. Ever. Levene understood music like nobody I've ever worked with, the guy was fantastically gifted; did a bit too much of the hard stuff but he wasn't doing that at first. He couldn't afford to at first. He seemed fine at the beginning, though – the whole band was great for about four months.'

Levene remembers the Walker audition rather differently: '[He] was number seven in line, in the queue of drummers who were auditioning for us that day. Lucky seven. And it turned out he was Canadian and we picked him and then he was in...'

That night, Walker returned to his shared house in suburban South London. 'I'd been able to practise before the audition because of this Income Tax payment from when I'd been working on building sites in Canada. That gave me the money to get this little house-share in Tooting which gave me the chance to drum,' he explains, 'and drumming is very athletic, you gotta keep at it. If you don't do it you lose your timing quickly. When your skill level drops, you're faking it and it's hard to fake being a drummer because it's very technical.

'It was a surreal band to join because it was a guaranteed success, 100 per cent guaranteed to chart after the Pistols. You were gonna go Top 20 no matter what.' And back in Tooting that night, Walker received a hero's welcome from his housemates: 'Their attitude to me has changed, because everyone's heard of Lydon, everyone's heard of Rotten, he's world famous now. And I'm different now, I'm worth a helluva lot more now, 'cos I'm in his band. It's like a light's shining on you, there's a difference, a distance. Already...'

04
number forty-five

Lydon's domestic retreat was located at Gunter Grove, near the World's End in Chelsea. Now terraced properties there cost in excess of a million pounds. In early 1978, Lydon bought part of number 45 with a £12,000 deposit. This was one further statement of his independence from the Sex Pistols, at a time when Paul Cook and Steve Jones in the Sex Pistols had continued to live in a house allegedly owned by Malcolm McLaren.

The move into Gunter Grove, believes Keith Levene, made Lydon reasonably content: 'John was relaxed a lot of the time there, I mean he'd moved around so much – different tours and squats and flats – and at Gunter Grove he finally had a base he could call his own.'

Reggae journalist, and Marley confidante, Vivien Goldman was a regular visitor at Gunter Grove. Described by punk chronicler Clinton Heylin as 'one of several substitute mother-figures' at Lydon's flat, Goldman remembered Gunter Grove as a great place to hear pre-release 12" reggae singles and dub platters on Lydon's powerful sound system. Huge state-of-the-art speakers would blast out reggae tunes at incendiary volume at all hours of the day and night.

Don Letts would hang out there a lot and took Dr Alimantado, whose 'Born For A Purpose' was a Lydon favourite, round to meet the PiL man. A more unlikely pair of reggae guests were Althea and Donna, then riding high with camp classic 'Uptown Top Ranking' who turned up at one of Lydon's many house parties.

Number 45 also had an accessible flat roof where more 'partying' could take place, although as Jah Wobble remembers, 'Considering the amount of drinking and larking around on that roof, it's a minor miracle that no one went over the side, 'cos they would've died, for sure. It was a long old drop.' Morris used the roof, and World's End skyline, as a backdrop for group pictures that went round the world. The still unnamed band cavorted, posed and mucked around in OTT costumes as their in-house lensman clicked away.

Lydon himself did indeed seem to love Gunter Grove, despite the peeling wallpaper and impromptu sofa – made from two old mattresses – partly because it was a magnet for all sorts of young Londoners. 'I love visitors,' he announced shortly after moving in, 'they're strictly here for my amusement, mind – I don't mind talking to people but I don't see why I should be a piece of public property all the time'.

Lydon even acquired a rat called Satan that he trained to fetch things. All the same, his place in the public eye, and all the attendant trivia, was something that Lydon wouldn't, or couldn't, ignore. 'He'd be looking in the mirror at two in the morning,' says Jim Walker, 'and he'd be going, "Oh shit, look, look there's a fucking wrinkle – shit! Shit!"'

The TV was permanently on, despite Lydon's frequent moans about British television's 'pathetic blandness', a blandness to 'hypnotise' the masses. Bemused visiting music journalists would find Wobble 'enthusing' about Edwardian soap opera *The Cedar Tree*, or dub reggae blotting out the sound on *Bruce Forsyth's Big Night*. 'I don't watch TV in the same way,' Lydon later claimed, 'I can see the humour in it, I love the bad acting!'

The problem with Gunter Grove was that the annexe wasn't part of the initial deal. 'Rotten bought the annexe flat later,' says Walker, 'and to do it he needed to borrow £15,000 off his lawyer Brian Carr. I stayed in that place for months, it saved me from coming up from Tooting so it was convenient, at least at first...'

As well as band members Levene, Wobble and Walker, a loose support organisation was operating around Lydon. This included his old friend Dave Crowe, and a new girlfriend, German publishing heiress Nora Forster. Forster, by now in her mid-thirties, was the very glamorous former partner of top session guitarist Chris Spedding. She was also the mother of the teenage Slits singer Ari-Up.

'Nora was the reason that I knew I'd made it,' says Jim Walker, 'she was a really cool broad. In fact when I met her, I really knew I was in a big band. She was this not-all-up-there German blonde chick but she was really nice.'

Nora's presence guaranteed home-cooked food, or failing that constant takeaways, although in her absence, the kitchen chez Lydon was a forbidding place: several Hells Angels were once literally served 'shit sandwiches', and omelettes were regularly spiked with dog ends.

Yet the whole PiL mood at this time was pretty positive. The four-man group were to split recording royalties and song publishing equally – 25 per cent each. Everyone was happy. 'Everything's to be shared equally,' Lydon told more than one reporter, 'we produce equally, write equally and share the money equally. There's no Rod Stewarts in this band. This is just the beginning of a huge umbrella organisation...'

'We were very, very close at first, 'cos we didn't have any money,' says Jim Walker. 'We worked five days a week, we had a rehearsal room that Virgin paid for... We were a proper little band – young kids, world at our feet – getting a set together. And we had all the drink we could drink – somehow.'

Walker also remembers the camaraderie extending to Lydon's family: 'I went to Finsbury Park, to the Sir George Robey pub with his family, these fantastic Irish people. I didn't even know I was part Irish at the time but you instinctively know, I liked them – they were just proper people. And I felt really sad for Rotten 'cos I knew that he couldn't walk the streets like normal people. I remember once he was asking his Mum to get him some spice or just something from the shop and my heart went out to him 'cos I'm this romantic kinda sad fool – punctuated by a ruthless son-of-a-bitch streak – but my heart went out to him 'cos I thought, "This poor fucker can't even walk the streets". I felt very protective of him as well and I thought, "Yeah, I'll fight for this guy, I'll do or die, I'll do what I have to do, if this is serious – I'm in for it".'

Seemingly, Lydon's past could only be distanced through violent means. On one occasion in August 1978, Sid Vicious and his girlfriend Nancy Spungen, both pitifully addicted to heroin, were chased away by an axe-wielding occupant of number 45. They left for New York soon afterwards. A day or so later, producer Dave Goodman arrived at the house: 'They greeted me with an axe and mentioned the incident. They were all really skint and hungry and I gave them my bus fare so that they could buy themselves some chips. Later on John came back and got annoyed 'cos they'd left the milk out of the fridge and it had gone off! He stormed off upstairs and I ended up walking home.'

Future Lydon collaborator Neil Barnes of Leftfield had visited the house aged just nineteen in the company of 'a mutual friend'. In 1995, he told *Mixmag* that Lydon 'was a right cunt, even worse than he is now. He completely took the piss out of me.' Not that this bothered the star-struck teenager: 'He was a total fucking hero? I mean, how could he not be?'

Simon Mattock, journalist and latterly film-maker, was another one who called round. 'I was just 17 then, up in Coventry, when I met Jock McDonald who said – well, implied – that he's PiL's manager. He offered to sell me this painting that John Lydon had done. It was called "Cat Shit" or something crazy. I didn't have enough cash to buy it but he told me Lydon's address in Gunter Grove.'

Having only passed his driving test two weeks earlier, Mattock borrowed his holidaying mother's car, and drove down to Chelsea. 'You could just imagine the pressure that came with that house. First thing I noticed was the graffiti [outside] – the words to "Religion" were gouged in the front door but there were words everywhere; door, doorframe, window-sills, walls. Some of it nice – a lot of it not so nice. The public, fans and enemies, were encroaching on your private life – I mean, they were within three inches of it, scribbling away.'

Spotting Nora after hours of waiting, he managed to 'work up the nerve to ask if John's in. And, even at the time, I felt like a school-kid asking if his mate can come out to play. She says, "No, but come in and wait anyway," probably 'cos I'm covered in PiL badges.' Lydon eventually returned and surprised Mattock with a series of gifts: 'John gave me a t-shirt, a single and a pair of trousers – "I won't be needing these anymore," he said.' He was also given a rather less orthodox free gift: 'A council rates bill! Which he suggested I pay, a notion that freaked me out for a minute. I thought he was deadly serious at first!'

That afternoon, with tea to boot – 'Can you imagine any big new star today inviting you in, giving you tea and clothes and stuff?' – was not the end of Simon Mattock's connection with PiL: 'Later on, after keeping in touch, I designed some clothes for PiL which they wore onstage, on album covers, on promo videos and on TV. I became good friends with most of them – especially Martin [Atkins] and Wobble.'

While Mattock remembers a hospitable, if eccentric, household, others recall the atmosphere in such surroundings as somewhat darker. X-Ray Spex singer Poly Styrene had a virtual nervous breakdown at Gunter Grove, bloodily hacking all her own hair off one endless night, forcing the others to call an ambulance. Shortly after, her manager appeared with two men in white coats and literally took her away. She has since spoken of a sinister, almost occult, mood at the Grove with crucifixes turned upside down and rooms in total darkness though Levene denies this is a realistic view. 'Poly was probably just very young at the time and took things the wrong way. I mean, if you got upstairs at Gunter Grove you'd find it was fun, people just having a laugh, having a chat, playing a bit of music, watching TV. Whenever I was there it wasn't that heavy – wasn't heavy at all, not really...'

THE ROYAL BOROUGH OF KENSINGTON & CHELSEA			
GENERAL RATE —			

			REFERENCE NUMBER
MR JOHN LYDON 45 GUNTER GROVE, S.W.10.			2414 072 03C

DESCRIPTION OF PROPERTY AND DETAIL	RATEABLE VALUE	RATE IN £	AMOUNT NOW DUE
	£	£	£
1ST AND 2ND FLOORS MAIS PLUS ARREARS	388	1.344	521.47 539.71

1 APRIL 1983	AMOUNT PAYABLE	1061.18

Lydon's Gunter Grove rates bill, 1983, £1061.18, and overdue

'There were three main drugs floating around – heroin, weed and speed,' says Don Letts. 'Me and John had nothing to do with the heroin, I know that, but there was just loads and loads of stuff. So, because of all this drug consumption, it's like every single person in the room, in the house, is always on a different level. Some people have said it was like a non-stop party but it was weirder than that, darker than that. There was more unsaid than said, y'know... I used to go round there myself to listen to music. John and me had become friends because of music, because of reggae and the love of bass thing. He'd be impressing me with his 12-inchers and I'd come up there with pre-releases. That's how we communicated. Keith spent most of his time down in the annexe part of John's apartment – it was like two separate parts almost. And Keith spent his time down there and did whatever he did. He didn't hang and socialise much upstairs. People say you have to suffer for your art. Well if that's true then Public Image really made it cos they really fucking suffered for their art – and some of them revelled in that suffering too. There was just so much attitude. Nice guys don't make great music, let's just put it that way.'

Letts wasn't the only 'non-punk' visitor to Gunter Grove. 'Little Debbie Wilson and Youth from Killing Joke were always hanging round,' he says, 'but I think I was the only guy there who also went round to see The Clash, the only guy who straddled both camps – I mean I only ever saw Joe Strummer round there once or twice though Paul Simonon would come round more often. But when the vibe got too dark and heavy at Gunter Grove that's what I'd do – I'd just get out and go see Joe Strummer.'

Jah Wobble agrees that there was increasingly a lack of warmth and empathy at Gunter Grove: 'Yes that started to creep in towards the end of 1978 and got increasingly worse through 1979. There had been a nice vibe around Gunter Grove to start with, we had some nice parties there and all that, but through 1979 things got dark and depressing, consequently for me it got quite boring. What did my head in was the torpor, as soon as I'd walk in there and sense the down vibe I'd want to walk out again and go back east to Stepney.

'This is my first band, I want to be working not sitting around Gunter Grove with a load of fucking freeloaders, so I'd piss off; I had a regular girlfriend and another life completely separate from PiL. The PiL thing wasn't something that I lived breathed and slept 24 hours a day. I don't actually think it was a terribly unusual scene as compared to other HQ's of big rock stars, except maybe there was even more lethargy displayed at Gunter Grove than in most other bands containing heroin users and heavy dope smokers. I bet that the vibe around the Stones two streets away a decade earlier had been in essence pretty similar to PiL. Basically what you have is a bunch of not very nice people, insecure misfits who for the first time in their lives can have people at their beck and call at all hours of the day and night.

'Consequently there would be all sorts of flotsam and vulnerable people turning up there, upper class junkies, or people like that Poly Styrene girl, please God things turned out okay for her. I remember that on a couple of occasions there'd be married women, a good few years older than us, who had kids somewhere, a home to go to and everything, hanging around, for hours on end, for no good reason, vaguely hoping to get closer to this, this thing, this fame, this power.

My only defence throughout that time was to take the piss to be honest. Humour is a wonderful antidote to decadence, even then I knew that. Towards the middle of 1979 I would only go to Gunter Grove to get my wages.'

However Wobble's sense of humour – and, possibly, his latent sense of decency – ensured that many of the more disturbing events occurred when he was absent. Others speak of violence and intimidation, of insults and humiliation, of soft and hard drugs – quite apart from the 'Sid and Nancy axe' incident, locals' pets were said to have been mutilated and scorched, one fan was assaulted and left bleeding, and another had their record collection burnt.

'To be honest, the atmosphere there always had an undertone of evil, that's the only word I can think of that describes it,' Jim Walker says now, 'an undertone that got stronger and stronger as time went on. All these hangers-on rolling John's joints for him, and desperately taking the piss out of each other. Squabbling over drugs. People humiliating themselves, people humiliating others.'

'It was like The Addams Family house,' Don Letts would recall in his 2007 memoirs. 'When you went round to Gunter Grove it was like a trial by fire. John would fuck with you. If you had a weakness, John would find it. It was almost like people were coming round for John's entertainment and would walk out of that place psychological wrecks.

'There was a real thing about trying to get John, keep John, get the ear of John,' says Wobble, 'like it was the court of King Louis or something. Everyone sitting round, taking drugs for hours and hours. And everyone needed a bath. And it's kinda frustrating 'cos I'm like, "John, trust me, listen to me, I'm speaking sense. Forget all the hangers-on and let's do this band thing properly". There's a lot of energy vampires out there, looking to sap your energy, looking to tap into power. Even though the power's usually a mirage. But John's kinda loyal and I think he's sometimes loyal to the wrong people. I suppose I made similar mistakes myself later.'

For Jim Walker the shocking change in mood was even more of a blow. He'd escaped an increasingly cold family atmosphere back in the Canadian mid-West – only to find that the initial Lydon welcome – with all its family warmth – was, in fact, an illusion. 'Hell is an absence of love,' he says now, 'and that [was] Gunter Grove – total indifference. I remember once feeling so low in that basement that I took some of Levene's heroin with him. We were hiding down there like little kids, and smack makes you feel as if you're a little kid anyway, that's part of its evil appeal, part of its shit.

'Anyway, when we came back upstairs, Lydon knew what we'd been doing and he made some "you're a junkie" joke remark about me 'cos I'd always been Mister Clean in his eyes. But he was only kidding, of course, he didn't actually give a shit if I became a junkie or not, he couldn't have cared less if I overdosed – me or anyone else. He didn't give a shit. Later that week one of the Arsenal fans came over, the guy was training to be an athlete so he could enter the Olympics, all that stuff – so, of course, everyone keeps egging him on until he takes stuff – speed or coke or maybe both. Then they give him more and more. That ruined that kid's whole week, possibly ruined his career, his life. It was horrible. I knew I had to get out...'

Dennis Morris sees it in a different, but equally harsh, light. 'The biggest problem was we suddenly had everything we'd ever wanted and we weren't really prepared for it. I remember sitting in John's lounge and we'd all made good money, and we were like, "Er, what we gonna do with it?" We couldn't spent it on Gucci clothes, because we had our own look, we couldn't spend it on a flash car 'cos that wasn't done, we couldn't go on some ski holiday. We couldn't even go outside sometimes as outside there were still people looking to attack you. We'd boxed ourselves in, basically.

'So at Gunter Grove, there was smoke everywhere, Levene was running round on his fucking skateboard half the time and he had bought all these remote control toys so there were foot-wide cars and helicopters whizzing past your ears and your feet all the time and John's got six kegs of Guinness going behind the sofa. Wobble was always full of his incredible energy and it was madness, so many mad incidents. Ari-Up came round once and John flicked a match at her – it hit the gel in her hair and went up, Whoosh! Half her hair was on fire. We just blew it, all the money, just spunked it away.'

Photographs of PiL in Gunter Grove at this time capture the mood – the earlier clowning around for the camera has all gone. Walker's girlfriend Carol no longer poses sitting on his lap, as Lydon has made it clear that she is not welcome there anymore. 'Lydon hated her 'cos she just wouldn't take any of his shit,' says Walker, 'She'd just insult and parody and bait him straight back. She sounded quite educated and that confused him too 'cos he wrongly assumed at the start that she was just this soft little Sloane Ranger girlie from some protected background and she's not. The accent's something she picked up in London; back in Glasgow one of her relatives was known as the Hard

Man of Maryhill. Tough fucking people that argue and fight for fun. In terms of intimidation, Lydon was small fry compared with that and she knew it and he knew it. So what does he do? He effectively bans her from the place. You have to laugh.'

This was just another indication that the game had changed. Others were more obvious – no one plays laughing games on the roof anymore. No one, in fact, bothers to even stand up for photos anymore. Instead Lydon stares defiantly at the camera, Don Letts hogs the sofa and a crestfallen Jim Walker stares down, avoiding the SLR's glass eye. All the while, both phone and front door would go unanswered.

For some of Lydon's neighbours, there was rarely a dull moment. Photographer Mary Harrison-Goudie and her husband Rui Castrovsky, a Portuguese radio presenter and journalist, also lived in Gunter Grove. In September 1978, they told *Sounds* reporter Andy Courtney that they had received three promotional copies of the 'Public Image' single through their letterbox. They had also accidentally opened a letter addressed to Lydon from the anarchist organisation Black Cross, who were asking his new band to perform at a benefit for three jailed anarchists.

Band members and visitors remember few complaints from neighbours – an allegedly 'deaf' couple living in the basement never seemed to object – although admittedly, the atmosphere could be so intimidating that such opposition would not dare to make its voice heard. Nora Forster later told the *Mail on Sunday* in 2004, 'We had terrible scenes there. A neighbour complained about the noise because John was banging up and down on the piano for a couple of hours. When somebody dumped water over his head, he came back with a knife.'

By early 1980, police raids were in danger of becoming commonplace at number 45. In early February, one such visit had, reported *Sounds*, made the place look 'less tidy than before'. Then at around 6.30 on the morning of Wednesday 13th February 1980, only hours after a PiL performance had been transmitted on BBC2's *The Old Grey Whistle Test*, the reality of the group's sullied reputation came crashing through the front door at Gunter Grove. A big police raid found Lydon waving a ceremonial sword from the top of the stairs. Despite the damage to the door, and the hour-long police search that followed, PiL were lucky that night – the property yielded no more to the cops than a tear gas pen...

Still, remembers Don Letts, 'John was taken down the cop shop, bare-footed in his dressing gown and pyjamas. He had to walk back down the Fulham Road and all the way back to Gunter Grove dressed like that. He was seriously pissed off.'

For the group, and Lydon in particular, the constant scrutiny and tension was becoming unbearable. Something would have to change. Don Letts maintains this incident would be instrumental in Lydon's eventual decision to relocate to New York.

05
unlimited supply:
theirs not to reason why

The first press interview with John Lydon's new group appeared in the *NME* on May 27th 1978, in an article called 'Johnny Rotten Doesn't Live Here Anymore', which was written by editor Neil Spencer. Jah Wobble, who claimed to have only seriously begun playing the bass a month before the interview took place, was quoted as saying that 'Rock is obsolete', and while enthusing about how rock music was starting to assimilate dub's adventurous tendencies, cited Elvis Costello & The Attractions as capturing this burgeoning style particularly effectively. The group even had a name – supposedly 'The Carnivorous Buttockflies' – although no-one was taking that one terribly seriously. For a *Sounds* interview published on 22nd July, punk champion Caroline Coon noted several other 'joke' names, including 'The Future Features', 'The Corney Various', 'The Windsor Up-Lift' and 'The Royal Family'.

But it was the headline for Coon's feature that contained the new band's actual name: 'Public Image: John Rotten and the Windsor Uplift'. As well as Lydon rather idealistically hoping that the band would be playing gigs within six weeks – Coon suggested six months would be more like it – he offered some kind of description of that most over-used of words: 'Punk is against hypocrisy, monotony, consistency. It's against the unacceptable face of capitalism, against religion, against any organised establishment movement. Basically they're all evil'.

The band's new name was soon extended to Public Image Limited before Dennis Morris threw in an idea: 'I suggested shortening it to PiL and then I added the aspirin logo with the reversed "i". I didn't have it ready until after the first single. I didn't do it all on my own either – I mean, John's a wonderful person to work with, to bounce ideas off in a really magical way.'

The same week as the *Sounds* interview, Lydon turned critic for the *NME*. Apparently paid £100 for his trouble, he penned a page of pithy comments under the headline of 'Would You Pay This Man Money For Writing The Singles?' Over-fond of feeble punning – renaming Steve Harley as 'Steve Hardly', for example – as well as sideswiping at sheer irrelevance like Simon Park's theme tune to the Noel Edmonds TV quiz *Hobby Horse*, Lydon's singles page rarely got any more cutting or savage than dubbing The Human League's 'Being Boiled' as 'Trendy Hippies' and reacting to Steely Dan's 'FM' with 'More West Coast dirge well below the level of human integrity'.

Meanwhile, the rumblings of PiL's very earliest material were taking shape. As with most of PiL's work in 1978, it was the rhythm section that had many of the most inspiring ideas. 'I think we kicked off a lot for them,' says Jah Wobble. Jim Walker goes further still: 'Me and Wobble started every song when I was in the band. Every single song that year. Either he'd come up with a bass line and I'd join in with a beat or I'd come up with a beat and he'd jump in. Then Keith would build on the riff we'd given him with his guitar and, when it was all done musically, Rotten would add the lyrics.'

But neither of the earliest numbers would ever see the light of day. 'The original "Cowboy Song" wasn't some joke number,' according to Walker, 'It was this fantastic Irish style ballad, this really moving song that, lyrically, John just improvised – it was the kind of thing that The Pogues or even U2 made a fortune with later on but Lydon's take on it was much, much better. It was phenomenal. Superb. But he suddenly didn't want to do the song anymore so that was it. End of story. I think there might be a rough demo somewhere but that's it, that's all that remains of this fantastic number.'

The second PiL song, 'You Stupid Person', also disappeared – and remains similarly unreleased at time of writing. 'That was a good one,' says Wobble, 'a really strong song.' Other PiL insiders rate it as one of their best-ever tracks but its lyrical content – which may have referred to Nora Forster – might have been just too contentious. In the end 'You Stupid Person' was quietly dropped.

But despite the false starts, and the quiet periods, a new sound was being forged. Levene's smoothly abrasive guitars were finding their perfect counterpart in Wobble's earth-shattering bass and Walker's fluidly pounding beats. As Walker puts it, 'We were four total maniacs making extreme music. We could do just about anything we wanted – musical nirvana!' Levene feels much the same: 'PiL was an extension of that punk attitude – the Pistols took things as far as those individuals could take them, and then PiL took things further.'

Anthony H. Wilson, the Manchester writer and music entrepreneur who first dared to put the Pistols on TV, sees it in broader terms. 'Obviously, one gives credit to Joy Division for creating post-punk. Because, in the end, all punk could say was "fuck you". Sooner or later someone was gonna need to use punk instrumentation and punk attitude to express more complex emotions. And that was what Joy Division did. I think what PiL began to express was more complex music without going pompous and the rest of it. To me it was very musical, it was very noisy but had real melody there, all the way through it.' His view is shared by another future prime mover in the music business, Alan McGee, then a teenager working on the railways in Scotland. 'The Pistols were a bog standard rock band,' he says now, 'except that it was genius bog standard, but to leap from that to PiL's avant-garde eclecticism was fucking amazing. If a band like Public Image came out now, they'd still be big – and they'd still be ahead of the game.'

Whilst PiL's diverse dynamism marked them out as 'post-punk', they shared punk's original vision of 'the outsider as artist'. Yet for Lydon, PiL's raison d'etre was simple and almost flippant: 'We only wanna be in a band in order to escape the boredom of everyday life. Being taken seriously makes the whole thing seem so ridiculous.'

At the end of July 1978, Lydon and the rest of the group arrived at Advision Studios to record the song that had given the group its name. 'Public Image' had been inspired by Muriel Spark's 1968 novel *The Public Image*, about the trials and tribulations of fame as experienced by a hyped but talentless actress. John Leckie, then the engineer at Advision, later told *The Independent*: 'The band all had new equipment, which hadn't been unpacked.' When both he and his assistant Ken Thomas briefly left the studio, they returned to find that 'Jah Wobble had turned every knob and pushed every button on the desk.' After two days recording the backing tracks at Advision, the track was completed at Wessex, the 24-track studio behind a Protestant church at 106 Highbury New Park, Islington. Two years earlier, Wessex had been the venue for the much-acclaimed early version of 'Anarchy in the UK' produced by Dave Goodman, which EMI had rejected. The engineer at Wessex, Bill Price, had not only already worked with the Pistols, but everyone from Mott the Hoople to Caravan, but his assistant 'Jerry' was to clash with Jah Wobble later in the pub.

'The guy really had been winding me up all day,' Wobble insists, 'ignoring me, giving me dirty looks, being rude. And I'm thinking, "Hang on, we're paying you good money for this, I don't need your shit." He was a martial arts guy who'd heard something about me and obviously fancied himself a bit. Anyway, he was a bit older and a lot bigger than me so when he starts being cheeky again in the Robinson Crusoe, I thought, "Right, that's it, you can fuck right off." But he really wanted a fight and so I gave it to him, gave him a bit of a hiding. It got messy, claret everywhere – his blood not mine, I hasten to add – but luckily Dennis Morris and his bird saved me from the police. They were in their motor and as all the Old Bill arrive with the flashing lights and the sirens and all that malarkey, I leapt in the back of Dennis' car and we sped off down Highbury New Park road before it got really silly.'

The next stop was to be Wessex, where the PiL tapes were 'liberated' in case there was to be any come-back over the night's trouble. Except that the tapes 'borrowed' weren't Public Image masters.

'What happened was we ended up going back to the studio after the fight,' Walker explained some quarter of a century later, 'and we ended up stealing, by mistake, these Dr Feelgood master tapes for their next album, which was *Private Practice*. We'd met them in the pub the night before and kinda got on. So then they phoned us up the next morning and said, you know, "You've got our tapes, we'll send a cab round".'

It might all seem like OTT high-jinks now but for the young Jim Walker both the fight and the tape 'theft' revealed a serious lack of professionalism. 'From that point on PiL was like being on a pirate ship. We weren't a real band anymore, 'cos I knew we weren't going to go back to Wessex. I never really liked the tape of "Public Image" 'cos I thought it wasn't quite good enough. I thought we were going to re-record it 'cos I thought we could do it better. But we didn't, we just did the vocals at Wessex and we mixed it – and I must admit that it sounded great. And I thought, "Great, we're gonna have a whole album at this kinda level". Some fucking hope!'

Despite the chaos surrounding its recording, 'Public Image' remains a startling debut single. It begins with Wobble's throbbing bass, sparse but catchy, and with a lighter touch than on the otherwise similar 'Boredom' by Buzzcocks. Before four seconds are up Walker's snare and ride cymbal crash in. After just two edgily perfect drum beats comes half a dozen defiantly cheery 'hullos' from Lydon, spoken in slightly different ways and mixed at different levels; they give the false impression of being in different places in the stereo field. It's also Lydon greeting a public that only knew Rotten. At once, Lydon's trademark cackle – an echo of his 'Anarchy in the UK' greeting – collides with Levene's thrashing yet chiming guitar, an insistent bravura piece of stringwork that's deceptively simple on first hearing. Then, the frontman launches into a dazzling lyrical attack – on his tabloid enemies as well as the one-note 'mohican punks' who only cared about the (dyed) colour of his hair.

French cover for debut single 'Public Image'

Apposite words for a former Public Enemy Number One: a public enemy with a large cult following who didn't, in the main, want him to change.

Levene's double-tracked note lacerations raise the stakes higher between verses, between Lydon's declaration that he will not be treated as property.

In the delivery of the choruses, Lydon's voice is always coming in a fraction of a second too late by normal standards. The effect, when combined with the track's 'reggae style' level of echo is surreal, endless almost, as the voice subliminally drifts into the next verse. Long after the track's finished the listener is half-convinced that, in some cavernous studio somewhere, Lydon is forever singing the smeared four syllables of the two word title.

The song, a debut disc remember, ends with the declaration that it is a finale, a 'goodbye' as tight reverb cuts it into short, sharp, fading slices.

One of Lydon's former bandmates – ex-Pistol bassist Glen Matlock was astonished: 'I don't know much about PiL, because I could never be truly objective about 'em, for obvious reasons, but when I heard their first single I thought, "Wow! This is really, really good".'

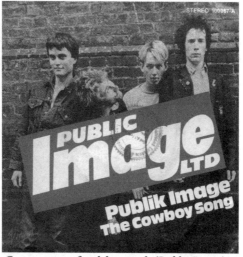

German cover for debut single 'Public Image'

According to Walker, when top Warner Brothers' music executive Bob Regehr heard 'Public Image' and three other songs he offered to fly the band to the USA where a million dollars would be spent promoting PiL and their completed album in October. It was an offer that Lydon surely couldn't refuse – but he did...

According to Dennis Morris, Keith Levene had initially wanted Public Image's first recordings to be produced by OTT metal guitarist Ted Nugent – famed for supposedly shattering wine glasses with feedback live onstage. Virgin were up for using Nugent, who did at least have some production experience, and even a reluctant Lydon was said to be considering it. This was despite the frontman saying about producers, 'Why should we give 25 per cent of our money to a music biz hippy who then tries to tell us how we should sound?'

There had also been talk of working with Dave Goodman as engineer. 'I said I was often in a studio full of weird instruments at midnight after some session and thought it would be great if he was there and just let loose on the instruments. He seemed really interested and said "Just call me when it happens, Dave"'.

But the collaboration would never reach fruition: 'Around that time I had to go up to Virgin to collect a gold record from Simon Draper,' said Goodman in 2001. 'Draper was this South African who was Richard Branson's second in command. He knew I'd caught a bit of some PiL rehearsals and asked me about it, basically asked me how good they were. Now I didn't even know then that they hadn't actually been signed by Virgin at that point – I thought they had – so I said that they were really good but maybe a little bit untogether – I was thinking of me walking home 'cos they'd eaten me bus fare! – but I said that I'd like to produce them. Anyway, as far as I can gather, Draper apparently then tried to turn what I said into a big put-down of the band. He wasn't a huge Public Image fan and I think he was using it as either an excuse not to sign them – or, maybe, he was just trying to get the price right down a bit. Anyhow, I then had them [PiL] believing I was trying to sabotage their Virgin deal.'

In the climate of the day, such a misunderstanding was dangerous – especially for Goodman. 'PiL came looking for me at the 100 Club when the Tribesman were playing. Wobble was a bit threatening – pushing his fist into my gut – though I wasn't seriously injured or anything. And then, later on the same evening, after we'd had a drink together, John Lydon was still really uptight and kept saying to me, "You're either working for yourself or you're working for McLaren!" When I said I didn't know what he meant, he just snapped, "You're full of shit, you're full of shit!"'

If Goodman had been alone, things could have turned even nastier. 'I was with my label partner Caruzo [Fuller] and, according to him, when I turned around Lydon raised this pint mug to glass me with. Caruzo grabbed his hand, calmed things down a bit. The main guy in the Tribesman said to me a few minutes later, "Let me deal with this, [Lydon] needs a good slap, I don't care who the fuck he is or who he's with."

'But I was just trying to calm things down at that point and told him to forget it. Thing is, I loved John and his work and I'd never have tried to damage his career – he should've looked elsewhere for his saboteur.'

Walker remembers that night too. 'I went along with it at the time – I was in the PiL gang, right? And that's when you have that gang mentality: "They're my boys, my mates, right or wrong, doesn't matter who they hit, doesn't matter who they hurt". But at the back of my mind I knew something stank that night – the way Lydon behaved, I knew it really stank.'

Walker's growing disillusionment with PiL was complete when the 'Limited corporation deal' was finally spelt out. Lydon's lawyer Brian Carr had drawn up agreements – the Public Image Limited company was not going to be split four ways equally as first envisaged. Lydon, and his legal representatives, were going to own a bigger share. The others – Wobble, Walker, Levene – were to receive £60 a week. Plus some publishing.

Wobble and Levene were mildly put out but Walker, with his commercial family background was outraged. 'We were meant to be a corporation – we were a corporation, or a limited company. We were meant to be shareholders, we were all shareholders, meant to be directors. But the shares were 52 per cent to Rotten and the rest of us got the dregs. I'm from a business family, I knew I was being robbed? And I phoned Levene and said, "Look, we're being robbed here, you know this, right?" And he's, "Oh, yeah, yeah, you're right, I'm with you" and all this. My idea was to get everybody together and say to Rotten, "Look, we've been discussing this, what the fuck's going on here? Let's work this out." At least we had something then, some kinda leverage. He was fucked without us. What was he gonna do without us? Look what he's done without us. Nothing. He hasn't really grown. Him and Levene are basically the same as they were 25 years ago.'

Having lost control of the Pistols and even, at one point, his stage name, Lydon was not going to allow more than the illusion of equality – for better or worse. 'Later, basically, we were in rehearsal,' continues Walker, 'and I never thought a rehearsal room was a place to argue about business – but Rotten just said, "That's it, right! Stop the rehearsal!" And Rotten has this big go at me in rehearsal. And Wobble has a go at me as well, saying, "We didn't know you from Adam, you lucky bastard, you got this great opportunity we let you in on and you start bleeding moaning"...'

As a trained musician, Walker was not impressed with such arguments. 'I'm not saying nothing, I'm keeping quiet but I'm thinking, "I don't need this band, I don't need anything, I'm not in this band 'cos I'm somebody's friend – I could walk out and join any band I like".' For Walker, the tongue-lashing from Lydon was one thing. Keith Levene's response was quite another. 'Levene just completely turned in front of me. There was no mention of the fact that he'd agreed with me totally just a few hours before – he just completely fell into line like a dog that's been beaten. And I more or less thought then, "Well that's it, I'm leaving – I'm leaving when it suits me".'

Despite Wobble's apparent support for Lydon, he too was less than impressed with the deal. 'I knew it was pretty bad, just about everybody that I asked thought that it seemed dodgy, but I thought, "Nah, I'll go along for the ride, John'll sort us all out in the end"...'

Despite Morris' wish to get the band to Island Records – a move Wobble and Walker had also supported – PiL signed to Virgin, an eight-album deal for £75,000. For Lydon and Brian Carr it made sense – although Branson's Virgin was hardly a hip label, they had grabbed the Pistols. For PiL, signing with them was the quickest, easiest thing to do in terms of possible legal complications, and it also ensured Carr got his loan to Lydon repaid promptly. Complications were multiplying anyway as Lydon sued McLaren for the Pistols' 'missing' millions. Things had reached such a low point between McLaren and Lydon that there was no possibility of them talking it out between them – it was an impasse that was to cost McLaren control of the band and *The Great Rock'n'Roll Swindle* feature film (and cost Lydon and the other Pistols hundreds of thousands in legal fees and receivership bills).

Meanwhile, just as Virgin in the UK continued its association with Lydon, so did Nippon Columbia in the Far East. Having previously signed the Pistols, the latter label secured a Japanese deal for PiL to the tune of £18,000.

There was also a £30,000 PiL publishing deal though this wasn't actually signed in 1978 – partly, perhaps, because there were not that many songs to be published, initially. 'There was a long time between doing the single and the album,' Morris says, 'maybe weeks, maybe months, maybe even more... at that time John and I used to get a lot of ideas from records, we'd always be exchanging records, singles, albums, 12-inchers, bootlegs, whatever. I had a more varied collection than him but he'd always have these really obscure reggae things. It was all very organic, generic – things were allowed to grow, ideas-wise and music-wise. It wasn't false and forced like a lot of music is now. PiL were left to their own devices a lot and the only person who could communicate with them all and with the label was me. In some ways I became the link to the label. I was also taking the album pictures and publicity pictures and coming up with the stage lighting.'

Morris' calm manner tended to dilute some of Lydon's hostility towards Virgin – or any other label. It was an angry, bristling front that many, even within the group, didn't fully understand. 'From the minute we signed with Virgin,' claims Walker, 'Lydon said we had to be at war with them. Now Virgin was really run by Branson's first cousin Simon Draper and he ran it like a plantation. It wasn't efficient, no files, everything stacked up on desks for maximum confusion – you go in there to audit them and forget it, it would take you a thousand years just to organise it and that, obviously, could be seen as part of the strategy. "Yeah, come and audit us, find it all – if you can". But John was like, "Yes we have to cause trouble with Virgin". It wasn't that intelligent an attitude really. Virgin were more than incompetent enough as it was.'

For some it seemed as if the band were being taken for a ride, screwed by Virgin and the music biz generally. Surely a big-time manager could have got a better deal? They weren't all as fast and loose as McLaren, were they?

'Peter Grant wanted to manage us from the off, you know?' Walker avows. 'Led Zeppelin were on their last legs and we were the biggest up-and-coming thing and Grant's no fool. Can you imagine what he could've done? That guy took Led Zep to the top, sold tens of millions of records, brokered movie deals. He'd have made us massive in the States. But Rotten had this anti-manager hang-up – and I suppose someone's gotta see it from his point of view, he'd been bitched up by McLaren and he had a lot of wankers around him. Sycophantic people – some in high positions, someone who worked for the *Daily Mirror*, and they were all going, "Oh, keep control, Johnny, keep control! You don't need any managers, you don't need anyone!"

'There were just so many wasted opportunities with Public Image. The interest in us was growing out there in the States and Warners would have spent seven figures on us there, back then, when a million bucks really was a million bucks. You've got to hit the American heartland and you've gotta work for a living. This is a business, it's not just sitting around a flat, taking drugs and being grey. If you want a career then you have to do it, to work at it. But Lydon was more interested in "communications videos" and sitting around and mismanagement...'

With the PiL money being kept, at one point, in cash stuffed in a cardboard box under Lydon's bed at Gunter Grove, Walker clearly has a point about mismanagement. He was also right about the publishing. It would take 16 years for Wobble to get the monies he was owed – and when they arrived they were considerably diminished by the simple fact they'd been kept in a non-interest bearing account all that time.

PiL, or rather John, had nominated Dave Crowe, another old Lydon pal, to collect receipts and be a free-form accountant. Former Acme Attractions beauty Jeannette Lee was to help out. Lee was to be the band's unofficial PR and organiser – she was also an ideas-woman who was hoping to shoot short films and videos to be inspired and/or scored by the band.

Jeannette Lee had previously been Don Letts' girlfriend and he brought her into the PiL mileu - they had met in 1975 at a soul night at the Lyceum. Six weeks later she was working with Letts in the legendary clothes store Acme Attractions. According to Letts's fine autobiography, Jeannette was the reason most customers came into the store. Later she ran Boy with Letts and introduced him to The Clash.

Jeannette [along with Lydon] had also helped Letts to edit his *The Punk Rock Movie* using scissors and sellotape. It was Letts, who shared a love of reggae with Lydon who introduced Lee to the ex-Pistol.

Neither Crowe nor Lee were fully qualified for their roles and the latter's was complicated by her affair with Keith Levene. 'Jeannette was always around, almost from the start,' Levene admits, 'she came in to do video ideas, and maybe film some things.'

'I used to go round there with Jeannette when we were still an item,' says Don Letts, 'but, increasingly she'd be hidden away with Levene in the annexe.'

'Later on she was my girlfriend, for a time,' admits Levene now, 'but she came in to Public Image mainly to do things on the video front. She had some great ideas for short movies, script ideas I suppose you would call 'em now. These ideas were mostly for 25-minute to 45-minute films, short films that could go to film festivals or TV channels or whatever – definitely not pop promo video MTV things. Brilliant ideas she had... but nothing really got finished, in the end. Which was a bit disappointing. We just didn't see it through in that way – Jeannette didn't ever seem to have time.'

Wobble takes a rather more jaundiced view of the 'video communications-short films angle' that PiL pursued. 'People like Jeannette Lee came in and Dave Crowe. I mean, God bless 'em and all that but... Jeannette - never really liked her that much at the time, thought she was a bit too clever by half. I just thought, "What's her job? What's she actually gonna fucking bring to the table?" you know. "What? It's her role to just look pretty and hold the Super-8 camera, is it? And pretend we're all in *Performance*? That's it, is it...?" And I don't really rate that film much to be honest. I actually asked her a couple of times, "Excuse me, Jeannette, but what do you actually do?" I remember her and Keith just glaring at me. But wisely they kept their fucking traps shut.'

For Wobble it was 'all play-acting... all crap. I know I did resent her at the time because I really wanted to get on with making music - and she wasn't really helping. She was also getting paid the same as the rest of us who were making the music that paid for it all. I think the general idea was to copy the sixties avant-garde, you know Andy Warhol and all that. However, there wasn't even much video shot. I remember thinking, "C'mon then, stop talking and get the fucking cameras out if you're really gonna make a film."'

The band's 'wages' were now regular and the cost of drink and drugs were no longer a big financial problem at Gunter Grove. Yet the mood there, even as the piecemeal recording of their debut album began, was hardly celebratory. 'Once we'd signed our contracts with PiL, once the money arrived that was it, Lydon didn't have to be friendly to us anymore. The whole mood began to change,' says Walker, 'we were just hirelings.'

'I kept looking for excuses, for reasons why I should stay with PiL,' reflects Walker, 'like when we were recording more stuff at that 16-track, Gooseberry, we all took loads and loads of coke, there were little dishes full of it everywhere and we all liked each other again. But, within minutes, I began to suspect that this was naive shit. I just knew it was only the drugs that were making us friendly to each other that day. Everyone hated everyone by then. It was all about hate and money. That's an awful vibe to try and make music in, it really is.

'And the sound was just so second rate there – I mean the bass guitar sounded OK at Gooseberry, that's why people went there I think – that and the fact it only cost £25 an hour or something – but everything else there was shit, basically, not in the same league as Wessex. Cracked equipment, mice, cockroaches. We were only using it 'cos it was so cheap, this hole in the ground in the middle of Chinatown. We recorded "Fodderstompf", "Attack" and "Low Life" there and, just listen to them, I mean really listen to them – it's terrible recording quality. Sounds like it was done on a dodgy 8-track or something. Terrible is the only word for it really. It was just so depressing being there.'

Before Walker got any more depressed there were other matters to attend to. Finishing off the debut album, the first gigs, the first public controversies. All of which were to bring fresh surprises, tensions and disappointments – and fresh headlines.

06
monopoly, public property: got what you wanted

Despite Jim Walker's growing anger and disillusionment, PiL were still on an upward curve in September 1978. On the 15th of that month, the promo video for the first single, 'Public Image', was shot. Don Letts claims to have directed the piece, although other sources place Peter Clifton at the helm, with Letts relegated to 'Art Director.' Whatever the credits, Letts played a pivotal role in making the video. The Branson-sponsored trip to Jamaica with Lydon had brought the two reggae fans much closer and Letts had started to hang out with the newly formed PiL. Letts was unique in the way he moved with ease between the PiL and Clash camps. Lydon asked the relatively green Letts to shoot the promo for PiL's first single at a studio in Olympia on 16mm camera with a full film crew. 'I was making the shit up as I went along,' Letts explained, 'having never been to film school.' Due to Letts' self-confessed 'total inexperience' he went for the 'safe option' of shooting the band playing in a dimly-lit studio. 'Again it was great of John to give me that job – he could have used anyone in the business and I'd never even shot a pop video before. And it helped get me loads of other work with The Clash and Bob Marley... It was one of the things that changed my life, basically.'

Still, it wasn't a straightforward process. 'Everyone in PiL was on different drugs,' Letts reflects. 'One person was up, one was down, one was coming in sideways.'

For the video John and Keith were clad in some wonderful gleaming zoot drape jackets, courtesy of Kenny MacDonald – 'People talk about Oswald Boateng as the black designer of all time,' says Dennis Morris, 'but Kenny was years ahead of him, was years ahead of his time – I'm sure he influenced all that Blue Rondo A La Turk crowd in the early 1980s, all of that slick suit thing.'

Wobble went in the opposite direction to the space-age zoot and appeared in the promo as a moody take on The Man With No Name, complete with round Western hat and gun belt: 'I was a big Clint Eastwood fan. So, of course, when you're a big kid like me and you're in a video, you dress up as Clint Eastwood in *A Few Dollars More*. Simple as that.'

With Dennis Morris snapping colour shots, Lydon sneering out the lyrics with his usual burning force as Levene swaggered beside him, everyone present sensed they were on the brink of something that would be both massive and fun. The video, while minimal, looked undeniably strong. 'I mean, it's no huge production, there's nothing that special about it whatsoever, it's just the band playing,' Letts said years later, 'but I think it works OK, I think I captured their performance, if nothing else.'

Even Lydon's somewhat aimless moves at the end couldn't disguise a superb promo that almost matched the song it accompanied.

The Public Image recording deal with Virgin had given the band an almost unprecedented level of creative freedom. 'It just wouldn't happen now,' comments Wobble, 'for a new band to be given the chance to control sound and artwork and everything, the industry just wouldn't allow it.'

There was even, Levene claims, encouragement for Lydon's wild side. 'Virgin wanted John to be even more outrageous. That was the kinda sub-text, it was made known to us that they were prepared to put up with a helluva lot from us. People have asked me if Richard Branson really hated the PiL stuff. He was quite into it really.' Jah Wobble: 'We invited ourselves onto Branson's boat... to play him demos of our stuff. On at least one of those occasions we couldn't even play the acetate to him 'cos his boat was listing to one side so much, that the needle kept falling off the record... Disorganised hippy shit, basically.'

But freedom's a double-edged sword – as well as classic releases it also allows throwaway nonsense like 'Public Image''s flipside 'The Cowboy Song'. No longer a modern but 'beautiful Irish ballad', it consisted of little more than painful screeching over a faint disco beat. Jim Walker remains embarrassed: 'We all sat round the mic drunk, did two takes screaming randomly, and without being too Joe Strummer about all this, there are kids out there with their 50 pence allowance buying this thing. They deserved better, they deserved a bit of value for money.'

Virgin's tolerance for outrageous lyrics, mad stunts and throwaway flip-sides didn't quite extend to the actual sound of the single itself. To ensure no label interference Lydon had been astute enough to be in on the mastering and to make sure the right metal masters made their way to the vinyl factory.

Within hours of delivery, though, the factory were contacted by Virgin who'd played their acetate copy and felt that the bass was way too loud and the vocals too low. A minor battle ensued but the group won the day, with Lydon subsequently labelling Virgin 'quite a little commune... the secretaries are groupies and they're all disorganised Hampstead hippies!'

In the midst of the PiL chaos, one member was already showing signs of breaking away. In October, the same month that 'Public Image' was finally released in the UK, Jah Wobble unleashed his first solo single, entitled 'Dreadlock Don't Deal With Wedlock'. 'It was better than sitting around all the time. When we started my attitude was, "I really wanna work, I can't understand why we're not working". No one in the band really objected at first because it was a novelty thing and I was known for clowning around. But it was me just getting on with it.'

At the time a heavy insomniac, Wobble would often be 'fucking about with short-wave radio and tuning into Radio Cairo'. His introduction to Arabic music, which would determine the direction of so many of his future solo records, came when he heard recordings of Egyptian singer Om Kalsoum, a performer so beloved by Egypt that when she had died in 1975, two million people reportedly attended her funeral. Wobble would later remember the impact of first hearing Arabic music as sounding 'so committed, so righteous, so awesome...'

By late September 1978, excitement was growing over the PiL debut. The forthcoming sleeve was whisked around one or two music press offices and caused a great stir – it was a mock tabloid newspaper that folded around the seven inch vinyl. The headlines and stories parodied current adverts as well as the various band members: Wobble had been 'wild with his chopper' until he joined PiL – a reference to the alleged axe attack on Sid – while Walker had to stand a dig at his middle-name, Donat, now printed as 'Dough-nut', and his relationship with long-time girlfriend Carol.

As far back as August, PiL had been offered a slot on ITV's new Saturday music show *Revolver*, which was presented by legendary comic Peter Cook and Birmingham-based DJ Les Ross. Made by the Midlands company ATV, *Revolver*'s concentration on punk rock scared the ITV network somewhat and after a teatime slot for the pilot edition in the spring, the series was banished to a late-night slot when it began in July. The producer of the series was prolific record producer Mickie Most, who had already expressed his admiration for John Lydon in a television interview. PiL's involvement in the edition scheduled for 19th August – two weeks after Sid Vicious had appeared – would have extended beyond playing a few live numbers, to actually selecting the other bands for the bill. But a lack of communication with Virgin meant that the label phoned the show direct, indicating that the group would be more than happy just to play the current single.

There are two versions of what happened next. According to 'official' PiL folklore, when the band heard the news they kept their annoyance under wraps – but just didn't turn up on the day of filming, preferring to get drunk at Camber Sands on the East Sussex coast instead. To add insult to injury they sent a few 'Having A Lovely Time – Wish You Were Here!' postcards to the Birmingham studios. Wobble later told a music reporter the band had used machetes to hunt down and butcher a cow in a nearby field, a story that, perhaps unsurprisingly, turned out to be fictional. Jim Walker's memory of the incident is, if anything, even more simplistic: 'Essentially, John had a bad case of stage fright.'

When Keith Levene was the only member of PiL to appear at ATV's studios, Mickie Most was, according to the national press, 'absolutely bloody furious' at the group's no-show, and said that Public Image would now be subject to an 'instant ban' from appearing on ITV, a situation that would last 'maybe 20 years'. A tight-lipped Virgin spokesman would only admit that the label felt a little uptight about it all. PiL win one – or two – bonus points on the street cred scale. Ironically, PiL's replacements on *Revolver* were the Rich Kids, featuring Glen Matlock, while Peter Cook, just three weeks later, improvised a brief Sex Pistols parody, entitled 'I Don't Care' for *Ad Nauseam*, the third and final LP release by his and Dudley Moore's obscene alteregos, Derek & Clive.

'He had a lot of friends,' says Jim Walker of Mickie Most, 'and that hurt us. We got very little radio play on "Public Image". I know we went Top Ten but we coulda been higher – you wanna be Number

One, don't you? If you're in the game you wanna win it, right?'

The single was finally issued on Friday 13th October 1978. The *NME*'s Julie Burchill was torn between adoring its 'lovely little sound' and cringing at its 'crummy lyrics', before concluding that it would chart 'on reputation' and that by 1988 Lydon would 'end up...like Iggy Pop'. Jon Savage in *Sounds* summed it up as 'rough, angry and right'.

In the event, the ITV 'life ban', threatened by Mickie Most, lasted just seven weeks. The 'Public Image' video was screened as part of LWT's *Saturday Night People* on October 7th in a filmed insert by Peter Clifton. While radio airplay was limited during daylight hours, a further screening of the video on BBC1's *Top of the Pops* five days later helped to propel the single to number nine in the charts and eventual sales of just under 240,000. In a way, no Public Image Limited single was ever again to sound so freshly innovative and yet so commercial. And the PiL line-up was to be shattered before another single could even be short-listed for release.

'Public Image' had reached the shops exactly a year after Jim Walker's arrival on British shores, when he had vowed to allow himself a year to crack it. Now he had, the 'victory' had a bitter taste. 'I was still looking for reasons to stay with PiL and not finding any. I was pretty much determined to leave, in my own sweet time, once the album was out and a few gigs were under my belt then that was it. I was so sick over being ripped off over the money...'

Wobble and Levene's financial worries were to be alleviated – for the moment, at least. Virgin could be scammed for a few grand if there was a new Jah Wobble 'solo' record. And the price would go up if Keith Levene and Don Letts – hip dread around town – were involved. 'I didn't even know they were recording me,' says Letts, 'I went into some basement toilet just to mumble some lyrics into a mic and hear what they sound like. I was talking about some serious stuff, some important themes, but then I'm waiting to get a call to do the record, and the next thing I heard is they've played with my voice a bit, stuck a track under it and put the whole thing out as a finished record. I was a little bit pissed off, to tell you the truth, because I thought we'd finish it properly.'

The result was the limited-edition 12" EP 'Steel Leg Versus The Electric Dread', issued in January 1979. 'I was supposed to be "the Electric Dread,"' Letts continues, 'Wobble was Wobble and Keith was down as "Stratetime Keith" – but I was still annoyed when they did the cover pictures so I refused to be photographed for the sleeve. Anyway, they stuck a paper bag over someone's head and photographed him as the Electric Dread! It doesn't really matter, there's no big grudge now and there wasn't then really.'

With Wessex Studios no longer an option, the rest of the first Public Image album was completed at various alternative venues, including Virgin's Manor Studio in Oxfordshire, as well as Gooseberry and the luxurious new Townhouse in Goldhawk Road near Shepherd's Bush. The latter formed the backdrop for further PiL 'piracy', according to Dennis Morris: 'We were in there after midnight, left to our own devices so we nicked all the cane furniture for John's place at Gunter Grove. He never had enough furniture so we grabbed everything, sofas and chairs and tables and stools and potted plants – the lot!' Meanwhile, Wobble recalls the excess at Gooseberry concerned drinking: 'Three large bottles of frascati, many lagers, plus a large bottle of brandy – plus, on most occasions, a fair amount of powder.'

Although such antics didn't amuse Walker he was pleasantly surprised at Lydon's artistic generosity in the studio. 'At the Manor we wanted a live drum sound and so we had to use the old billiards room. It was set up so it was just me and Rotten, eye to eye as I drummed and he sang. I think he was doing "Annalisa" and we improvised a lot, tried a lot. And later on [he] encouraged me to mix my own drum sound. So we mixed democratically as well and that is down to Rotten.

'It was a great experience. People don't realise that most of that album was done in one take. We'd always leave a recording studio with a finished track – incredibly efficient compared with a lot of bands today who take three months to finish one single. "Theme", "Annalisa", "Religion", all of them, all the ones that worked took just a day – except for "Public Image" that took a week because we were fumbling around, finding our feet.

'Everybody was fine as long as they were sober which in the early days was pretty much the case because we didn't have money. Until the drugs started coming in four or five months into it we were a proper band; I mean we worked everyday, just about. Rotten was usually at his lawyer's so he'd come in late. But the three of us would work things out... it worked really, really well...'

Keith Levene would tell *Perfect Sound Forever*'s Jason Gross [quoted in Heylin, 2007] 'We thought we were doing something quite radical, by making the songs up literally as they went along.' Mistakes would be left in. 'We were getting away with being audacious and saying, "We can do whatever the fuck we want. We're PiL, fuck you." People never knew if we were serious or playing a joke on them. But we were serious.'

Vivien Goldman, who was a regular visitor to PiL recording sessions, recalled to Clinton Heylin how Keith Levene later somewhat hubristically said 'he didn't want to play guitar in any way that anybody had ever played in the past. Otherwise it wasn't worth it.'

With the album finished, Lydon and the band clocked up a few more interviews including a two page special in *Record Mirror* in early November. Within the double spread Lydon seemed to talk of the Pistols' demise with serious regret. There was, it seems, 'no reason' for the Pistols to split – no reason beyond McLaren's 'deranged' determination to drag the band down to meet 'failed bank robber' Ronnie Biggs.

It was around this time that Lydon had talked about 'Religion', saying it was a song from the Pistols' days that Sid Vicious wouldn't stand for. It was hard for Sid to answer back, given that he was then in an American jail, for the alleged murder of Nancy Spungen, who had died in the early hours of 12th October. Yet transcripts of the Pistols' last radio slot with K-San in San Francisco the previous year reveal Vicious actually revelling in the 'new song we got' about God, a song 'that's a real attack' on the Almighty. To those who knew the whole story it was one of the first glimpses of the Lydon attitude to consistency. The *RM* piece also had Wobble promising that the best was 'yet to come' and it ended with John towing the party line – the Pistols were far 'too limited' anyway – but, with his obvious regrets, it must have been an unsettling interview for his new PiL colleagues to sit through.

The forthcoming album was entitled, minimally enough, *First Edition* – it was scheduled for release during the first week of December 1978. With typical panache PiL had booked two gigs to celebrate the album's release – instead of being a day or two before the issue date the live events were booked at the Rainbow for three weeks later; Christmas Day and Boxing Day, the two days of the year when London rarely, if ever, sees gigs (partly because of little available public transport in the capital).

With the fans having to make such an effort, Virgin were worried that PiL – having still never played a live date – would not be able to deliver the goods, and so arranged an eight-show tour of Europe, consisting of two gigs each in Holland, West Germany, Belgium and France. Lydon cancelled these almost as soon as they were set up and would agree to only two – one in Brussels on 20th December and one in Paris on the 22nd. And even these didn't quite go according to plan.

'First thing that happens when we get into the hotel in Brussels,' Jim Walker explains, 'is that Rotten suddenly says, "It's all off! I'm not doing the gig. Fuck it, why should I?" And this whole pathetic argument went on, with Rotten being awkward and Keith Levene pleading with him. It took an hour or more to talk him into it, it was ridiculous.' But Walker also comments that PiL's lack of experience as a live unit had an exciting advantage: 'It felt like a rehearsal with an audience watching. We'd look at each other and smile, it was really cool.'

A ticket for PiL 'avec Johnny Rotten', Paris, 1978

Totalling a mere six songs, though – 'Theme' , 'Low Life', 'Annalisa', 'Religion', 'Public Image' and the infamous 'Belsen Was A Gas' – it was a 'rehearsal' that Walker concedes was bound to cause trouble: 'At any gig there's always a lot of catharsis, of wish-fulfillment. But just doing six songs [is] a bit of a rip-off. There were over 700 people there. And no security – and I mean virtually no one. There were cans and bottles flying in from the start, but Rotten just soaked it up and kept singing. I was right behind him with the kit, of course, so I'd be watching these bottles coming towards me in slow motion. I had a couple of real bad knocks that night, bad bruises, but I was just too high – on beer and adrenaline – to notice the pain until much later.'

Wobble found his first night as a professional musician – which comprised two sets two hours apart – memorable too. 'I ended up kicking the head of security in the face – he'd been looking at the band, bad-mouthing us and pushing a few people about. And so there was a riot, and we ended up barricaded in the dressing room.'

'There were about 35 or 40 big bikers who wanted to kill us all,' Walker remembers, 'so we ended up locked in this big concrete bunker, waiting until they'd gone, [at] three in the morning. Some fun, huh?'

Walker's first-ever visit to Paris two nights later was to prove similarly disappointing: 'Where's Jeannette booked us into? Some suburban motel that's miles from the centre of town, some dive used by travelling salesmen! I said to her, "What the hell are we doing here? We're miles from the action?" And she gave me all this stuff about all the central hotels having rats and cockroaches and fleas. So I said to the guys, "I'm gonna check out the town, who's coming in with me?" And not one of them could be bothered leaving the hotel. They're all just drinking beer and watching TV, that was it.'

The actual gig was at Le Stadium, with French girl group The Lous watching from the wings. Don Letts, shooting a Super 8 film of proceedings, remembers 'a dark, intense affair. John had this real manic presence, that meant no one would fuck with him. He could fart and no one would dare say a thing. I rolled loads of film that night, and later on, but the low lighting meant much of it had just this murky feel.'

With anti-fascist protestors demonstrating at the inclusion of 'Belsen Was A Gas', it was another blood-splattered event – for Wobble in particular: 'This huge heavy fucking thing came flying through the air and knocked me out. It was this severed pig's head! A fucking pig's head!'

The minimal stage lighting used in Paris was 'designed' by Dennis Morris: 'It was lo-fi lighting. Black plastic, minimal. The idea was so that it would all fit into the back of a van so you wouldn't have to cart all these huge lorries around. It was supposed to create an atmosphere – and it did, it looked great. Although there was one guy in Paris who came up to me and said, "Are you doing the lighting?" And when I nodded "yes" he took off his glasses and offered them to me, saying, "Here, take these – I think you need them!" People always felt a bit short-changed by it all, it was all so experimental for the time. So ahead of its time.'

The Paris gig received a few good notices but the set – at still only eight songs – remained very short, even when padded out with Pistols oldies like 'Problems' and 'Belsen Was A Gas'. As if to typify the confused and detached sense of the evening, PiL's after-show party was at a venue miles away; unfortunately, no transport had been laid on for anyone except the group.

07
first blood first issue

The debut album *First Edition* – 'produced and written by PiL' – was released in the UK on December 8th 1978 and took two weeks to reach the LP listings. Its inability to edge any higher than 22 was probably due to the greatest hits and seasonal cash-ins that were clogging up the Christmas and New Year listings. Although an 'extended version' of 'Public Image', with no less than 'twelve verses', was predicted to be included in the LP's running order, the single version appeared instead.

First Edition's surprisingly slick colour cover featured Lydon on the front and Wobble on the back, photographed in glossy magazine style with typography to match. Inside the cover were a sly, foxy looking Levene and a pristine, shirtless Walker (again in expensive magazine mode). Lydon's picture parodied fashion bible *Vogue*, Wobble's – featuring him sprawled all over the executive desk – was there to mimic the news chronicle *Time*, Levene's conjured up the comic *Mad* while Walker's was not unlike the gay magazine *Him*.

All four portraits featured the band name PiL – though Wobble's actually read 'Public Image Ltd' – and all four had, of course, been shot by Dennis Morris: 'That first album had a really nice sleeve. When *Mojo* used some of the first album shots for their cover in 2004 they asked, "Are these ones really old?" They thought they were new because a lot of that stuff is timeless. And they were polished. You see, I was also taking pictures for a time with Rose Royce – they were massive then with "Car Wash" and "Wishing On A Star" selling millions – and their make-up girl was great. I asked her to help me with that first album cover for PiL. She loved the idea of meeting Johnny Rotten and agreed instantly.'

Aside from strong echoes of 'Public Image' in both 'Low Life' and 'Annalisa', PiL's debut 45 was no real guide to the album's overall sound or tone. The gloriously stoned, but punishing nine-minute ramble 'Theme' was the opener, where Levene's guitar blizzard collided with Lydon's repetitive yet compelling mantra of 'I wish I could die...I will survive'. At the other end of the LP lay the mad joke voices and subsonic bass of the disco-punk "Fodderstompf" – which was initially only created in order to extend the LP's playing time beyond the thirty-minute mark, as requested by the record company. Some critics, for instance Simon Reynolds in his excellent post-punk study *Rip It Up And Start Again*, believe its instinctive nature and improvisational nerve to represent the highpoint of the album.

First Edition, *released 8 December, 1978*

If some of the lyrical content, like 'Religion', belonged in sixth-form poetry class, the pounding 'Annalisa' took on the German religious fanatics who'd killed their allegedly 'possessed' daughter. Elsewhere, some assumed that the target of the acerbic rollercoaster 'Low Life' was Malcolm McLaren. Others, including some at Gunter Grove, wondered if its subject was the still living Sid Vicious. Keith Levene is uncertain to this day: 'That song was about Malcolm McLaren in theory, but at one point, I think it was about John Gray. Lydon's usually got the hump with someone. And he usually writes with someone in mind, someone he's not too happy with. Malcolm was always his default villain, of course – he hated him, really hated him.'

Musically *First Edition* was as improvised and free form as the best avant-garde jazz yet as edgy as the wildest punk single. Levene shot sparks everywhere and while Lydon sailed over the lot, underpinning it all was the astounding Wobble-Walker rhythm section – the Sly & Robbie of the Blank Generation. It all added up to a truly different debut, the most shocking and unexpected album release by a major act since Lou Reed's stab at avant-garde commercial suicide, *Metal Machine Music,* in 1975.

Reviews for the LP were mixed. The nationals ignored it and the music papers nearly all thought that there was a surplus of studio gimmickry and a lack of production control. *Zig Zag's* Kris Needs was virtually alone in giving the set the thumbs-up. It was perhaps a wise move anyway, given that the same issue of the magazine had dedicated four complete pages to a PiL article by Robin Banks. Nonetheless, Needs' words seemed sincere and he wrote passionately of songs that were 'compulsive and danceable'.

Nick Kent, in the *NME*, was widely expected to give *First Edition* a vicious pasting, partly because of his much-exaggerated 100 Club run-in with Vicious and Wobble two and a half years earlier. But Kent actually gave it a balanced write-up that only damned, if it damned at all, with faint praise for the longer, more experimental numbers. Simon Frith in *Melody Maker* described Lydon's attack on religion as 'banal, reminiscent of Jethro Tull's *Thick As A Brick*', and although likening Lydon's delivery to that of John Cooper Clarke, commented that 'he lacks Clarke's love of language', settling for 'neat but static' rhymes. *Sounds'* Pete Silverton – later to be Glen Matlock's co-writer on his *I Was A Teenage Sex Pistol* book – was less impressed however, quoting a colleague who thought it sounded like sound effects being played riotously by a band who were going into the studio 'for the first time'. A comment that was more accurate than Silverton may have actually realised at the time...

In the US the British version of *First Edition* was not to appear either that year or the next. Warners, who had earlier been prepared to offer $100,000 – £60,000 at the time – for *First Edition* rejected it out of hand as far too raw, after just one hearing. They were, however, prepared to pay a similar figure if it was all recorded again, preferably in a quality 24-track studio. PiL's studio economies had proved false, completely false.

The LP had been released too late in the calendar year to make showings in many critical lists that Christmas, although critics' polls at both *NME* and *Sounds* voted 'Public Image' the second best 45 of the year, only beaten (respectively) by Buzzcocks' 'Ever Fallen In Love' and Patti Smith Group's 'Because The Night'. Listeners to John Peel, meanwhile, placed it at number nine in that year's Festive Fifty, with the two-year-old 'Anarchy in the UK' remaining triumphant.

With the album out and the Francophile shows over, it was time for the Rainbow Christmas gigs. The Rainbow was a 2,000-seater North London venue that was a stone's throw from Finsbury Park and Lydon's family home. Tickets for the Christmas Day and Boxing Day gigs had gone on sale on 3rd November at the venue itself, and at Jock MacDonald's Beaufort Market record stall on the King's Road. Not even this could happen without some kind of minor controversy – in this case, ticket touts turned up to try and sell tickets for £5 rather than the marked price of £3.50. Infuriated, Lydon called the police.

The *NME* had reported that younger bands were being approached to appear in the support slots, as well as 'family entertainers like Arthur Mullard...' The latter did not materialise, but the gigs were to be newsworthy in other ways. 'Let the animals in!' Lydon had said after the soundcheck and, for much of the crowd, his words weren't inappropriate. MacDonald's security wasn't sufficient to deal with the trouble that flowed like spirit from a broken bottle.

'A guy got glassed, whacked with a vodka bottle just a few feet from where I was standing,' according to music memorabilia dealer George X who was present the first night. 'It was very tribal – skinheads, football hooligans, mods, punks... the most violent gig I'd ever been to.'

'I never really liked it there,' says Wobble of the Rainbow, 'The bouncers were always heavy. Even before the punk days the vibe there wasn't very nice. There was an anti-feeling on those nights, lotta people hating the band as a lotta critics hated the albums. For me, playing me first gig in me own country, it was like – in at the deep end. It's like you've never played a game of professional football and now you're representing your country in the World Cup in front of a 100,000 plus spectators. And it had an effect on me – all that criticism. It really made me focus on my playing – "I will get this right, I will not make a mistake". And I'm still like that.'

Much of the fighting at the Rainbow seemed to stem from a clash between those who'd just discovered the punk bandwagon – and who were grimly clinging on – and those who were embracing something new.

'I'd moved on from punk and so had PiL moved on and so had Warsaw-Joy Division and so had the Banshees,' says George, 'but a lot of idiots in mohicans hadn't moved on. And they made their presence felt that night at the Rainbow, spitting and shouting. I was a bit wasted 'cos me and my mate had done a crate of lager and various 'herbal medicines' before we'd arrived. When we got in, Don Letts was blaring dub over the sound system. They had some big speakers at the back and there was a big sense of anticipation but also, like the later Pistols gigs, a bad violent atmosphere. Something's gonna happen here, that was the feeling.

'Then it went very, very dark – black – the house lights came down and this thunderous bass kicked in. I'd been to millions of reggae concerts but I'd heard nothing like that bass, it was like a fuckin' earthquake. And on they strolled, Wobble sitting down in his bandido outfit, Lydon in his glittery jacket. But from the moment the stage lights came up, the violence started. There was just waves and waves of people steaming into each other. There were mohican-types shouting, "You've sold out!" and all that. Lydon started handing out lagers to the crowd, some came back at him – all very nasty though he gave as good as he got. It was like being at a football match without the police. It was packed, it was chaos. PiL were fantastic though. It was a good idea, a Christmas gig, but like a lot of good ideas from PiL it wasn't fully followed through, it slightly didn't work. It was very much a shame that the violence marred it – it was a great show, exciting, an historic night but slightly disappointing for that reason. The rows. Apparently the next night it all went off without any real trouble.'

The Boxing Night gig was later captured on the bootleg LP *Extra Issue*. While the version of 'Belsen Was A Gas' is little more than pure hysteria, 'Annalisa' and the two performances of 'Public Image' show plenty of messy energy and snap. Levene's exquisite rawness is perfectly counterbalanced by Wobble's supple basslines and Walker's amphetamine-fuelled rhythms.

For Jim Walker, though, this second Rainbow gig was the date of his fourth and final PiL concert. His gigging days with PiL had lasted less than a week: 'Another incredibly awful gig. It was pathetic organization, it was like a 10-year-old running Microsoft. The fans were kept waiting 'til midnight – there was no thought for the transportation, no care about the fans, no consideration, just this mess... The opening act was Linton Kwesi Johnson – can you imagine a reggae poet trying to do a serious reading in front of 3,000 drunken football fans? And then next on were this awful group called Les Lous, this girl group from Paris. We'd met them there just a few days before and Levene says, "Why doncha come and play the Rainbow with us?" It was that kinda nonsense – and they were crap!'

It was the last straw for Walker. In early January 1979, after months of 'genuinely looking for a reason to stay – and not finding one', he finally dropped his bombshell: 'There were no other gigs lined up, not one. And the atmosphere was terrible. And still they hadn't sorted out the publishing. Soon as I left, the first thing I did about that was get a lawyer and he said go to Warner Brothers today. And Rob Dickens there gave me some money [but] PiL were busy writing my lawyer letters saying, "Oh, he had nothing to do with anything, nothing to do with writing anything".'

Jah Wobble initially thought that it was his endless pranks that had driven Walker out. 'He'd said a few things before but I wasn't sure how serious Jim was. I just said, "Stick it out a bit longer, see how it goes." And then he just left. So I said, "We can't just let him go, he's a great drummer, we've got to get him back". John was indifferent, "Maybe, maybe not". But Keith seemed to agree with me so we went looking for Jim. We found him in Bonnington Square [a notorious hangout for junkies in Vauxhall, South London]. But Jim wouldn't see us. Later, I think Keith got to see him but Jim didn't come back.'

'[Levene's] main pitch to make me return was to say that John and Wobble didn't care about me at all,' recalls Walker. 'Only he, Keith Levene, cared. This naturally decided the matter for me! Later [he] said in the press, "Oh, we just hire drummers, we tell them what to do..." We'd been the centre of attention, but you only get a year in England, and then you're just another semi-big band, one of dozens. You're no longer so special. That's why I was always trying to get us to America. That's where you make your big money.'

Walker's departure led to the cancellation of a gig in Dublin on 16th February. A new drummer was recruited in time for a concert at the King's Hall in Manchester a week later, although there seems to be absolutely no record of who it actually was. No review of the gig identifies the drummer by name, and Dave Humphries, who would join PiL in March, was not the man. The fact that the King's Hall date was an anti-racist event made PiL's presence there somewhat ironic for those who'd read Lydon's anti-Clash putdown of bands who put out 'cliched garbage with intellectually trendy words and Rock Against Racism slogans...' The *NME*'s Paul Morley attended the gig and was astounded. In the 3rd March issue, he wrote: 'PiL play it blank and cryptic, offering no easy clues or anything tangible to grab hold of. They satirise, ridicule, delude and elude...'

The records that PiL were to release during the rest of 1979 would reflect all of these contradictions and introduce still more on to an unsuspecting listenership. While the now-late Sid Vicious (who had died of a drug overdose on 2nd February), along with Jones and Cook, appeared on the biggest-selling Sex Pistols singles to date, their reliance on cover versions and sheer reputation would be dwarfed in quality by PiL's extraordinary sense of adventure and confrontation.

08
seen it in your eyes

Eileen Lydon died in the first half of 1979. Her eldest son later described witnessing her death as 'vile', but she was to be remembered in one of the angriest, most alienating tracks of that year. A track about 'last times', 'Death Disco' / 'No Birds Do Sing' was unleashed on June 29th. In 1987, Lydon would tell the *NME* that he had played the track to her shortly before her death: 'She was very happy. That's the Irish in her, nothing drearily sympathetic or weak.'

For many, 'Death Disco''s whole package of sound, vinyl and sleeve – a startling, and uncredited, Lydon painting of himself, Lee and Levene as caricature animals – came to embody the daring threat of PiL. Lydon's intense, haunting vocals are ably supported by a rumbling Jah Wobble bass that is practically subsonic, in turn accented by Levene's sparkling Swan-Lake-inspired guitar riffs. Dave Humphries, on his only recording with PiL, tops off the sound with brisk hi-hats. By the time of its release, he had left the group, and Keith Levene had recruited Richard Dudanski, formerly of Joe Strummer's pre-Clash band The 101ers, who had left Bank of Dresden.

Dudanski joined the band at The Townhouse to throw himself into work on the new sessions, but in spite of some exhilarating music, it was to prove a dispiriting experience. 'In fact [over] the next ten days, we recorded like five songs,' Dudanski told Clinton Heylin. 'The tape was just left running. Basically, me and Wobble would just start playing, and maybe Keith'd say something like double-time. But it was a bass drum thing which Keith would stick guitar on, and John would be there and then write some words and whack 'em on once we'd got the basic tracks. I think the first day we did "No Birds Do" and "Socialist". Then we did "Chant", "Memories". [But] the whole thing ground to a halt. Apart from those first recordings at The Townhouse, [and a session at] a studio in Bermondsey, [where we] recorded "Graveyard" / "Another" we never, ever played. Jah wanted to do something. We'd try and set something up. But it would just not happen. Keith would not turn up. It could have worked but we seemed incapable of actually doing it.' But in the meantime, as the fruits of the Dudanski sessions began to emerge, such behind-the-scenes discord was unapparent. 'Death Disco''s ferocious howl sounded like the work of an inspired creative force.

The accompanying promo – like its predecessor – had a nightmarish, lit-from-below quality. It was a post-punk film noir that added to the single's impact. Most remarkably of all, it climbed as high as number twenty in the UK singles charts, and actually gave the band a slot on the all-important *Top Of The Pops* on 12th July. It is to the BBC's credit that they gave peak-time exposure to such a coruscating record, especially given that Lydon performed the song with his back to the jollied audience, and Wobble sat in a dentist's chair throughout the performance. Simon Reynolds in *Rip It Up And Start Again* recalls host Mike Read embarrassedly mumbling the song's title.

The 'Death Disco' 12-inch version – limited to 15,000 copies – also contained '1/2 MixMegamix', an instrumental mix of 'Fodderstompf'. It was another first, a groundbreaking sound mix years before 'acts' like Stars on 45 and Jive Bunny devalued the term 'megamix'. Death Disco is also now the name of the New York music movement that encompasses bands such as The Liars and The Yeah Yeah Yeahs.

Ian Birch in *Melody Maker* tried to untangle the conundrum of 'Death Disco' when he considered 'It's more than possible to loathe and love them at the same time. Every time you look for a point of entry into the song all you get is a slap across the face.' *NME*'s Roy Carr was even more undecided: 'It exists, it irritates, it intrigues...'

On Saturday 30th June, Lydon had also appeared as a panellist on BBC1's revived series of the record review show *Juke Box Jury*, introduced by Noel Edmonds. Clearly, glancing at the guest lists for the rest of the series, booking Lydon was just one of a rollcall of 'wild-card' or 'controversial' critics. Bob Geldof had appeared in the very first show two weeks earlier – professional irritant Jonathan King would appear the week after Lydon. But while Geldof and King articulated their displeasure with the records at length, Lydon's sullen approach made for uneasy and sporadically hilarious viewing. Seated on the left-hand side of the panel, which was completed by Elaine Paige, Alan 'Fluff' Freeman and Joan Collins, Lydon peppered conversation with sarcastic remarks about new releases from Showaddywaddy, Abba and Donna Summer. The inclusion of Siouxsie & The Banshees' 'Playground Twist' was perhaps deliberately problematic, but Lydon sidestepped it, firstly by asking the audience their opinion, and then holding up the 'hit or miss' card prop sideways, so that only the edge was visible to the camera. Possibly the highlight of the half-hour occurred when The Monks, recently hitmakers with the execrable 'Nice Legs Shame About Her Face', appeared as mystery guests to promote their latest single, 'I Ain't Getting Any', which was to flop. Freeman, who had finally tired of Lydon's sarcasm, told him to shut up, and when the band appeared, Lydon held out his hand and declared, 'Pleased to meet me.'

Subsequently, Lydon commented: '*Juke Box Jury* is the most godawful show in the world and it's about time someone said so. I got a reaction – even if it was only "ignorant lout" or "sell out" or whatever. You don't have to like it as long as it gives you some kind of motivation. Telly is so bland it really is pathetic. One monotone, one level. It matters not what you watch. It's no wonder people don't think for themselves, they've been hypnotised out of it.'

If anything, PiL's appearance in Newcastle on Tyne Tees' late-night pop show *Check It Out* on 2nd July was even more confrontational. The interviewers Lyn Spencer and an 18-year-old Chris Cowey (who twenty years later would be producing *Top Of The Pops*) possibly didn't help matters – their idea of a rigorous opening question was, 'Where did the name Public Image come from?' The interview lurched from bad to worse when the group was played a film insert of The Angelic Upstarts' Mensi berating Lydon for selling out, whereupon Lydon stormed off, tailed by the rest of the band. (The transmitted version carefully substituted a blizzard of bleeps for the barrage of swearing.)

PiL's TV forays had also brought Lydon into contact with the man who'd first dared to put him on television back in 1976 – Granada Television's Tony Wilson, who not only read the news on the magazine programme *Granada Reports*, but also booked bands for groundbreaking late-night pop shows. On 18th June, he combined both roles and booked PiL for the early evening magazine. 'Like any other Pistols' fan, I was aware of what had happened in America in '78,' Wilson later said, 'and the splitting up of the group. And then – suddenly there's Public Image and that first record was very, very exciting. So, obviously, I rang up Virgin and said, "You know, if ever PiL wanna come and do something we'd love it". And sure enough, they eventually turned up and played "Death Disco".'

Anthony Wilson
© Tony Wilson collection

The Granada appearance was to show another side to Lydon's attitude to performing. With the pressure off – with things truly underground and unexpected – the PiL frontman positively welcomed live shows, as Wilson soon found out: 'The interesting thing was we always recorded that three-minute slot between two and four in the afternoon and when it was halfway through rehearsals – about to record the number – John looked down from the studio stage and said he wanted to do a gig.'

Wilson and business partner Alan Erasmus arranged the gig for the very same night, and several hundred locals turned up to see a stunning PiL gig. Lydon visibly relished the ecstatic mood at Russell's – a Manchester venue already known by its nickname, The Factory. 'A Certain Ratio supported,' says Wilson, 'and PiL, quite simply, were amazing.'

Lydon was to expound later that month on why the only three Public Image gigs of 1979 all took place up North. 'That Factory gig was damn good. All done on word-of-mouth. Only up there word-of-mouth ain't like London – a load of arty-farty intellectuals or big-mouthed goons with the attitude of "Huh, it better be fuckin' good, entertain us!" Northern audiences are just so much more open to things. They don't have pre-conceived ideas and pre-conceptions and prejudices. It's alright.'

A normal tour, even of the North, was still out of the question though as it would be like 'a prison sentence – I can't sleep until seven in the morning after a gig and then you've gotta leave for the next venue a few hours later so you get no sleep and end up feeling like shit.' And even spontaneous one-offs lost some of their sparkle when the fourth estate attended. 'I don't like it when the press find out. There's not one paper you can open and feel happy about. You just pile-drive through a load of drivel. If you enjoy music how come journos throw out gloom and depression with every issue?'

So why, it was asked, did Lydon himself do so much press? 'I only do interviews because I don't wanna fade into oblivion – all forms of communication are important, people need to know you exist. That's why I was determined to do *Top of The Pops* even though it was pure hell. There's no point hangin' on to your morals and convictions if nobody in the fucking world can hear a single word you're saying.'

There was no doubt that a Lydon music press interview was already an attractive, if uncomfortable, sideshow. Endlessly quotable and memorable, Lydon was a slippery individual to characterise. Occasionally, a journalist would eschew cliché when writing about the band – take for example the *NME*'s Danny Baker. His feature 'The Odd Combo', which appeared in the paper on 16th June 1979, marks him as another one who is hard to pigeonhole. Initially clashing with Lydon over the assumption that all 'journalists are stupid', Baker leaves the scene of the interview claiming it as 'My most satisfying meeting with a pop group to date. Then I was a carping, cynical disbeliever, ready to make news with a showdown. Now I'm a fan, an unreserved supporter, and I hope they get a hit single.'

Despite the triumph in Manchester in June, PiL remained a shaky live attraction. On 8th September, they topped the bill in Leeds at 'Futurama '79: The World's First Science Fiction Music Festival', above the likes of Joy Division, Orchestral Manoeuvres in the Dark, Cabaret Voltaire and A Certain Ratio. They took the stage at the Queen's Hall at two in the morning. As the final UK gig that Jah Wobble would ever play with PiL, it was a poor epitaph. With terrible acoustics aggravated by a two-stage set up, PiL chose a particularly challenging selection of material, including 'Chant' and both sides of next single 'Memories.' The audience responded aggressively and Lydon turned his back on them, performing most of the set facing the backline. Writing in the following week's *NME*, reviewer Andy Gill commented: 'It is dreadful. Lydon stalks off midway through the ninth number without so much as a backward glance. In fact he's a model of clockwork predictability, he behaves exactly as I expected. Wobble spends most of the set in his armchair, a posture which matches his bass-playing perfectly, and Levene wanders aimlessly about the stage, a manner which matches his.'

Lydon himself described the Leeds gig as being 'shit,' and even hardcore fan George X, who'd travelled all the way up from London, wasn't overly impressed. 'That Leeds gig sounded terrible, the mix was crap and the place was like an aircraft hanger,' he says, 'but it was still worth seeing. It was still exciting, Wobble and Lydon are always worth seeing.'

The Leeds gig was to be Richard Dudanski's last. '[Futuruma] brought everything to a head,' Dudanski would tell Clinton Heylin years later. 'Again, no rehearsals, shitty sound. John was in an awful mood, Keith was out of it, and [we were] hanging around all day. And I had a big row with Keith after it - we hadn't played for about four months.' Dudanski left the band within weeks, sending a cryptic message to the music press that ended, 'the really good ideas behind the band will never be more than just that. I hope not for JR's sake...' It was a shame because Dudanksi had been really impressed by Lydon's genuine love of music. In addition to Lydon's beloved reggae, Dudanski told Heylin how the leader and newest member would swap all sorts of different music and listening at Gunter Grove to 'a little madrigal, or Renaissance music, a lot of Irish folk music. Bulgarian voices, Indian stuff, a lot of Islamic percussion stuff.' Nonetheless, his use of the initials 'JR', Johnny Rotten, showed where Dudanski felt most of the blame lay for the group's growing malaise.

To finish the upcoming album, a drummer was once again desperately sought. One of those that got asked for advice was Anthony Wilson. 'I got a phone call, and someone said, "We need a drummer, got any ideas?" And I said, "Well, Mark E. Smith has just sacked Karl Burns from The Fall and he's a great drummer". And I rang up Karl and sure enough, Karl was interested. I drove him to London some sunny Sunday afternoon, to some studio south of the river, somewhere around London Bridge way. John was in a snarly mood but

The first PR shot of Public Image Limited with, from left: an unshaven Jah Wobble, Jim Walker in trainers, and John Lydon in white tux. An over-fringed Keith Levene holds the bottle.
© Dennis Morris, 1978

Ex-Furies drummer Jim Walker and long-time girlfriend Carol caught mid-drinking session before the latter was banned from Gunter Grove (and before the former left PiL). Summer, 1978.

© Dennis Morris, 1978

John Lydon onstage in typical hunched pose, with Jim Walker behind, just weeks before the latter left PiL forever. December 1978.

© Dennis Morris, 1978

Bassist Jah Wobble, playing the cowboy with no name, shoots his cool for the first PiL promo video, September 1978.
© Dennis Morris, 1978

Guitarist Keith Levene onstage at London's Rainbow Theatre, December 1978.
© Dennis Morris, 1978

The Good, the Bad and the Ugly. PiL on set for their debut pop video, September 1978. From left: Jah Wobble, Keith Levene, Jim Walker and John Lydon.

February 1978 and John Lydon, fresh out of the Sex Pistols, soaks up the sun in Jamaica - his 'entourage' included Richard Branson, Don Letts and Dennis Morris - the latter replacing David Bailey on photo duty.
© Dennis Morris, 1978

PiL on the roof of Lydon's Gunter Grove residence during July 1978 - with Lydon in hand-painted shirt, Walker posing as a mad biker, Wobble as a spiv while Levene camps it up.

© Dennis Morris, 1978

that was quite good. My main memory of that was me saying to John, "Have you heard that Neil Young song then, John – 'Hey, Hey, My, My?' [from Young's *Rust Never Sleeps* LP. Later to be quoted in Kurt Cobain's suicide note, the lyrics themed on the idea 'It's better to burn out than fade away' included the line 'This is the story of Johnny Rotten.']." And John goes, "Fucking shite!" And Jah Wobble says, "Oh yeah, if it's fucking shite why'd you play it to everyone who ever comes round your house then?" And John looked at him and walked out of the room. John was caught in that moment.'

After passing the audition, held in September 1979, Burns was hurried to The Manor studio in rural Oxfordshire. 'Block booking of almost a month', sighs Wobble now, 'Branson probably charged us 25 grand for that, what a waste!' But within 48 hours of arriving at The Manor, Burns had resigned from PiL. Having made the crucial error of falling asleep with Lydon and Wobble when they were high on acid, the drummer awoke to find his bed-cover smouldering – and his mattress surrounded by burning pieces of paper soaked in lighter fluid.

In October the unbelievable happened. A desperate John Lydon approached PiL's original drummer, Jim Walker, by now a member of Kirk Brandon's early group The Pack. 'They've tried to stop me getting any publishing, saying I did absolutely nothing composition-wise – [and] neither me nor anyone else I know has ever received recording royalties. Levene's being slagging me in the press, [and] you've got this kind of campaign against you to try and wipe you out of history. I was a non-person, I didn't exist. And then Lydon has the fucking nerve to call and say "Er, we've had a bit of trouble with drummers, we want you back. Let's have a meet, face to face, and let's get it all sorted out".'

But the meeting did not run smoothly: 'So I turn up in the pub alone and Rotten's not alone, of course. He's in there with his bloody lawyer. If Brian Carr was dragged along to intimidate me it certainly didn't work – I said the same thing I'd first thought of when Lydon had called the night before. "Sure I'll come back but I want the 25 per cent I was promised. I don't care about the other suckers, you can go on giving them 60 quid a week for all I care, but I want my 25 per cent in writing. And that's it – take it or leave it". And Rotten-Carr sat and nodded and agreed and said, "Fair enough, that's fine, let's do it" and all that bullshit. And, of course, the next day they biked over this snotty lawyer's letter, "Dear Mister Walker, I'm afraid in the interests of fairness we must reject your ludicrously greedy demands..." Something like that. The same old bullshit, basically. So that was my last contact with Rotten.'

If Virgin's Simon Draper was alarmed by PiL's revolving door policy on drummers, not to mention the group's erratic gig schedule, then he certainly didn't show it. According to Wobble, 'Draper was like: "If only these horrible low life people would listen we could milk a lot more money from this thing... but whatever – we'll still make money from it. Keep it going, gotta keep the dough rolling in," no matter what...'

PiL's next drummer would be its longest-serving: Nuneaton-born 19-year-old Martin Atkins. 'As a kid I'd drummed along with a lot of Beatles which you're not supposed to,' Atkins now admits. 'Bill Weekland, who is now drummer with REM, once told me that when we were warming up for a Ministry show. It was, "You must never never practise along with Beatles records." This was because George Martin used to increase the tempo of the choruses as a production technique, to make the chorus more triumphant and he'd slow down a melancholy instrumental section to make it more melancholy and gradually speed up an outro to keep it more interesting and so on. And I thought, "Oh My God, I'm finished," 'cos that's all I did, I practised along with *Abbey Road* and *Let It Be* and all those albums.'

By the late 70s, Atkins had moved with his family to Durham, and had joined covers band The Hots. 'We were professional but I decided to spread my wings a bit. In early May 1978, he had journeyed down to London 'for some auditions. Just as I was leaving *Melody Maker* comes out. I remember sitting in a Chinese restaurant with my last £4, I was getting a ride back to Durham, and I found the ad that said "Drummer Required For Band With Rather Well-Known Singer", which was the ad for PiL. And I called up and it was Virgin Records and I said "Look, I'm, er, I'm your man – I'm pretty good, y'know and I understand what punk is all about and, er..."'

Over the next 18 months, Atkins had persisted, a tactic which was eventually to pay off, but not without its share of agonising patience: 'I just kept calling, talked to Jeannette [Lee] a lot, I talked to her mother a lot too when Jeannette wasn't in. So they got to know me as "that Northerner". And I called up, and Keith said "Well, we're gonna be at the Townhouse on Sunday, around four, we'll call you." So, of course, from two o'clock Sunday afternoon onwards, I sat by the phone – well, I didn't sit by the phone, I lived in the attic of a three storey building in Willesden and there was a pay-phone on the ground floor – anyway, four o'clock rolls by – nothing. Five, six, seven, eight, nine... eleven o'clock at night I went to bed. At four in the morning the phone rings... and by the time I got down the stairs it'd stopped ringing. I didn't have a number for the Townhouse.'

Meanwhile, PiL's third single – 'Memories' – was issued on 12th October 1979. After the chartbusting antics of its predecessors, there would be no TV exposure this time round; it struggled to number sixty. Garry Bushell in *Sounds* resorted to weak punning, as is still his wont – 'I thought Wan-Kin was a town in China until I discovered PiL'. Danny Baker in the *NME* proved his declaration of support for the group in June had been no mere bluster, and scorned his undecided colleagues: 'Enough of this "confusing" and "intriguing" guff... The power beats hotter than most anywhere, it's as plain as the nose on your face.' Baker made 'Memories' his Single of the Week.

Metal Box *CD reissue in replica film can*

Hot on its heels came PiL's second album, which conceptually as well as musically left the competition far behind. And the man who knew all about spotlights, Dennis Morris, was the man who came up with it: 'The idea of using that metal film can for *Metal Box* hit me because I was by then living by this film can factory. People said, "Oh you must be the band's creative director" but we were against titles like that. We were a unit... or, at least, we thought we were.'

Metal Box's innovative film can packaging was matched by its contents, twelve tracks smeared over three twelve-inch 'singles'. This came about partly to confound the accepted 'order' in which album tracks are supposed to come, but also because the thicker, broader grooves of 12-inch 45RPM records allowed for deeper bass and a more solid mid-range. The records were all wrapped in protective metal, although a plan to seal the cans with 'PiL' tape did not materialise, despite hundreds of metres of tape being made. In a final break with tradition, no review copies were dispatched and music journalists were obliged to buy their own.

Budgetary costs for the set had spiralled to the point where plans for a lyric sheet had to be abandoned. As an alternative, PiL placed a full-page ad in the music press on 24th November 1979, which displayed the lyrics to the entire LP, at first entitled *The Metal Box*. The *NME*'s Angus Mackinnon was so fulsome in his praise for PiL's latest venture that it led to a front cover that week, even though there was no interview to promote it. The review was the cover story. Over at *Sounds*, Dave McCullough gave it five stars – 'a broad, rich album, a sizable nod in the direction of a real rock'n'roll future' – though other music magazines weren't quite as enthusiastic and those few newspapers that bothered to cover it regarded the set as a tasteless joke.

Selecting highlights from such an extraordinary record is a tricky business. *Metal Box* was not to be a retreat from the strangeness of the group's debut but instead, an extension. A smouldering, mesmerising bass part kicks off the eleven minutes of 'Albatross' – part drunken leer, part po-faced nightmare, and a harrowing but compulsive epic in which Lydon found himself pursued by his past legacy. 'Memories' and 'Death Disco' reappear, the latter under the new name of 'Swan Lake', after the origins of Levene's guitar motif. The shimmering, surreal 'Poptones' boasts a unique circular arrangement over which Lydon contributes an unsettling vocal. Lyrically the song concerned the real life case of a kidnapped, blindfolded girl whose attackers were later traced because she could recall the strange tape they kept playing – it was still playing in the kidnappers' car when the police stopped them. Ironically, 'Poptones' was itself reportedly written in a car, a blue Nissan carrying Lydon, Wobble, driver Joe de Vere, and copious amounts of illicit substances...

Many years later, in the pages of Simon Reynolds' book *Rip It Up And Start Again*, Levene compared 'Poptones' to staring at a white wall. 'If you look at it for a second, you'll see a white wall... If you keep looking at it for five minutes, you'll see different colours, different patterns in front of your eyes – especially if you don't blink. And your ears don't blink.'

The closing instrumental 'Radio 4' was similarly eerie, a feast of layers of synths over a slow evocative beat. It sounded not unlike the soundtrack of some art-house extravaganza. Alan McGee, founder of Creation Records, was to borrow the titles of both 'Poptones' and 'Radio 4' for his own projects many years later. The former became the name of McGee's low-key successor to Creation in 2000 – the latter his own nightclub in West London's Notting Hill.

The clanking, soulless 'Careering' and the skidding shuffle of 'Bad Baby' both sounded like extracts from film scores too – perhaps some Euro-trash disco horror movie. The latter featured the first appearance of new PiL drummer Martin Atkins, whose actual audition for the group at the Townhouse Studio, was included on this track. It was not a session Atkins would easily forget: 'Studio A at the Townhouse, to someone who was 19, looked big. Like a basketball court with a mixing desk at the other end. They said, "Oh, here's that Northerner," you know. And then they said "There's the drum kit, go and do something." I just sat down and did it,' played "Bad Baby" with Jah Wobble playing along.' 'There was attitude galore,' Atkins told Clinton Heylin, 'and gleeful excitement at messing with people. There was disregard for the rules.' It was Atkins' only contribution to *Metal Box*, most of which had been completed prior to Richard Dudanski's departure, with Levene, Wobble and Dave Humphries having some additional percussive input into the LP.

'*Metal Box* was a defining moment for me,' says Alan McGee, 'It's still great now – I still haven't fully got my head round that album. I mean Rapture and Primal Scream and people have done some really interesting shit since but, for me, *Metal Box* is still 500 miles ahead.'

Some who had been more than accommodating towards *First Edition* were taken aback by the content of the new record. Alan Parker, punk journalist and author of *Vicious: Too Fast To Live*, was nonplussed. 'The Pistols fan will lap up that first LP with a soup spoon. It's "punk rock", it's "new wave". But with *Metal Box*... my first steady girlfriend Alison bought me the original tin box. I never ever got further than side three. I was like, "What the fuck is this man trying to sell us?"'

Shortly before Wobble's departure from PiL was announced, Keith Levene would tell Chris Bohn of the *NME* that he regarded *Metal Box* as 'mood music' in that 'It doesn't have to be mood music, if you're not in the mood for it'. Bohn was startled by this comment, believing that 'even those tracks that sound superficially easy, like "Chant" and "No Birds Do Sing", [are] too turbulent to take a passive role'.

In 1983, Jah Wobble would liken PiL's second album to having the value of a time capsule, 'to be dug up in a thousand years time'. Now he regards it as 'a quantum leap, really of its time. In some ways I prefer the first album because I tend to like the albums that are on their way to somewhere, I like the searching rather than the arrival.' Despite concentrating on 'me own heavy duty bass-lines' he was also taking a growing interest in structure: 'Take something like "Bad Baby" and it's almost, with a guitar going over it, you're reading left to right, you're moving forward. It's like a song structure – here's the beginning, the middle and the end. But if you take something like "Poptones", it's different, it stands still – it's truly a fixed form, it's all octaves, chromatic, beautiful...and very modal. It's just such a rounded, perfect snowdrop of a bass line, like a perfect DNA code.

'Technically, it shouldn't be hard to play those notes accurately, but there's a certain feel there that's kinda tough to get right. Musically, it was similar to *Dark Magus* by Miles Davis [recorded in 1974]. I've got a feel, like Miles has got a feel on trumpet, it's quite a delicate feel actually – will Miles make it? He always just got there and that's the beauty of it. You couldn't mistake Miles for any other trumpet player, [like] Keith Richards has [also] got his own sound, [although] I don't really like the Rolling Stones. And I've got my own sound – I've still got that.'

'As we were going into *Metal Box*,' Wobble would elaborate to Clinton Heylin, 'what we were doing really became something else. It was a partly industrial sound, which was quite appropriate.'

For Wobble, the industrial sound of the music was reflected in its unorthodox packaging: 'I mean, a metal box? You can't get much more industrial than that, can you?' Keith Levene agrees: 'It worked, as an idea. It got a lot of attention for the album – and still does. People still ask me about it. It's become almost a kind of icon or something. Of course, when we went to America we saw how we'd been ripped off. Virgin charged us £33,000 for the film can covers – because they had to get them specially made up – and there were only supposed to be 50,000 ever made, a genuine limited edition.'

But this was to turn out to be another 'unlimited' limited supply, as Levene later discovered in the US. 'In America you'd see copies of the *Metal Box* in loads of places so that limit was obviously broken – even though they were going, unofficially, for over $25, which was a lot of money back then. And even with the over-runs there were not enough to go round. Little record shops would get, like, 12 or 15 copies and the kids working there would buy 'em all up and sell 'em for twice as much under the counter or to their mates. With hindsight, what we should really have done was make it just a little more expensive and then have it as a continuing ongoing thing.'

Meanwhile back in 1979 Jah Wobble was noticing that all was not well. 'Well, when I joined I was the novice of the band but by this point suddenly I can see that it's Keith that's getting out of his depth. You see, he had on occasion been musically brilliant, there's no doubt whatsoever about that, but now he was doing a lot of heroin, and that lead to a vicious circle, where he was out of the game for long periods. However, the band still moved ahead without him, and so he would get even more insecure, and feel inclined to have another hit sooner rather than later. He was on a merry-go-round. I think that is just one example of how addictions feed off themselves, with an appetite that's increasingly voracious. So lots of times on *Metal Box* he'd suddenly be struggling to keep up – and then he'd just slip into "Swan Lake" or make some ambient noise on a synthesiser. Which worked but was a bit of an easy option, there were other paths he could have taken. Really it was the latter day equivalent of sticking a sample over a backing track. Even then I knew what was going on. Under the surface he was absolutely full of insecurities. He'd got lost and he could no longer keep up. To be honest I don't think that he ever found his way again. If you disagree with that statement tell me what guitar parts he has done since then that compare to "Poptones" or "Public Image."'

Recording sessions, fuelled by speed, could drift on into the small hours and after dawn. Not that the group ever worked nine to five, as Wobble remembers: 'A lot of time got wasted. The studios and engineers were booked, but they would just be sitting there idle for hours on end. I think that's criminal. Studio time should never be wasted. That used to happen a lot at the Manor especially. I couldn't stand that so I would always just initiate things and start something off. Even when we were booked in the Manor I would go down to Gooseberry and do stuff and then take it up to The Manor and drag John out of the TV/Video lounge and get him to listen to what I had done. That would often get the ball rolling. John would sit under the piano [or] a table for ages, writing the lyrics. And he could be a bit uptight with the sound guys, "I said less reverb!" They'd be some poor engineer sweating away. He would certainly let them know who the boss was.

'But once he was faced with a backing track to something like "The Suit" he would take notice. I had worked on that track at Gooseberry with Mark Lusardi. I had put the lyrics to "Blueberry Hill" over that.

'However, I thought that it was also a must for PiL. That track features an analogue drum loop that Mark and myself put together. So much for me nicking PiL backing tracks heh? It was totally ahead of its time that track. John freaked out when he heard that. I had forced him out of the video lounge. I was going mental for him to listen to it. He was galvanised into action and within a few hours "The Suit" existed. John's lyrics on *Metal Box* are amazing; those lyrics suit the music so well. The way the music felt was often so near perfect, there wasn't that much to do mix-wise. There was a minimum amount of movement needed on the faders, a touch here, a touch there, it wasn't what you would call complicated music.

Second Edition *released as a double-vinyl LP*

'Of course that didn't stop a lot of needless pissing about in regard to mixing, but so what; we were a youngish band learning our way. I learnt so much at that time, not only with PiL but also on my solo stuff; it was like a crash course in how to use the studio.'

In the meantime, others in the PiL coterie were gradually being eased out of the equation. Earlier in 1979, Dennis Morris had been offered a job by Chris Blackwell at his record label Island. 'I said, "To be honest, you've got nothing I'm interested in, if you want me aboard you'll have to sign The Slits and Linton Kwesi Johnson" – the PiL support team basically. And he says, "Well, I've never heard of them but I'll sign them if you look after them". And he did and it was great – I was my own God, I had a huge office, four TVs and, finally, a stereo to match John's. He was round all the time, smoking in the office all afternoon with Island thinking, "What the hell's Dennis doing?"'

Although both Johnson and The Slits racked up above average sales, Morris felt that Island 'still didn't really trust me'. But another Island signing, Marianne Faithfull, about to release her *Broken English* album, needed a photographer for her sleeve: 'They'd tried everyone, Bailey, Lord Lichfield, you name 'em, but they just couldn't get the right shot of her face. Then they finally said to me, "Go on, Dennis, you give it a go". And I did and it looked OK, she looked good on that *Broken English* cover and that was it – they trusted me.'

Suddenly, Morris claims, Chris Blackwell now expressed an interest in signing PiL to a US deal: 'There was a midnight meet with Tommy Mottola – which had to be secret 'cos Virgin weren't supposed to know – and he said "We can cut a deal with them but Dennis has to oversee it". And then there was a second meet with the band – again secret – and the deal for the US was done and Chris Blackwell said, "This wouldn't have happened but for Dennis and so I really think you guys should give him a couple of points". At which point Keith Levene went crazy saying, "If that fucker gets any points then I'm leaving the band right now!" And John said nothing, not a word. He just hates being put on the spot and that was it, he wouldn't support me and so I was no longer in the inner circle.'

'I wasn't there at that meeting,' says Wobble, 'I'd already gone home. Dennis told me later. I had been very excited about Chris Blackwell getting involved. I was beginning by that mid-1979 period to feel very pessimistic about PiL. When Blackwell got involved I got very excited. At that time he was a very dynamic entrepreneur, who had a reputation for being hands-on and getting the job done. When I met him I took an immediate shine to him. To this day he is the only record business tycoon that I ever liked. Of course it all worked out in the end for me personally, I ended up signed to Island off and on for the next twenty years.

'Allowing Dennis to walk was such a mistake by John Lydon. I was also shocked that he (John) would treat a mate like that. To be honest

I viewed him (John) in another light after that. I couldn't see any possible excuse for that behaviour. Dennis was such an important member of PiL; as important as anyone. I observed the PiL camp's reaction to Dennis going. Of course no one bar me had a word to say about it. It was quite Stalinistic, Dennis was airbrushed out of PiL's history.

'Obviously Keith was pleased as punch and I think Jeanette read it as a possible opportunity for her on the artistic front. But alas she never did make her mark in that respect. Remember that this is the bloke (Dennis) who put all those great covers together and he's gone just like that. I remember saying to him "Den watch this space mate, I'll be next. Once we have done America I'm off an' all."'

Dennis continues, 'Keith did the same thing to Wobble later on. I think Keith had always been a bit jealous of my closeness to John and he'd also freaked out when he realised he was gonna be on the inside of the *First Edition* LP sleeve and not the front or back cover. He never really forgave me for that and vetoed the original standard issue *Metal Box* sleeve for the same reason, the album they called *Second Edition*. They didn't know though that there was a clause in the American contract so they got dropped in the next year anyway. I didn't really shoot any more photos of 'em after that. That was it, all over after some 18 months.'

With a retail price of £7.45, *Metal Box* was issued on 23rd November 1979, and did well to reach number eighteen in the British album charts, in spite of a radio ad for the album where Lydon described it as 'twelve tracks of utter rubbish from Public Image Ltd.' But the sales were boosted by a rapturous critical reception. 'Light years ahead of the Sex Pistols,' said *Sounds*. The *NME* described *Metal Box*'s effect as 'pulverising', concluding that 'PiL are miles out and miles ahead.' When the initial pressing of 50,000 ran out in February 1980, Virgin issued a conventional album version entitled *Second Edition*. Dennis Morris's original cover – a chilling picture of Lydon in shades, surrounded by darkness, was replaced by distorted black and white images – the faces of Lydon, Wobble and, gracing the front cover, Levene. The reissue would enter the album charts in March, peaking at 46.

Although the young Martin Atkins had only played on one of the album's dozen tracks, he joined the group on their session for Radio 1's John Peel. Three versions of tracks from *Metal Box* – 'Poptones', 'Careering' and 'Chant' – were recorded at the BBC's Maida Vale studios on 10th December 1979, and transmitted one week later. But Atkins' place on the band's touring itinerary had already been assured prior to the Maida Vale session. After the 'Bad Baby' rehearsal/recording in October, he had heard nothing 'for three weeks. Then Wobble called and I had my second audition at some rehearsal room.'

This audition had turned out to be brevity itself: 'Wobble would just say "Religion" and I would – we would – then play like thirty seconds of "Religion". He was like, "Yeah, okay, er – 'Annalisa'... Okay, now...'Low Life'." Then he just called Jeannette and said, "Book the Paris show – he's in." And at that point I hadn't really sat and talked to John or Keith.' Although Atkins' stint in PiL was no plain sailing – and would be interrupted for a few months during 1980 – he would eventually outlast two of the band's founder members in its ranks.

09
paris in the spring...
is this all there is?

PiL's innovatory 'corporation concept' was 'one of the things that first attracted me to them,' Martin Atkins said later. 'Because, you know, by the time I hit 19 I'd been playing my drums for nearly ten years so I was kind of… jaded as well and I could see, you know, big changes everywhere – The Undertones were releasing a seven-inch in a folded-up poster, everybody was putting out their own records starting their own labels and it was… a revolution.'

But if Atkins was expecting a revolutionary set-up – or even just a competent one – he was soon to be disillusioned. 'We rehearsed somewhere twice after I'd joined, in places where there wasn't really a PA and there wasn't really any equipment and it was just ridiculous. I realise in retrospect we were trying to stay out of the way. Not that we felt any commercial pressure. There wasn't a manager there going, "Alright boys, quick, put these pants on – we've gone tartan!" We just did what we wanted to do. We might have benefited, actually, from a bit more structure, you know, a bit more of a work-load.'

Atkins, meanwhile, had made a friend within the group. 'Wobble befriended me there, John Lydon was kind of – I don't think John was distant at all, I think I was a little bit intimidated by him – and Keith was on heroin which I thought was a bit too heavy.'

'Next thing you know we're on a plane to Paris,' continues Atkins, 'there were some drugs around, I know that for a fact 'cos people travelling with us got arrested on the plane before we even took off from Heathrow. I still have my temporary passport from that trip, my plane ticket, my Virgin itinerary, my backstage pass... everything.'

The mayhem continued upon the group's arrival at their Parisian hotel on 16th January, the night that Blondie had played a concert at Le Palace. Atkins recalls, 'I remember they were all hammering on my door, "Hey, we're the guys from Blondie!" and I just didn't believe them, because who the hell was I? And then I can hear these footsteps coming back and now there's even more of them and these guys are like going:

"Who am I? Tell this guy who I am!"

"This is Frank Infante from Blondie! I'm standing right next to him!"

"See, I am Frank from Blondie!"

So then I finally let them in.'

PiL played two shows at Le Palace on 17th – 18th January, which were recorded by French radio. Atkins: 'I said, "We should release this" – I think more out of my desire to be on more than one song on a PiL album than anything else'. The performances would eventually surface nine months later on the live LP *Paris Au Printemps* (Paris In The Spring).

After Paris, PiL returned, somewhat inevitably, to Gunter Grove. Martin Atkins remembers 'buckets of drugs' and 'watching *Apocalypse Now* on John's system, you know, incredibly loud. We'd regularly be over [there] from Friday night 'til Monday morning – non-stop'. The drug reliance, coupled with internal band politics, could make planning anything something of a challenge. A live outing on BBC2's *The Old Grey Whistle Test* was scheduled for 6th January, but apparently postponed due to Keith Levene's 'blue flu', a phrase that some took to being a hard drug reference.

PiL's ramshackle but genuinely exciting two-song spot was transmitted on Tuesday 12th February. 'Seeing Public Image doing "Poptones" and "Careering" on *Whistle Test* was unbelievable,' Alan McGee declares now. 'Lydon totally charismatic. Wobble couldn't really play but he was a genius, doing this jazz rock free-forming thing. Levene was a Yes guitarist in a punk band, off his nut but inspired and inspiring – a bad advert for good drugs...'

Lydon was clad in a blood red coat as he barked out his lyrics while Levene occasionally jabbed at a Prophet Moog synth, and Wobble posed menacingly. Perhaps the biggest surprise concerned Wobble, who unusually was standing up to play bass. 'The host Annie Nightingale came along and she was really warm and really into us. She stayed most of the night with us, drinking and talking.' Lydon spent most of the rehearsal refusing to believe that Nightingale's fulsome praise was sincere.

Although no one knew it at the time, this appearance was Wobble's swansong with PiL on British soil. He had started to tire of the inherent laziness of the group, and was itching to record more and more. He raved to the *NME*'s Angus MacKinnon in February 1980, 'I used to see the studio as a kind of fourth instrument but now I see it as a vehicle for all the instruments you're playing yourself. It can allow all sorts of attitudes and leeways to creep in and that's very positive.'

Lydon in red; PiL do BBC TV's **Old Grey Whistle Test,** *February, 1980*

Even before the quartet departed for their first tour of the United States in April, Keith Levene's condition was a cause for concern. Wobble: 'He was more and more on the smack by that time, it was everything to him, absolutely everything. But to be perfectly honest the writing for me was on the wall way back in mid-1978. I got on the Northern Line at Bank on my way to our Tooley Street rehearsal studio. Keith was on the train comatose; smacked out of his nut. I couldn't wake him. I remember that as a reality moment. I remember thinking "Make the most of this my son, 'cos it (PiL) probably won't last too long."

'When we reached the London Bridge, I just got off and left him. He didn't turn up at rehearsal that day. I didn't say anything to the others. I wanted to see what Keith would say. He came out with some nonsense story about getting locked in a squat with no phone.'

Wobble's early fears about Levene's heroin use were realised: 'Yes things got worse and worse, when we left New York and the East Coast on that tour Levene started to suffer heroin withdrawals. So we ended up paying for his smack supplier and another to fly over on Concorde to come and see Keith with some gear. So there's thousands and thousands of pounds wasted on getting Levene's dealers over to the States - and I'm getting 60 quid a week. That was so wasteful and stupid - so annoying. I always thought that was a pretty drastic measure to take; was he paranoid about buying stuff from drug dealers in Mid-West America, or did someone else need to be "looked after?"'

'That American tour was just crazy,' reflects Atkins, 'I mean we flew everywhere so we had no idea of the sheer scale of the country.'

A few days after arrival, Lydon told journalists, 'The Pistols finished rock'n'roll, rock'n'roll's shit and it's gotta be cancelled. We don't consider ourselves rock'n'roll at all...' Certainly, PiL made some stringent attempts to subvert the band vs audience dynamic. Lydon would hand the mic to young kids in the audience, and even pulled them onstage for song after song. 'A gig is something that the band are meant to enjoy too,' according to Lydon, 'You should get some kind of entertainment.' Keith Levene: 'What we were trying to do was get the crowd up off the floor and out onto the stage, and then get the band out into the crowd. Break down all the barriers. When it worked it was good.'

If nothing else, this tactic did keep together the 'new' rhythm section – at least when they were genuinely playing live. 'Martin was a hard-working drummer,' says Wobble, 'He was actually some company for me on the road, some company for me otherwise I think I would have just fucked off even earlier – even though me and him were getting loads of plaudits. I was getting loads of plaudits myself for playing at the New York Palladium [the tour's second date] – this novice bass-player playing for 20 or 25 minutes solo at the start of the set and the crowd's rocking to it. But I wasn't happy, 'cos I'm like, "Where's the rest of the fucking band?" I said "If you don't wanna play, fine, gimme me passport back. Now." And Jeannette was like, "No, no, no, don't go".'

The tour consisted of ten shows over three weeks, beginning in Boston on 18th April. Warner Brothers' 18-month-old promise – that they'd spend a fortune promoting PiL Stateside – was made good. 'Somebody lost thousands of dollars,' says Atkins now, 'I know we did the Detroit City Roller Rink [on 28th April] to less than 300 kids out on a [Monday]. But we played to 10,000 people in Los Angeles so maybe that show alone might have covered most of it.'

The day before the Los Angeles show, on May 3rd, PiL recorded an appearance on the venerable pop show *American Bandstand*, made by the national network NBC. Already in its 23rd year, the programme, hosted by Dick Clark, was as much an institution in the States as *Top Of The Pops* was in the UK. Also appearing that week, in a bill that only mainstream pop television could juggle, were The Doobie Brothers, Mary McGregor and Jermaine Jackson.

Atkins was unaware of how significant the performance was: 'I thought it was a cable TV show, I had no idea.' The record company, probably for reasons of time, had re-edited the two lengthy songs, 'Careering' and 'Poptones', which caused Lydon, in Atkins' words, to be 'running all over the place, all over the set. And I think the reality of that – though he might like to say differently – was that he didn't know the re-edit that Warner Brothers had done. So he was just running away from the cameras to hide his mouth. You couldn't see his lip-syncing 'cos he didn't know where the words were gonna come.'

Prior to the show's taping, Dick Clark had greeted the group in their dressing room with the words, 'I'm Dick Clark', only to be told by Wobble, 'Good, well fuck off then.' *Sounds* journalist Sylvie Simmons wryly observed that, to Americans, this incident was 'akin to spitting at the Queen Mother'. Even so, Clark would later place PiL's performance as eighth in a retrospective of the show. 'If we'd been better prepared for *American Bandstand* they wouldn't still be showing it now,' argues Martin Atkins now. 'But you create that kind of happy accident by chance. Which is not to say that PiL's success was an accident. There was attitude galore – and gleeful excitement at messing with people. There was more disregard for the rules, and the fact is when we accidentally disregarded the rules in America we created a backdrop that helped us get away with it all.'

The *American Bandstand* appearance was broadcast on NBC on Saturday 17th May, by which time PiL were back in Britain. On the 10th, the last date of the US tour which took place at the South of Market Cultural Centre in San Francisco, Lydon and Levene had held a major press conference. The future direction of the group was spelt out here when Lydon told the assembled reporters, 'We're doing our own videos, we own our own cameras, we're building our own studio.' Levene backed him up; 'We're into getting around the film unions, not working within the film unions – we think they're a restriction. Hopefully the video album concept might help that.' Union busting was not the controversial subject in the US that it would have been back in Britain then but the reporters present still managed to confuse Lydon and Levene with their next question. Asked how they intended to project and distribute their own videos, the best retort they could muster was 'er...dunno...'

Jah Wobble's growing, and maybe understandable, disillusionment with what PiL had become was almost complete: 'Keith had heroin withdrawals as we got on a flight, and there was Jeannette carefully putting a blanket round him, and then John and Jeannette helped him down the aisle. All the stewardesses were fussing around, remember this was in the days that they still pretended they cared. John and Jeannette were politely telling the stewardess and the passengers that he's just got a bad case of 'flu, poor boy, and don't worry he'll be okay. But I suddenly did a loud Basil Fawlty voice: "It's Alright Don't Be Concerned, It's Just Heroin Withdrawls, We Will Locate A Street Dealer At Our Next Destination And Everything Will Be Tickety Boo!" 'I'd really had enough of all the smack bullshit.'

In America, Lydon and Levene had also made a particularly belligerent guest appearance on Tom Snyder's NBC programme *The Tomorrow Show*, which was broadcast on 27th June. After a first half in which Lydon alternated between blanking questions and emitting monosyllabic grunts, Snyder exploded during the commercial break. 'What the fuck do you think you're doing?' shouted the mild-mannered anchorman, 'You're making a fucking fool of yourself.' Part two began with the director poised to pull the plug, but while the rest of the interview was a thinly-veiled exercise in mutual aggravation (Lydon: 'You went into a bit of a tantrum'), at least Lydon started to bother to answer Snyder's questions. Declaring rock and roll to be a 'disease', he went on to claim, intriguingly, that 'We have our own interests and we are also making our own film right now in England'.

No-one has ever since acknowledged the existence of any such film. Finally, Lydon declared that 'We tried to break down those barriers [between performers and audiences]. But it's not working so we have to think again. In the meantime we have to pay attention to something else... That's the trouble with America, you're all so regressive.' Snyder then apologised – sarcastically, of course – for himself and the rest of the world being out of step with John Lydon and the silent Keith Levene.

Before the cameras cut away for the last time Lydon baited his host about US President Carter's recent stumbles – both politically and physically – and then surreally sang a few words from *The Wizard of Oz*'s 'Somewhere Over The Rainbow'.

Jah Wobble, meanwhile, had tired of the PiL dynamic, and believed that music was no longer Lydon or Levene's number one priority. 'I sort of sensed towards the end of *Metal Box* that they (Lydon and Levene) were falling faster and faster into a morass of nonsense. All the bollocks about umbrella organisations and making videos was coming thick and fast. I knew one hundred percent that it was all bollocks and wouldn't ever come to anything.'

For Wobble, Levene's heroin addiction had reached such a level that it made any possibility of the band progressing null and void. 'It wasn't only the heroin addiction itself but also the resulting duplicity and arrogance that caused problems for the band. Keith was a typically manipulative two-faced addict who needed to be confronted. Instead we let him go on feeding his habit. I told John a few times that we had to act. In the end I had to come to the conclusion that John liked it that way. I couldn't understand that at the time; how could John benefit from that?'

It is a valid point. Why did Lydon, who had told reporters and friends time and time again that he 'disliked junkies and hated heroin', then tolerate the addiction of Levene rather than try and force the latter to treat it?

According to *The Face* in 1983 - in a Lydon piece that led to the glossy magazine being banned from Public Image press conferences for almost half a decade - Lydon actually enjoyed the company of addicts because he 'could feed off their weakness'.

'However', says Wobble, 'ultimately I didn't blame Keith, he is after all a typically immature addict. If I had held a grudge I would not have remained friendly with him up to the early nineties, at which time I did fall out with him. In PiL John was the guv'nor, it was his call, and like so many of John's decisions concerning PiL it was a bad one. And of course it wasn't just Keith and his heroin addiction that I was fed up with; the business affairs of the band were being run in a chaotic fashion. It was obvious by then that the chaos was a deliberate tactic. I think that it helped when it came to not paying people properly. It was very similar to how McLaren run the Pistols. But the biggest problem I had was with John himself; to be honest the last residues of respect that I had for him were fast fading away, his behaviour on the American tour had seen to that. I wanted out before the last bit evaporated.'

The reception towards Wobble's actual departure was, on the face of it, more indifferent than acrimonious: 'I went around to Gunter Grove and banged on the door until Dave Crowe answered. I told him that I had come for money. He just nodded and stepped aside. Dave was actually a nice bloke, I could tell that he was uncomfortable with his position in things. I went in and took away the shoebox full of money. There was a few grand in it. I took my girlfriend to America for three weeks or so and then when I came back I phoned John and said, "John, it's obvious this is not working out, so I'm gonna go up the road, okay?" And he was like, "Yeah, yeah, okay", not unfriendly. And I then said, "I don't wanna get into a slanging match, I'll just give [lawyer] Brian Carr a call."'

Lydon acknowledged this, again in friendly fashion. Says Wobble, 'It was unusual for him, or anyone, to pick up the phone at Gunter Grove. I got the impression that he had company and didn't want people to know who he was talking to.'

By August 1980, PiL's official line towards Wobble had been made public, even though Levene had emphasised to the *NME* only a month earlier that 'If any one of us left, then PiL would no longer exist'. Wobble's 'crime' was that he had used some *Metal Box* sessions as backing tracks for a solo project, namely the LP *The Legend Lives On – Jah Wobble in Betrayal*.

The album had been released by Virgin in early May, while the group was still touring America. The story that Wobble had 'stolen' the *Metal Box* tapes disappointed the straight-talking Stepney boy: 'I had been on poxy fucking sixty quid a week, and even that had become intermittent. I had signed my publishing over to PiL. John hadn't sorted me out. He wasn't to be trusted. At the beginning I owed him. But I had repaid the debt with interest. So I went off and made my solo stuff. In fact and I swear to God this is true, I gave PiL my backing tracks like "The Suit" for instance, that started out as "Blueberry Hill". I recorded it at Gooseberry and took it up to the Manor. I never snuck in and stole tapes from PiL. I wasn't going to be like the others and get fucked off empty handed; I was going to fucking well make sure that I came out of it (PiL) with something.

'The meeting with the lawyer did not start well: John and Keith were supposed to be at the meeting I had with Brian Carr but they didn't turn up. John really blew it there, we could have finished it amicably there and then like geezers.

'First thing the lawyer wants me to do is sign this thing, which basically signs away all cash advances from Japan for all my solo stuff. And I was like, "Er - no, I'm not signing anything like that," and he was like, "Er, okay then, fair enough... his hands were shaking. I think he was afraid that I'd go mad and smash his office up. In fact I just wanted to get away from the place. Although at least by going there I found out that Nippon in Japan were attempting to pay me a nice advance. When I left Carr's office I walked up Cheapside in bright sunshine. I remember that I did a little hop and a skip. I felt so happy.'

For Martin Atkins, news of Wobble's departure was closely followed by an unpleasant surprise closer to home. 'A couple of weeks after the American tour I went to get my money from Gunter Grove and it was like, "Oh, Wobble's gone, you know, he's out now".' To his horror, Atkins realised that he'd been unwittingly working on sessions for Wobble's solo album.

Wobble says: 'Yes that's true but all he needed to do was invoice Virgin as they had agreed to pick up the tab for session fees, but whatever he can't complain because I went and did his Damage Manual thing for a fraction of my normal fee, so we are quits now.'

Atkins continues, 'A week after Wobble's departure Keith said, "Oh yeah, by the way Martin, you're fired too!" He fired me three weeks after the American tour... I suppose if I'd been in charge of things and I thought that the band wouldn't be doing anything live for well over eight months then I'd probably let everybody go as well. I kind of understand it now though it was an unpleasant shock at the time - I hadn't really been fired from a band before.'

Lydon himself seemed to have forgotten that one of the grudges he – and, later, the other Pistols – developed against Malcolm McLaren was based on the fact they were ignorant of their finances, being paid just £50 a week while Glitterbest raked in five- and six-figure cash advances. Of course, there were a few major differences too: primarily,

Lydon was a key member of the creative musical process, far more than McLaren ever had been with the Pistols.

Anthony Wilson takes up Wobble's tale: 'When PiL finished, his Virgin contract had him screwed every which way. I remember we used our lawyer Paul Rodwell, who was a heavyweight ex-CBS lawyer, a legal eagle, a real Rottweiler. [So] we put [him] on to Wobble's case and got him out of his contract in a couple of weeks so he could get on with other stuff. I think he remembers that to this day. I think we paid for it ourselves, it was a favour to him, because he was well-liked by us all.'

'With that whole Sex Pistols scene,' says Wobble now, 'most of the people you find who were connected with them were very disappointed with the way things turned out in the end. There was a feeling they'd been ripped off in some ways - a feeling based on truth, on genuine grievances, in a lot of cases. And it's exactly the same with PiL. There's a disproportionate amount of people who are really disappointed - who felt they did not get what they thought they should get. And, funnily enough, I ain't one of 'em, not at all, 'cos I came in out of the blue and it's OK. It's like some kind of love affair, you hope it's gonna work out but it doesn't. I came out of it with autonomy, and a solo career, it all turned out for the good. You can't ask for much more than that, now can you?'

The power struggle within the group was becoming clearer: Keith Levene's actions, plus Lydon's attitude, had helped force out Jim Walker. Levene's actions had forced out Dennis Morris. And now John 'Jah Wobble' Wardle had had enough too. In many ways this suited Levene - PiL without Wobble could be a lot more 'video-centric', giving him and girlfriend Jeannette Lee a lot more room to be avant-garde visually. That, at least, was the theory.

By July 1980, then, PiL had lost five key members of 'personnel' in less than 18 months – Morris, Wobble, Walker, Atkins, and Dave Crowe (who quit shortly after Wobble's departure). Only three remained – Lydon, Levene and Jeannette Lee. The Public Image company seemed to have a lot of powerless, but angry, shareholders.

10
flowers behind the screen

Lydon's spur-of-the-moment decision to visit Dublin – city of his Irish roots – in early October 1980 soon proved to be a disastrous error. He was ostensibly there to see a live outing by the short lived band 4 Be 2, featuring his younger brother Jimmy, although he was also planning to scout out tour possibilities and/or re-location venues for the PiL organisation. But on Friday 3rd October, Lydon was arrested after a scuffle with two publicans from the Horse & Tram public house. The singer had been refused entry from their bar, and they had tried to throw him out – hardly a warm Dublin welcome.

Although he was the only one with any bruises, Lydon was taken to court. Charged with offences carrying a three month sentence, District Justice John McCarthy decided the two men offering to pay Lydon's £350 bail were 'unsuitable characters' whose money was not, apparently, good enough. When Lydon's Irish lawyer Myles Shevlin pleaded that the judge 'was being a little hard' on Lydon, McCarthy snapped back, 'No, I am not, I am giving him every chance! The question here is will he be available to the court on Monday or not?'

Lydon spent a long uncomfortable weekend at the city's Mountjoy Prison, before being granted bail and a postponement. He immediately returned to London to embark on sessions for PiL's next LP. At the actual trial, held in early December, District Circuit Judge Francis Martin dismissed the case against Lydon in under ten minutes. The accused seemed to shrug the incident off but, coupled with the numerous police raids on Gunter Grove, must have thought that his cards were indeed marked in the British Isles. Lydon would later reveal he had been attacked several times during his short stay in prison, and that he would never return to Ireland.

Following his sacking from PiL in the summer, Martin Atkins had returned to the States to tour with Brian Brain, a group that featured bassist Pete Jones, his old bandmate from The Hots. On his return to Britain in the autumn, he found that 'PiL were working on the *Flowers Of Romance* album. And they said, "You should come up, Martin". And I thought "I can't wait to hear everything you've done over the two weeks that you've been up there in the studio." And there was nothing done.' Nothing except some recordings of bizarre golden oldies: 'John sang "Twist And Shout" and John and Jeannette did a duet on "Johnny Remember Me", the old John Leyton hit. Which actually sounded fantastic.'

When Atkins and Levene weren't being locked out of studios over unpaid bills, original material for the album was recorded in 20- to 30-hour marathons at The Townhouse in London and the Manor in Oxfordshire, where a ghost seemed to be experimenting on Lydon and Levene's nerves. 'It would', according to Levene, 'suddenly go cold, freezing cold.' Levene would subsequently tell the *NME*'s Julie Panebianco in 1983 that the recordings happened during the closing stages of his three years of heroin addiction: 'I tried to make the session coincide with the part of the day where I really had the least amount in my system'. For his part, Atkins claims that his drive saw it finished: '*Flowers* was me and [engineer] Nick Launay going mad. "Nick, Nick, Nick," I said, "I'm going to sleep every night listening to this Mickey Mouse watch and there's rhythms inside of it that I want to drum to." [So] we'd put a big mic on it. Then Nick would say "Let's put it on a floor tom and it'll resonate even more." So we'd record that onto 24-track then I'd go play, "ding, da-ding da-ding" and take the time signature from the watch. Then Nick would put the harmoniser on there, we'd get something really going. And then we'd say, "Here John, come and have a listen to this." Or then I'd just leave and the next day I'd hear what John had added on the vocals. The drums, the Mickey Mouse watch sound effect, the backwards trumpets, that's all me...'

Not that Atkins' role was, by then, confined to drumming alone. 'I did a bit of bass myself on a couple of PiL things, just tinkering around. I was more into reading things onto quarter-inch tape and slowing the tape down to create sound textures.' This formed the basis for 'Vampire', a track from the *Flowers* sessions which remains unreleased after 25 years. Meanwhile, guitarist Levene was, remembers Atkins, 'upstairs playing Space Invaders a lot. His contributions, [like for] "Hymie's Hymn" were quite separate.' For Levene the fact that it works so well – for him at least – is partly due to studio technicalities at the time, technicalities affected by time. 'The thing to get in a studio is, as with *Flowers*, is to get a ten day lock-in or something. A week, ten days, two weeks, three weeks. Whatever you can get, whatever you can afford because then you can really get things done.'

Atkins left the PiL fold once again before recordings were complete, as he had to return to America for more Brian Brain dates: 'I just left 'em to it, I wasn't really involved in the mix. I wasn't even back in the PiL band anyway. I just played 'em a bunch of stuff and said, "Look, here's some more beats for you while I'm gone – if you use 'em, give me a co-write, OK? See ya!" I had trusted them, and I thought that was pretty crap of them 'cos they used that drumming for Timezone['s "World Destruction"] with Afrika Bambaataa'.

Writing credits on *Flowers Of Romance* list Martin Atkins on three of its songs – 'Banging The Door', 'Four Enclosed Walls' and 'Under The House'. 'Home Is Where The Heart Is', which became the B-side to the 'Flowers Of Romance' single, erroneously listed Jim Walker as a co-composer. In Atkins' words: 'Virgin admit to that mistake now.'

Atkins claims that a meeting with Lydon in 2003 revealed that he'd been even more involved in the finished work than he'd previously thought: 'John told me that I actually played on and co-wrote the song "Flowers of Romance" as well. And I said, "You know, I always felt that that was my drumming." Whether he steps up to the plate and tells Virgin, or not, is up to him.'

With PiL still recording the new album, there had been no new product from the group during 1980, save for an inconsequential item, 'Pied Piper,' that appeared in late October on a Virgin Records sampler *Machines*. Ian Penman in the *NME* was scathing both about its content – 'vituperatively empty noise at odds with the rest of the album' – and its cynicism – 'worth none of your money and 1'38" of no-one's time'.

Virgin's next solution to the drought of PiL product came with that reliable standby, the live album. Credited to 'Image Publique S.A.', *Paris au Printemps* ('Paris in the Spring') was a compilation from the two performances at Le Palace in January, and was released in November. With next to no promotion, it barely grazed the album charts, creeping to 61. Yet despite poor sound quality and so-so performances, reviews were relatively kind. Admittedly, Dave McCullough in *Sounds* regarded it as 'more Virgin's album than PiL's...

more pre-Xmas artifice than Lydonian hand-on-heart lettin' it all out.'

But *Melody Maker's* Lynden Barber revelled in its 'dangerous nightmare music that'll make you worry'. And Vivien Goldman in the *NME* – hardly a neutral voice in the debate, given she had recorded with Lydon just months earlier – explained that there were no overdubs on the album, with only, to quote Lydon, 'some reverb to drown out the booing'. In another section of the review that resembled a press release rather than a critique, Goldman also wondered rhetorically, 'What will PiL be minus Wobble? The answer is seven or so tracks already recorded for a new album'. Apparently, 'the Company's created a new kind of rhythm, a definite danceable rhythm not based on bass and drums'.

Paris Au Printemps (Paris In The Spring)
released November, 1980

Virgin were less convinced by this new direction. Although *Flowers Of Romance* was completed well before Christmas, the record company hated it, and delayed it until the spring of 1981. Even then, there was talk of only pressing 30,000 copies, and at one point, they had even suggested preceding its release with a re-issue of the single 'Public Image'.

Instead, *Flowers Of Romance* was anticipated with its title track, released in a slightly different mix as a single on 27th March. It had hints of the 'Burundi Black' beat that Adam & The Ants and Bow Wow Wow had already charted with, but also built in a nicely unsettling fashion, topped by Lydon's wailing tones and some surreal backing vocals. The references to 'starting again' and 'so-called friends' seemed to hint at the recent departures of Walker, Wobble, Morris and Crowe, but soon those words would have an even wider application. Once again, radio gave the song an extremely wide berth, but the *NME*'s Paul Du Noyer awarded it Single of the Week, and *Top Of The Pops* actually asked PiL back for its 9th April edition – Keith Levene was dressed in a doctor's white coat for the performance, while Lydon donned a dog-collar. The single climbed to 24.

Flowers Of Romance, *released April, 1981*

By then, the LP was in the shops, and despite her protestations, the publicity-shy publicist Jeannette Lee appeared on the sleeve as the sole cover star. Wobble's unifying bass was much missed, although the tracks with Martin Atkins' excitable drumming offered compensation for some. Opening track 'Four Enclosed Walls' seemed almost bloody-mindedly similar to the title track. After a startling beginning of squealing feedback, followed by a Tudor beat and a spray of Balinese bells, 'Phenagen' quickly fizzled out after barely two and a half minutes, despite Lydon's mad nursery-rhyme delivery. Levene's brooding 'Hymie's Him' was a look back to *Metal Box*, a threatening rhythmic soundtrack to some stylised nightmare. 'Track 8' was a shriek of sexual disgust, whilst 'Go Back', subsequently dismissed by Lydon as 'too throwaway, not good enough', had been recorded in the immediate aftermath of Lydon's release from prison. Lydon continued: 'It's horrible to listen to that kind of paranoia.'

Jah Wobble not only dismisses the first PiL album after his departure, but also questions the very essence of the group: 'An album which flatters to deceive. You listen to it and sonically it's not all that. To be brutally honest, we all know that the name PiL, after *Metal Box*, meant shite.'

His former rhythm partner Martin Atkins takes an opposing view: 'I think *Flowers Of Romance* is so strong – I dunno if you remember but it was slagged off at the time it came out. It's very difficult to work on an album that resonates 25 years later and remember that when we did it people were just like, "Oh my God, this is so awful"...'

In fact, the critical response was varied, even adulatory in places. John Gill in *Sounds* awarded the LP the maximum five stars, describing it as 'Absolute music!', and the band as 'The only savages ever to have invaded the avant-garde and triumphed!' *Melody Maker*'s Lynden Barber praised how 'at first it intrigues and on successive plays seduces' before promising 'If there's a more innovative record released during the next 12 months, I'll be astonished'. Though Ian Penman in the *NME* was unimpressed. 'PiL seem to be so retentively, forlornly hung-up,' he wrote, 'to a blinding neurotic degree – on their anti-rock'n'roll crusade as to lose sight of where this crusade might actually be taking them.' Bemoaning the 'lyrical and vocal slide into self-parody and laziness', he also wondered about the double-standards he perceived of the group: 'If lofty avant-garde types sit around at their leisure making messy noises it's pretentious, if we do it, it's honest, innit?'

The album entered the charts at number eleven, PiL's all-time peak position. After its release, Lydon explained that he never expected nor even wanted it to 'top the charts'. That kind of acceptance would mean that people had either caught up with PiL or that the band 'had gone three steps back!' This act of constantly shifting the goalposts was initially clever, but ultimately self-defeating, an attitude that the standard of future LPs would underline.

Meanwhile, the *NME* issue dated 4th April 1981, but published three days earlier, contained a news story that former Cream drummer Ginger Baker was joining PiL, and that the band was now in 'intense rehearsal' for a 'soon-to-be-confirmed tour of Northern Ireland'. It was an April Fool joke on the part of the paper's staff, presumably based on the notion that PiL had, by now, seemingly recruited most working drummers at some point.

PiL's life as a live entity remained in the balance. In May, they agreed to play two nights at the Ritz club in New York City, ironically in place of Malcolm McLaren's latest protégés, Bow Wow Wow, who had been refused entry due to visa and work permit difficulties. 'It happened because I was seriously into video technology,' explains Keith Levene. 'Back then, the Ritz had one of the very first big video screens in America. It was rare in 1981 for anywhere to have that, let alone a nightclub. So I went for it and talked John and Jeannette into it.

Bootleg of the infamous 1981 'Ritz Riot'

With a line-up that also included a rhythm section of Ed Carabello and Ariel Lucas, PiL began the gig behind the screen. Video cameras projected this image on to the huge screen, as a baying crowd, each member of whom had played $12, were constantly asked by Lydon, 'Are you getting your money's worth?'. Finally Levene provocatively said, 'This is your chance. If you destroy this screen, we will destroy you. We have the power up here.' Cue a hail of bottles, and a performance which ended after barely fifteen minutes. Whereupon, according to David Fricke, New York correspondent for *Melody Maker*, the Ritz DJ started playing a track called 'Rip Off', although it is unclear whether or not this was the Sham 69 song. Commented Richard Grabel, reporting for the *NME*: 'PiL had finally succeeded in really overturning the old rock and roll applecart. But just for one night. A somewhat futile gesture.'

Levene: 'I told the Ritz management, "We'll do two gigs here, back to back, but only if we are completely in charge of the video gear". The Ritz management said "Yeah, great, fine, whatever – as long as nothing gets broken, as long as the screen doesn't get touched." And what was the first thing to get trashed, of course? The screen.' The management had agreed to pay PiL $12,000 for the two nights – but the video screen alone cost more than that. The planned second gig on the Saturday night was cancelled.

A little over a year later, John Lydon told the *NME*'s Neil Spencer, 'It was never meant to be a gig at all. We agreed with the club that we'd do their videos for them and they went and advertised it as a PiL show. Then they completely over-reacted to the trouble... There was no audience riot. It was all so over-played.'

Levene subsequently told the same paper's Julie Panebianco in late 1983 that the performance at the Ritz had been deliberately curtailed by the group. '[John and Jeannette claimed] that I was treating them like puppets, then the morning of the gig they had their suitcases packed ready to go home.' Levene pleaded with them to stay, saying, 'If we don't do this gig we'll fuckin' get our legs broken'.

'We didn't want to do any place that was too arty or avant-garde,' Levene says now. 'We wanted to see what the Friday night gig crowd would make of such an event. And a lot of 'em got into it, as well as the boos there were loads of people cheering and even the kids who got a bit cut up were laughing afterwards, saying, "Wow, man that was great, the wildest thing ever". I still get people even now saying "I'm so glad I was there, that was so different, so unlike anything else". That's one thing we always tried to do with PiL, make every gig a big deal, make every gig relevant – a real event... It was mostly a fun event, it wasn't a heavy duty riot.'

'That New York Ritz riot was more like a joke, wasn't it?' Lydon himself claimed years later, 'they [the crowd] had fooled themselves into thinking it'd be just like the record – and then the record jumped.'

It was during the summer of 1981 that PiL relocated its nerve centre from London to New York. Just before departing, Lydon recorded contributions for two editions of London Weekend Television's regional youth magazine programme *20th Century Box*, presented by *NME* journalist Danny Baker. Screened at Sunday lunchtimes on July 26th and August 2nd, they were featured as part of 'The Rise of Independence' and 'Record Producers'. In July, the Lydon collaboration with Vivien Goldman, 'Launderette', had also been unleashed as a single.

In October, PiL finally left their American label Warner Brothers 'by mutual consent'. Lydon later remarked: 'It was like, "Give yourselves up to us so we can manipulate you." It was a, "We'll make you stars if you don't ask for much money" situation.'

'I just say to bands, if you want help breaking America then fine,' said Atkins years later, after starting his own indie label in the US, 'but that's a five-year commitment and how do you expect to get a huge commitment out of me without making one yourselves? If you wanna do a one album deal with a one-year option then forget it, it's not worth anybody doing anything. Bands have to commit and they have to really tour or nothing happens. Who wins? You know.'

By the time PiL and Warners parted company, Jah Wobble and original PiL drummer Jim Walker had teamed up in acid-jazz pioneers The Human Condition, with Dave Animal (ne Dave Maltby) on guitar. Their recordings were only issued on cassette – 'I like small contained things, they're more refreshing', said Wobble – and sold very well, averaging '7,000 to 8,000'. The first cassette, simply called *The Human Condition* and a live recording at Collegiate, London on 13th September 1981, was released only days later. A second live collection, *Live in Europe*, was recorded in Holland in November, a set that according to Wobble, was 'on sale before the gig was finished. Great gesture, great idea – if a little pointless'.

While in the Netherlands, the monumental drinking sessions sometimes took their toll. 'We were knocking back so much,' confirms Wobble, 'we once had this huge food fight at the home of this Dutch promoter. Anyway, Jim was so drunk that night he forgot to blink when I threw a bread roll at him and this hunk of bread detached his retina! Had to take him to hospital and everything and then I was helping him across the road for weeks.'

'We were drinking a lot. Wobble once said that when I'm really drunk he's only known one person like me,' says Walker, 'I mean I go completely insane. I totally let go – I'm just not a human being anymore. I become a caveman, completely psychotic.'

'Another time,' remembers Wobble, 'we were rehearsing in some church and me and Dave Animal went and hid in the belfry. Jim comes looking for us and it's totally quiet and totally dark – our eyes are used to it, of course, so we can see him searching for the light switch. Just before his hands reach it me and Dave give the bell ropes a great yank – and then we gave out a big scream, "Aaah!", as the bells started ringing. Jim was so surprised he fell backwards down this flight of stairs. He didn't get hurt that time though.'

Audiences for The Human Condition were appreciative, although critics were, in the main, indifferent to their charms. 'Levene and Rotten were jealous of Human Condition,' Walker said later, 'so we must have had something going for us.'

Nineteen eighty-two saw no new material issued by Public Image Limited. Rumours that the group were splitting up in late January were quickly quashed, but it was May before the band began recording material for a new album. After seeing a Brian Brain gig at New York's Mudd Club on 10th May – during which the group played a cover version of 'Careering' – Martin Atkins was once again lured back to the PiL fold. Just as well – Virgin threatened to cancel the advance on the new record if sessions did not begin immediately. A new keyboard player, Ken Lockie, formerly of Cowboys International, augmented the line-up, and recordings began to emerge from South Park Studios in Manhattan. Later that summer, a second member of Brian Brain – bassist Pete Jones – joined Atkins in the group, shortly before the ousting of Lockie.

In the midst of money shortages, Lydon was therefore glad to accept $10,000 cash when he landed the role of a psychopath by the name of 'Leo Smith' in a new feature film directed by Roberto Faenza, and starring Harvey Keitel. It was Lydon's acting debut. On release in 1983, the film – which began life under the title *Psycho Jogger* – would be known variously as *Corrupt* (USA), *Copkiller* (Europe), and *Order Of Death* in the UK. Clearly, Faenza – or maybe the casting agent Bonnie Zimmerman – had a preference for a rock star in the role – the part had already been rejected by Sting, Elvis Costello and, reportedly, Phil Collins. Filming for Lydon consisted of initial shoots in New York, followed by six weeks at Cinecitta Studios in Rome.

Lydon himself had fun, later telling journalists, 'Me and Harvey took the piss out of 'em relentlessly. Once the crew walked out on strike after we did that Italian Army Salute joke (raises hands in surrender gesture).' When asked if he liked the murderous character he portrayed in the movie, Lydon replied. 'Yes, because he's a swine. But he won through, he was just so convinced he was right that he was right, in the end. He was kind of positive, in a kind of negative way...'

By the time Lydon returned to the USA in August, Jeannette Lee was no longer a member of PiL. Instead she was working with her husband Gareth Sager in Rip, Rig and Panic, a Bristol-based quintet that mixed pop, funk and jazz. Its lead vocalist was Neneh Cherry, who would become a star solo performer at the end of the 1980s.

An American tour followed for PiL as 1982 gave way to 1983. One of Levene's final gigs in the group was at the Paramount Theatre, on New York's Staten Island on 26th March 1983. Later immortalised on the bootleg LP *Where Are We*, the concert is a fascinating time-capsule of the sheer startling power and swagger that they could still muster on a good night. After a spectral opening with 'Where Are You', the diamond-hard funk-rock of 'Mad Max' and 'Under The House' bring the crowd to its feet. 'Chant', with Lydon's yelps alternately hinting at sarcasm and desperation, is a tremendous showcase for Atkins' pile-driving drumming. Some of the most innovative aspects of PiL are long gone, but the mediocre recording quality cannot hide the dark atmospherics of the performance.

In November 1982 John and Keith's PiL had held a press conference at Le Dome, on Sunset Boulevard in LA. Lydon explained that, 'It's PiL at this table, right? But it's also PEP and it's also MIC. Public Enterprise Productions and Multi Image Corporation.' When asked what these fancy new acronyms actually did, Keith had a decidedly pat answer: 'MIC is an extension of the original PiL idea. It's not a group whatsoever. It produces PiL's music and artwork. It facilitates a multitude of people going in a multitude of directions...' Within just six months, these directions were to irrevocably ruin relations between PiL's last remaining founder members.

11
this is what you get

In the absence of PiL releases, Jah Wobble had flourished. During 1982, he had founded his own label Lago, and released two singles under his own name, 'Fading' and 'Long, Long Way', the latter co-written by Dave Animal. In early November, he had also joined forces with former Damned drummer Rat Scabies in the group Bartok – a single 'Insanity' was released by On Records. None of these got anywhere near the charts, but Wobble also got some TV exposure in early 1983 when he gave an interview to a youth series called *Whatever You Want*, hosted by Keith Allen, and made for the just-launched Channel 4. Live performances of 'Slow' and 'Get Carter' from the Brixton Ace venue also featured.

In a way, the 'cottage industry' of many of Wobble's releases throughout the first half of the 1980s served as a first attempt for what would be the founding and maintaining of his 30 Hertz record label from June 1997 onwards. 'To my delight,' he wrote in the *Independent on Sunday* in 2003, 'I found that I could record an album in my bedroom for virtually zilch. You could spend another £100 cutting it before ordering 2,000 pressings at around 35p a shot. I'd pick up the records from the manufacturers and deliver them all myself to various distributors, exporters and wholesalers, as well as specialist shops. I found that I'd come out of it with a good few quid.'

Punk rock already seemed a very long time ago by 1983. The adventurousness of post-punk had inevitably been diluted into mainstream pop, although many of punk's original movers and shakers were continuing to make some of the more interesting records of the time. Buzzcocks' Pete Shelley had diversified into electronic music, while the surviving members of Joy Division had, with the addition of Gillian Gilbert, become the innovative New Order, whose electro-funk single 'Blue Monday' was one of the most striking and memorable chart hits of the year. Even industry bête noir Malcolm McLaren, thanks partly to producer Trevor Horn and keyboard player Anne Dudley, had struck gold, via the groundbreaking LP *Duck Rock*, which juggled square-dancing anthems, hip-hop rhythms and South African township chants. Seemingly, the charts of 1983 could feature almost any type of music – except, ironically, punk rock itself; Virgin Records' reissue of 'Anarchy in the UK' on 3rd June ('to commemorate the General Election') flopped miserably.

Significantly, the template of the 'PiL organisation' had also influenced several examples of subversive pop. The British Electric Foundation (B.E.F.), formed by ex-Human League members Martyn Ware and Ian Craig Marsh, had gained critical plaudits, then some commercial success, with singer Glenn Gregory, in the socialist pop trio Heaven 17. Following his adventures with Malcolm McLaren, Trevor Horn founded his own record label, Zang Tumb Tuum (ZTT), whose first hit, the suggestive 'Relax' by Frankie Goes To Hollywood, became the biggest single since the Pistols' 'God Save The Queen' to have been banned by the BBC.

Back in New York, Public Image Limited, still working on a new record, were reaching irreconcilable differences. Keith Levene remembers the project going well – to begin with, at least: 'I was playing with this 24-track, getting things down... I think it was sounding good – Richard Branson came along and he agreed with me.'

Around the spring of 1983, a new composition, 'This Is Not A Love Song' emerged from sessions. The remixing of the track in June was the catalyst for disaster between Lydon and Levene, who argued bitterly over its direction. Finally, only days after bassist Pete Jones had quit, Levene announced he was also leaving.

'If things get too far away from how I want them to be,' reflects Levene, 'then fuck it, I'll just walk away from it, no matter how big the deal is. At the time I did say that PiL belonged to me and Wobble as much as John. It didn't all belong to John. But I never really thought about it seriously, not once I was out. After I'd left that was it – on to other things.'

Levene's departure occurred just prior to a PiL tour of Japan: 'I suppose I really should have gone with John and Martin. That would have made everything simpler, maybe kept us together but... there was the tension over the album – and I'd just got married and my first kid was on the way and all that.' When asked about the departure of Lee and Levene – and, indeed, why there were just so many PiL persons who'd walked away from him – Lydon snapped, somewhat simplistically, 'There's an awful lot of weak people in the world.'

Levene didn't go quietly. In November, he would tell the *NME*, 'John was my best friend for years; it was me, John and Sid. Sid died, and John has now died as far as I'm concerned. I think he really does need to see a psychiatrist. He's completely out of touch with his feelings.' On Martin Atkins: 'I cannot tell you how much I despise him.' Levene went on to denounce PiL's new manager Larry White 'who used to manage Davy Jones of The Monkees' – although he had previously been manager on PiL's American tour of 1980. The embittered guitarist, who had come to resent the over-dominance of the frontman in interviews and portrayals, implied that a lot of the internal wranglings were exacerbated by a basic lack of funds: 'If you are in the Stones or Fleetwood Mac making millions, I guess you can work with people you don't like; in PiL's situation, it couldn't have carried on because we had come to hate each other's guts.' He also claimed that he was offered just $10,000 to relinquish his rights on all his PiL compositions, and then told of future plans to open a studio with Mars Williams (of The Waitresses and Swollen Monkeys) and short-lived PiL keyboardist Ken Lockie.

Drummer Martin Atkins, needless to say, has a different perspective: 'Keith stole the tapes and released *Commercial Zone* – and there were some songs on there that he didn't even know existed, like "Miller High Life" – that was Pete Jones playing bass, me playing drums and Bob Miller, our sound man. We were experimenting with feeding the entire drum-kit through a synthesiser and I don't know if Keith was in the room – or even in the country.'

The public perception of *Commercial Zone* – released on Levene's own label PiL Records in November 1983 – added to the 'Levene legend' but irritated Atkins. 'There's all these misconceptions – attitudes like, "Keith's a genius and 'his version' was so much better". I mean, Keith is a genius. But that's not his version.'

Because of Lydon's disapproval, *Commercial Zone* only officially appeared in the United States, although thousands of copies were exported to the UK and elsewhere. Biographer Clinton Heylin considered it the last real PiL album, with most of it recorded in 1982 with Levene still in the group's ranks. Certainly, the original versions of 'Bad Life' (original title: 'Mad Max'), 'The Order of Death' ('The Slab'), 'Solitaire' ('Young Brits') and 'Where Are You?' ('Lou Reed II') are far more exciting and intricate than the rehashes on Lydon and Atkins' *This Is What You Want, This Is What You Get.*

To this day, Lydon refuses to acknowledge *Commercial Zone* as anything to do with PiL. Levene's comment is something of a rhetorical one: 'It annoyed certain people, but what can you do?' Despite promising plenty of fresh music, Levene would take four long years to reappear with any new post-PiL recordings. He later told the *NME* in 1989 of legal wranglings which 'took me a year-and-a-half. One minute, I didn't have to think about money and I was, without thinking, directing my energy in the right places. The next minute, I was broke.'

Suddenly with no guitarist or bass player, and with a tour of Japan pending, Lydon and Atkins had to fill a huge hole at the centre of PiL. The first replacement was bassist Louis Bernardi, a member of a covers band at the Holiday Inn at Atlantic City in New Jersey. Atkins arrived there to meet Bernardi, and found the band covering The Clash's 'Rock The Casbah'. Joseph Guida on guitar and keyboard player Tom Zvoncheck completed the line-up. The new trio had barely played outside the state of New Jersey.

With very little time to rehearse any new songs, PiL's first show with a new line-up – a warm-up for the tour of Japan at the Hollywood Palladium in Los Angeles on 10th June 1983 – would necessarily reactivate some supposedly unlikely but very familiar material. Atkins: 'When we did "Anarchy In The UK" at the Palladium, I was shocked. It was like a moment in a movie – you'd see the first twenty rows pogoing...all the way to the very back of the room, four thousand, five thousand people... Everyone was moving. And I thought, "Oh my God. We'll never be able to not play this song again, we're stuck with it." We couldn't get away from it. It was an easy Get-Out-Of-Jail-Free card which just got out of hand.' When a TV reporter later asked Lydon why he was now singing the Sex Pistols songs when he'd always said he wouldn't, the PiL frontman replied: 'I felt pressurised into having to do them and so I wouldn't. But now no one shouts for it I thought it'd be quite nice to do it.'

In fact, the 'Holiday Inn boys' had joined PiL without perhaps considering the logic of being in a group with the former Mr Rotten, as Martin Atkins explains: 'In LA I said, "Look, go on onstage, get plugged in, I'll be there in a minute". Ten seconds later, Louie Bernardi came running back into the dressing room saying, "Oh my

God! Oh my God! Somebody spat at me!" And I thought, "You're playing with Johnny Rotten, for God's sake! What the hell did you expect?" And from that moment on they just cowered at the back of the room.'

Atkins and the rest of PiL flew to Japan in mid-June to begin the tour at the Nakano Sun Plaza in Tokyo on the 21st: 'Japan was bizarre. I think the first [show] we were just trying to get through it – but then we realised we'd sold out seven nights [there] – a 3,000 seater. We thought that means 21,000 people wanna come to see us but no... it means 7,000 or 8,000 people wanna see you two or three times. A couple of thousand of them came every night to exactly the same seats. So we tried to change the show around a bit and respond to that.'

Although the group also played dates in Nagoya, Osaka and Kyoto, the Sun Plaza dates dominated their itinerary. 'Highlights' from the fifth and sixth nights – 1st and 2nd July – were captured live for both video and a double live LP. The latter was the lacklustre *Live In Tokyo*, released in October, and already PiL's second live album in five releases. Even though the 32-track recording had been excitingly 'state-of-the-art', utilising a Mitsubishi X-800 recorder – one of only three in existence at the time – it was a wasted experiment.

The group had not made serious money in Japan, according to their agent. Food, drink and accommodation were then pricey in Japan. But PiL's problems were also more basic, according to one source. When Dave Goodman took a royalty cheque for Lydon down to Heavenly Management – from sales of one of Goodman's Pistols' productions – 'Rotten's agent or manager told me that they really needed the money as they were broke and still hadn't paid off their whore bill from the Japanese tour! I've actually still got a signed receipt for that cheque!'

The next PiL single had to sell. Perhaps against all the odds, it did. 'This Is Not A Love Song', the very track that had finally driven Lydon and Levene apart, was released in early September 1983. Penned in response to Virgin's constant request, only half in jest, that PiL could supply some kind of love song they could peddle, there wasn't much to it in all honesty, beyond a deliriously catchy sneering chorus and crisp funk backing. The fact that its B-side was 'Public Image', now nearly five years old, didn't seem to be a hindrance. Indeed, the single climbed to number five in the UK, their highest-ever chart placing, and caused the most extraordinary ticket demand for their very first British and European tour later in the year.

There were more personnel changes in the meantime – Arthur Stead had replaced Zvoncheck on keyboards, while guitarist Joe Guida had been dropped then hastily reinstated. Lydon himself was supposedly on fine form. On 26th October, he held a London press conference at the Royal Lancaster Hall, Bayswater. Entertaining and newsworthy on one level – his petulant responses were broadcast on every news magazine programme that was having a slow day – one or two music press journalists were a little more questioning of the set-up. Lynden Barber of *Melody Maker*, who had probably given PiL's actual music the best reviews in the previous two years, was at the press conference and was torn between its complacent subject and the baying journalists competing to ask the most imbecilic questions. Initially curious to ask why the newly-released *Live In Tokyo* was so 'pathetic', Barber instead relates how 'I thought I'd got him when I asked whatever happened to his much-trumpeted plans to get into video...' Lydon's response was, of course, sarcastic and non-committal: 'It was a load of mouth. Sorry.'

Barber was sufficiently aware to know that Lydon was playing a game with no fixed rules: 'As always with Rotten, it's not that he's always ironic, more that it's impossible to know whether he is being ironic or not, and it's this knowledge that no-one can figure out a way to pin him down that adds to his inflated sense of confidence and endearingly humorous arrogance...' Not that this could excuse some of Lydon's bleatings, which Barber likened to the opinions of 'yet another ghastly media bore'. Or the actual quality of the recent single, 'a song of almost cretinous banality'.

Two days after the press conference, PiL performed on the first show of the second series of Channel 4's live music show *The Tube*. Transmitted from Tyne Tees' studios in Newcastle-upon-Tyne, the occasion was something of a reunion for Martin Atkins, who had now been resident in New York for over two years: 'I remember my sister coming up because she was living in Durham and some of my schoolfriends came'. New presenter Leslie Ash, who had starred in *Quadrophenia* and would later feature in TV sitcom *Men Behaving Badly*, conducted a quite excruciating interview with Eurythmics, but did confide her utter relief to a *Melody Maker* reporter that at least she hadn't had to interview John Lydon. PiL's performance horrified just about anyone who saw it – 'cabaret' versions of 'Flowers of Romance', 'This Is Not A Love Song' and – already inevitably – 'Anarchy In The UK'. What's more, the studio audience seemed to be populated by a tribe of third generation punk rockers – the 'mohican' brigade that

Lydon professed to despise.

The following week, Faenza's *Order Of Death* finally opened in British cinemas, eight months after its European premiere. Although slammed at the time by the British press – *Time Out* magazine decreed that Lydon was about as threatening as a 'wet poodle' – it received good reviews elsewhere and the then influential *Maltin's Movie & Video Guide* (USA) described it as 'entertaining and intriguing' and the two leads were further commended for their 'fine' performances. Patrick Zerbib in *The Face* went so far as to say that Lydon was 'far more fascinating on screen than Keitel'. In 1986, Lydon cited its failure in the United States by saying, 'They ruined it at the premiere, they showed the end first and it was reviewed as such. Terrible.'

In late November, PiL preceded a lengthened British tour with a week-long jaunt at selected European venues. First stop was the Paradiso club in Amsterdam, a small church-like venue that Lydon had last played as a Pistol in January 1977. CS gas canisters were set off by various punk headbangers before a knife-wielding yob jumped up onstage and tried to stab PiL's frontman. After the group left the stage, fights engulfed the club. Journalist Simon Mattock went backstage to find 'Nora in hysterics. The knife incident had really freaked her out. She kept asking John if he was alright as he walked out of the building, face like thunder. Everyone associates that kind of mayhem with the Pistols, but PiL copped it far worse.'

The tour wound up in the UK in December 1983. On the 11th, it reached King George's Hall in Blackburn, where teenage punk fan Alan Parker and his friends had excitedly snapped up tickets. 'We'd never seen Lydon,' says Parker. 'And you thought, "Fucking hell! John Rotten's coming to Blackburn!"' The gig itself, however, seemed to establish a pattern of calculated spontaneity, as Parker claims: 'Because of the age it was, there was a lot of gobbing going on. Lydon said, "I didn't come out of a nice warm flat in LA to come to this piss-hole in the snow to be gobbed at!" When I got home that night, Dad said, "Was it cancelled?" because we'd come back so early. I later heard bootlegs of that night and PiL lasted less than 26 minutes. And [apparently] every night he'd moan about piss-holes in the snow. Every night he'd storm off for five or ten minutes and come back on with the neon halo on a wire over his head [to perform 'Religion']. And after 20 minutes, he'd finish...'

Lydon, Atkins and bassist Louis Bernardi began 1984 at Maison Rouge Studios in London, working on what became *This Is What You*

Want, This Is What You Get. Also present for the sessions were guitarist Colin Woore, keyboard player Richard Cottle and sax player Gary Barnacle. For Atkins, who was now Lydon's closest collaborator and co-producer, it was an eye-opening experience to work on an entire album alone. 'When it comes to production, John has amazing ears. He has the ability to listen to a mix [while] he's drawing all over the console in chinagraph pencil, suggesting techniques to dim down a sound before you reach for all the effects. Just use the EQ and the stereo field – stuff that I do now naturally.'

Lydon also demonstrated how his knowledge of reggae had some practical applications: 'He would amaze me with some Jamaican dub techniques, like feeding stuff through a pair of headphones in a metal sink and recording that back – which takes all the tone out of the hi-hats and puts them in a very different place. It's almost like a lo-pass, hi-pass filter. [Then on] things like "Tie Me To The Length of That", we just jammed – John played this thing that was like a cross between a mellotron and an electric organ – and we got some great sounds out of it. He played this walking, ever-changing bass line and I drummed to it and I felt that we were just totally connected at that point. Every time he changed, I was there with him, I'd change and he'd be there.'

The brassy riffs and multi-tracked vocal effects, which had helped 'This Is Not A Love Song' become so memorable, were revisited for the LP, giving its overall sound a rich density that made much of the previous few offerings seem sparse and lazy. However, Lydon subsequently bemoaned that there was no conflict, no tension and therefore no creative fulfillment: 'There was no feedback. If I had a crap idea, the crap idea would go on to vinyl almost directly.'

Released in early May ahead of the album, the single 'Bad Life' only reached 71 in the charts. Adam Sweeting in *Melody Maker* was contemptuous enough of the A-side – '"This is what you want, this is what you get", caterwauls Lydon as though it's somehow our fault...' – but positively harangued its flip, the previously-unreleased tape-loop excuse 'Question Mark'. Described by Virgin's press officer as 'extraordinary', Sweeting settled instead for 'shatteringly dull'.

This Is What You Want, This Is What You Get reached the shops on 9th July, during a summer that boasted an even quieter record release schedule than usual. Not even this desert of new product could propel the LP any higher than 56. Lynden Barber – yet again reviewing a PiL album for *Melody Maker* – was pleasantly surprised and amused, branding it the 'most consistent' LP: 'Lydon is making us rattle the rib-cage again. His wit has always been honed sharply enough to carve the stupidity of his inquisitors into strips, and have the audience collapsing in fits, but thankfully he's now got it back on record'.

Keith Levene, whose *Commercial Zone* project (in slightly revised form) had begun to turn up on import in the UK by September, was unsurprisingly underwhelmed by PiL's new 'official' long-player. He told *Sounds* reporter Andy Hurt that the same paper's (one-and-a-half star out of five) review of *This Is What You Want* 'made me feel a lot better! I went straight out and recorded a new track!' Not that any 'new track' would see the light of day for some considerable time. Levene mentioned in the same interview of his intention to record a 'heavy metal rap' collision under the moniker 'The Ninja'. A song called 'Rap City' was pending for release, but seemingly never surfaced.

For PiL, another tour loomed, and this time round, its line-up was not going to be completed by 'cabaret artists'. Martin Atkins: 'We went back to LA to audition. We auditioned like 80 people for each job – Flea from Red Hot Chilli Peppers came down to audition for bass.' In fact, he was offered the job, but declined, reportedly saying he only wanted to jam with the band. Eventually, the vacancies were filled by Canadian guitarist Mark Schultz, and by Americans Bret Helm (bass) and Jebin Bruni (keyboards). Atkins remembers they 'were just huge fans and it was "Oh John, can we play 'Bodies'? Can we play 'Bodies'..?" all the time, so we started playing [it].'

For Atkins, the second touring trip east, in December 1984, rapidly became a nightmare. 'My relationship with John had just deteriorated to the point where I thought that my only option – to try and level things out for the last two months – was to tell him that I was leaving. "Just gimme a break, it's eight more weeks 'til I leave – I'm outta here." But that just made things worse. He felt tremendous disrespect for me, which I understand now – anybody in that position is going to feel betrayal. Because it was our band at that point, our band and nobody else's. To say you're leaving 'our band' is a real slap in the face to its founder.

'At the same time you've got three new guys in the band who are huge Lydon fans – who given the choice of being nice to me or being nice to John, are gonna be nice to John. So it was a fairly awful touring situation to be in, I felt quite isolated and I remember John suddenly screaming at me onstage in Australia that I was playing "Religion" too long or too slow or something. And I thought, "But those songs have never had a set tempo or a set length or structure – why is he freaking out now?" It was time to go...'

But Atkins was already too aware of how little his departure would affect the overall identity of Public Image Limited. 'I knew PiL, and John, would go on without me,' Atkins commented. 'John's a very powerful person, you know – I didn't think for even one second that me leaving PiL would stop it. On balance I'd actually rather have it continue and be glorious than fail.'

12
anger is an energy

At the end of 1984, John Lydon joined in a growing chorus of anti-Cold War protest with Timezone, a collaboration with hip-hop prime mover Afrika Bambaataa, who had already scored club hits with the legendary James Brown, and with the Kraftwerk-sampling 'Planet Rock'. Together the bad boys of London's Finsbury Park and New York's Bronx conjured up the chilling 'World Destruction' single – a jerkily rhythmic classic that came with some uncredited drumming from a percussionist called Martin Atkins.

Although the terrible twins picked up a fair amount of radio airplay, the single only just made it into the Top 50. Critics, however, were underwhelmed. Danny Kelly in the *NME* could not hide his disappointment: 'The Bill Laswell organised rhythm track is back without saving grace and backs a staggeringly inappropriate Nicky Skopelites HM guitar strut and the worst synth-bits in the career of the great Bernie Worrell. All this and another gutless display of opportunism by Lydon we don't need.'

Nineteen eighty-five was a particularly quiet year for past and present members of PiL. After 'World Destruction', Lydon returned to the studio with Laswell, this time to contribute vocals to 'The Animal Speaks', a track by the American band The Golden Palaminos. Wobble was probably the busiest, notably on his collaborations with Ollie Marland. 'Love Mystery', a single release in April, featured an early vocal cameo from Shara Nelson who would later grace some of Massive Attack's most dazzling recordings in the early 90s. Wobble also joined Levene on the Dub Syndicate album *Tunes From The Missing Channel*, issued in June. Nevertheless, the flow of gigging was becoming a trickle, and after May 1985, he was to undertake no live work for three years.

In the autumn, recording sessions commenced in New York on the next PiL studio record. Laswell remained on production duties, and recruited several session stalwarts. On keyboards, in came Ryuichi Sakamoto, formerly of Japanese techno-pop pioneers Yellow Magic Orchestra, who had also collaborated with David Sylvian and scored the soundtrack to the film Merry *Christmas Mr Lawrence*. Former Zappa collaborator Steve Vai was brought in on guitar. And to replace Martin Atkins on drums – amusingly, for those who were aware of that *NME* April Fool of 1981 – was none other than Ginger Baker. Atkins is flattered: 'That's very complimentary, to be replaced by a legend like Ginger Baker.'

Early in 1986 Lydon had something to celebrate: a court victory over the auld enemy, Malcolm McLaren. In a way, ex-Pistols Cook and Jones had made the verdict inevitable when they'd deserted McLaren by swapping sides way back in 1979. But the legal wheels of Britain grind slow and it had taken seven more years for the legal battle against McLaren to be won. The triumph gave the band – and Sid's mother, Anne Beverly – access to over £880,000. Minus the hundreds of thousands of pounds that went to the various solicitors, barristers and receivers... Lydon was triumphant but pragmatic in victory: 'I'm pleased it's all over. I'm glad the hassles are behind me. Now buy the record. It's called "Rise".'

Unquestionably PiL's most outstanding single in many years, 'Rise' (or 'Single' according to the sleeve) was released five days after the outcome at the high court. Reviewers were ecstatic. One 'Mr Spencer' in *Sounds* reminded readers, 'This man's talent is immeasurable'. The *NME*'s Simon Witter regarded it as 'truly refreshing', and Adam Sweeting in *Melody Maker* described it as a 'thumping, mesmerising stretch of luxurious noise'.

'Rise' reached number eleven in the singles chart, thanks partly to an unprecedented amount of radio play (considering that it was a PiL record). With Lydon almost singing in the verses, and unleashing unforgettable refrains like 'Anger is an energy', the record's meaning, at face value about the torture methods employed by apartheid police in South Africa, was still complex and haunting enough to beguile anyone who heard it. An appearance on *Top Of The Pops* followed on February 20th, featuring Don Letts and Leo Williams – both of Big Audio Dynamite – and Bruce Smith, formerly of Rip Rig and Panic.

The eponymous trick on the sleeve of 'Rise/Single' was repeated for the long-player, released in early February; depending on what format you invested in, PiL's seventh LP was called *Album*, or *Cassette*, or even *Compact Disc*. A *Melody Maker* cartoon, published at the beginning of March, took this joke to its logical conclusion, when it depicted Lydon signing a fan's copy of the LP with the word 'Autograph'.

The effective and startling 'Rise' was the standout track on *Album*, although 'F.F.F.', saying goodbye to 'fair-weather friends' complete with chuggy and whining guitars, was another highlight. 'Bags', meanwhile, was a paean to Lydon's own vertigo – with the 'bloated body' image representing 'the end result when somebody falls off a cliff or building and the black rubber bag is what they take you away in'.

Neil Perry of *Sounds* was full of recommendation for *Album* – 'a wonderful, stunning and equally confusing record'. Other critics were less convinced – The Stud Brothers at *Melody Maker* branded it 'complacent, sluggish and apathetic', and went on to scoff at the way in which the session players 'indulge their most notorious cliched extravagances', in particular Vai's solos of 'unparalleled silliness, really going absolutely bananas on "Bags"'. Their conclusion was a sober one: 'Lydon must still revel in criticism, his past leading him to believe it a result of controversy. What he may fail to realise is that, whoever you are, you can be boring and criticised for it.'

Perhaps even more damning than the Studs' critique was the review written by Gavin Martin in the *NME*. Although complimentary about the LP itself, Martin wrote the review as if it were a Lydon obituary, published in the year 2003. It suggested that *Album* was a full-stop, an ending of sorts for Lydon and PiL.

One thing could be relied upon – Lydon's impeccable quotability, as demonstrated by a rush of front cover stories in the UK music press. Now comfortably resident with Nora in Los Angeles, he expressed enjoyment for the cutting-edge British TV comedy of *The Young Ones* and *The Comic Strip Presents...* He admitted to enjoying the argumentative nature of interviews, particularly when it came to being provocative: 'Even though I'm utterly bland is shocking in itself', he told Adam Sweeting in *Melody Maker*. On singing, he confessed to Jack Barron of *Sounds*: 'I still don't know how to sing. It isn't the point I suppose, but that's my own insecurity. When I hear voices like Sam Cooke's...they can humble you. It's very good to be humbled from time to time'.

He claimed to have little patience for the impending tenth anniversary of punk rock, and said of the ridiculous and much-hyped video-punk band Sigue Sigue Sputnik (featuring Tony James of Generation X), 'They're a joke, they're like something out of Boots the Chemists really'. Following his appearance in *Order of Death*, some film roles had been suggested, although none appealed. 'They wanted me to play a bounty hunter from Mars who comes to Earth to look for escaped convicts from Venus,' he giggled to Andy Strickland from *Record Mirror*. 'The minute I land I turn into a Johnny Rotten-type character with a ray-gun.' It was in the same interview that he told of rejecting a request to appear in the American TV show *The A-Team*: 'Boy George is doing the episode that I turned down!'

In contrast to the glowing response towards 'Rise', its follow-up single – 'Home' – was released to almost no interest whatsoever, peaking at 75. A British tour in May was well-attended, however. Anyone expecting a commemoration of the punk rock's ten years may have been surprised by the cover of Led Zeppelin's 'Kashmir', but satisfied by the climactic reading of 'Pretty Vacant', even if Lydon had only actually penned a few lines of the Glen Matlock composition.

When critics told Lydon he was pandering to the more retarded punk fan – and verging on self-parody – he had answered with his usual defiance: 'I'm pandering to no one except myself. PiL's concerns are mine – mine and nobody else's!' Nevertheless, such bluster tended to betray that PiL, even as a concept, was fast becoming nothing more than The Johnny Rotten Backing Band. In spite of this, its touring line-up was one to be reckoned with. Bruce Smith was on drums, the keyboardist was Lu Edmonds and the bassist Alan Dias. The guitarist was none other than John McGeoch, formerly of groundbreaking acts like Siouxsie & The Banshees and Magazine.

As was becoming traditional with PiL live outings, the tour was dogged with trouble. At the opening show – Hanley's Victoria Halls – Lydon was hit by a billiard ball, and at the final gig, London's Brixton Academy on the 27th, the usual hails of spit and glasses from unrepentant punks rapidly escalated into a bloody riot. The lighting rigs were tugged over with rabid fervour, PA stacks quivered, and fighting caused a dozen arrests. Lydon ordered PiL offstage but that only seemed to make things worse. With the violence getting out of hand the Academy's management pleaded with the band to go back on. They did so but during the encore a punk leapt onstage and took a swing at the PiL singer. After the intruder had been manhandled offstage, Lydon lashed out, verbally: 'I was looking forward to this gig but you really don't deserve it. Go back up North! You deserve all-out nuclear war, you really do...'

But London's reception seemed almost friendly compared with the mayhem that was to greet PiL in Europe in 1986. Its nadir was reached on September 12th at the Donauinsel Festival in Vienna, Austria. Within minutes of starting, a huge two-litre bottle of wine flew through the air and smashed into McGeoch's head. His scalp opened almost instantly, pumping out blood. He required forty stitches and the rest of the European tour was immediately cancelled.

PiL roadie Roadent, who'd performed the same task for the Clash in 1976-77 before becoming a minor German soap star, was present at the time. 'John and everyone else were too busy to deal with it so I – though I was blind drunk – had to take John McGeoch to the hospital. He was in a right state, completely soaked with blood from his head to his toes – which sobered me up pretty quick. Then at the hospital they had to hold his scalp apart to pick out all the jagged bits of glass. I got to see his actual skull. To get him back together took dozens and dozens of big stitches....'

During McGeoch's recovery, the rest of PiL took a few months sabbatical. Smith played on some of the sessions for Terence Trent d'Arby's debut LP *Introducing The Hardline*. Edmonds toured Germany with 3 Mustaphas 3. In the spring of 1987, they reconvened to record the next PiL LP with producer and Art of Noise alumnus Gary Langan. During the construction of new material for what became *Happy?*, they also laid down re-recordings of several PiL classics, intended for a compilation called *Renovations*. Lydon later justified the planned collection by saying, 'Won't be full price and, if you don't want it, you don't have to buy it', but it never materialised, save for 'Religion' and 'The Suit' which would creep out as B-side fodder. 'Flowers of Romance', 'Banging The Door' and 'Tie Me To The Length of That' were also reworked, but remain unreleased to this day.

Happy? itself arrived in the shops in September 1987. 'Seattle' was a tightly tuneful rant about the industrial wasteland cities that Thatcherite Reaganomics were spreading across the Western world. Thatcherism got another back-hander on 'Save Me' where Lydon compared it with religious fanaticism. The driving 'Angry' was a return to familiar themes but it had a dark, yearning arrangement of its own – as well as being an attack on an indifferent audience. The juddering 'The Body' showed the guitar skills of John McGeoch at their best, which dovetailed impeccably with the chorus's female backing.

For the most part, though, it was an unremarkable set. *Rolling Stone* put a brave face on matters, describing Lydon as a 'visionary' whose best work may be 'yet to come', but it was in the shadow of critical and commercial indifference. 'Their humour has withered on the vine,' yawned the *NME*'s Biba Kopf. Ron Rom in *Sounds*, peculiarly, gave the record credit for talking down to its audience and believed it to be 'as cynical as the question mark that supports it.' Simon Reynolds in *Melody Maker* – thoroughly intoxicated by the Levene/Wobble era of the group many years earlier – rated the album's final cut, 'Fat Chance Hotel', 'with a (literally) nagging hook and a strange sound like a Mexican brass band disappearing down a massive plughole', but found all that came before it 'New Wave at its most colourless and asexual'. In particular, Reynolds found the groaning weight of expectations and the historical perspective of Lydon's career and persona rendered the record 'almost impossible to listen to'. Lyrically, Lydon had cornered himself with 'trite rhyming, chaste stuff about "uniforms", "mindless ants"...But with that voice these are the only kind of words that Lydon can sing...'

Even in interviews, there was something exasperatingly pat by now about John Lydon – contrary for the sake of it, it appeared. *Melody Maker*'s Mat Smith confessed in his (edited) August 8th cover story that the original 'blueprint was far more exhausting', a litany of targets buried in a yah-boo-sucks approach. While it was faintly refreshing to have someone, anyone, in 1987 describing U2 as 'mediocre pub rock on a grand scale', or the tabloids as 'a manipulation by extremely tedious spiteful third-rate people', when it came to Lydon's opinions on the likes of Curiosity Killed The Cat, frankly, who cared? The only kind words Lydon could find about the contemporary music scene were for, of all things, 'the new Wet Wet Wet single', although he immediately tempered this (deliberately inflammatory?) remark by describing the grinning quartet as 'absolute goonybirds'.

For the most part, however, one was left wondering about which flecks of his vitriol were sincere, which were ambiguous and which were simply taking the piss. A musing on PiL's chart positions – 'Whether there's a Number 1 single on there, I wouldn't know. That's up to the general public. I think everything I've done should have been Number 1' – could have been any one of the three options. Whether or not Lydon worried about record sales, Virgin must have done, and there was good reason to worry. *Happy?* reached number 40 in the album charts, and just a fortnight later, had disappeared.

'Seattle', when released as a single in August, had not even reached the top forty. 'The Body', its second 45, was the first ever PiL single to miss the top 75 completely.

Other former members of the Public Image Limited clan had similarly fallen from grace. Jah Wobble had enjoyed critical and artistic success for three years after his departure from PiL. However he had finally succumbed to alcoholism and addiction to cocaine. But, by 1986 he was in recovery and began working for London Underground, tackling everything from ticket collecting and sweeping platforms to eventually driving the trains.

An oft-repeated story is the one he has told about a tannoy message he delivered at a tube station. 'One day I just walked up to the PA microphone at Tower Hill station and announced in formal train announcer style to all these commuters, "I used to be somebody, I repeat, I used to be somebody."

'Then I just smiled and went back to sweeping. The funny thing is no one seemed to notice. I actually wasn't upset. I'd said it for a laugh, that was my feeling at the time. Musically I used to be someone, a contender, and that was all over now, but funnily enough I felt more alive than ever. I was very happy to be off the bottle - and to still be alive.'

Reading matter for Wobble addressed this sense of relief and his discomfort with his past. In 1986, he read *The Strange Life Of Ival Osokin*, the sole novel to be written by P. D. Ouspensky. 'I'd made a lot of fuck-ups and was off the drink and drugs. It made me feel a lot better about my past. This fella goes back in time armed with the knowledge of what he's done and finds he makes all the same mistakes over again. Deep, funny and very comforting.'

Musically, he was also inspired by Salif Keita's *Soro* album, and thinking, 'I still fancy this job.'

In early May 1988, Wobble used a fortnight's leave from the Underground to tour what was still West Germany with the Invaders of the Heart. It was his first foray into live work for three years. The most important member of the group was perhaps Jaki Liebezeit, formerly of Can, whose rolling rhythms were the ideal counterpoint for Wobble's basslines. The two had met in 1980 when they made Island record's 'How Much Are They' with another Can member, Holger Czukay.

Wobble later recalled to *The Birmingham Post*, 'I was obsessed with playing this new heavy modal dub, based on intuition and working in musical codes. Jaki understands this perfectly.' Later in 1983, they worked together on 'Snakecharmer' with the Edge from U2.

Meanwhile, in America, a name from PiL's past had started to hang out with John Lydon. But the brilliant young designer Kenny Mac-Donald was now using large amounts of hard drugs – something that Lydon was no longer prepared to put up with. Perhaps partly because of all that had gone on before with Keith Levene and PiL. Perhaps because MacDonald was a non-musician, whose eccentricities and habits no longer had to be tolerated. Either way, within weeks Kenny was edged out and his phone calls – perhaps understandably – were returned with decreasing frequency. At the time of writing, MacDonald is serving a life sentence in a UK prison for the alleged murder and mutilation of his girlfriend.

After a month of supporting INXS on a lucrative American tour in March 1988, PiL spent the summer preparing to record a new LP with Bill Laswell in New York, but sessions would dissolve into arguments within a week. Following fruitless attempts to remix the tracks with other producers, including reggae producer Scientist, the recordings were abandoned, and PiL returned to the UK having incurred recording debts of $80,000.

In the late summer of 1988, PiL toured the Eastern half of Europe. Live shows included entertaining a 200,000-strong crowd at the 'Soviet Peace Festival', staged in Tallin in Estonia on 26th August, and a Greek 'Rock Festival' in Athens nine days later. The latter ended, increasingly predictably, with the audience storming the stage, and anarchists throwing rocks and petrol bombs. The latter also set fire to rubbish bins and several rare trees, eventually causing some $2 million worth of damage. Following these dates, Lu Edmonds left the group, due to tinnitus.

The questions regarding PiL's identity and credibility still refused to die down. Hadn't they originally said they were never going to tour, let alone tour endlessly? And, now, who or what were PiL anyway – without the founding members who had made those original ideological decisions in 1978 and 1979, what was left? Bass player Alan Dias may have insisted to a reporter from *Sounds* in 1989, 'This ain't no backing band', but surely it was now just the John Lydon show and so why, many wondered, didn't he just call it that? Surely the whole point of PiL was collaboration and co-operation, 'democratic mixes' and 'new communications'? Such rhetorical questions were raised in Clinton Heylin's enlightening and critical biography of the band – *Rise/Fall* – that appeared in 1989.

Lydon's inconsistencies were summed up by a non-plussed Martin

Atkins. 'I'd have to be a fool to be surprised by anything a personality like John Lydon did.' Neither praise nor put-down, it was merely a plain old-fashioned statement of fact. Lydon himself continued to claim in interviews that he had moved on from punk rock's clichés – he reacted with horror to the news that Guns'N'Roses were long-time Sex Pistols fans with the words 'That band really have misunderstood us. It was all about opening things up, not closing things down'.

What became the 9 album was eventually completed in London and Los Angeles, and released in May 1989. The new producer was American Stephen Hague, who had achieved massive success with Pet Shop Boys, New Order and – on his 1984 pop-opera album *Fans* – Malcolm McLaren. A strange hybrid of stadium rock and tepid disco, Keith Cameron of *Sounds* would describe the resulting effect as 'like Mark E. Smith fronting Simple Minds', but declared that 'Too often, 9 is in thrall with style for the sake of it.' Jack Barron, who by now had defected from *Sounds* to the *NME*, applauded the choice of Hague for producer: 'He has teased out all the strengths of the current PiL and amplified them.' But despite some smart lines – for instance, 'Same Old Story''s 'Who gets the mansions? We get the ruins?' – much of it sounded tired. Even the positive reviews – Steve Sutherland in *Melody Maker* being one prime example – wound up mirroring the sloppiness on show, as if self-importantly writing 'Complacency count: nil' as a pay-off somehow legitimised both the standard of the record and the critique. Essentially, critics were back to describing PiL records as 'intriguing' without really explaining, or perhaps even knowing, why.

Before PiL departed for a US tour in the company of New Order and The Sugarcubes, the usual swathe of interviews to promote the record were (superficially at least) far more interesting. Chris Roberts of *Melody Maker* managed to amass a list of who Lydon currently admired – 'Edwina Currie, Jonathan Miller, kd lang, fresh air, anyone who gets a reaction, Hiawatha, Mike Leigh, Lindsay Anderson, Alan Bennett, sly wit, Janet Street-Porter' – amongst the vaguely predictable sideswipes at the ubiquitous (of Jonathan Ross: 'a useless plank of wood').

Former guitarist Keith Levene's disgust with what PiL had become had not dimmed with the passing of time. Speaking to *Sounds* in the final weeks of the 1980s, he claimed the entity to be 'a travesty, a disgrace. I've got far more of a right to that name than the man with the current responsibility. I don't think that the man is hungry enough these days – he's too tied up with the lawyers...'

Otherwise, though, Levene seemed relatively content with his lot by this time, even more so in an interview with the *NME* that was published the very same week. He was generous towards those who had undeniably borrowed his distinctive style of guitar playing: 'I just say, "Good luck to him". I put it down to good taste.'

He had just released the LP *Violent Opposition*, the title of which had originated from a quote by Albert Einstein which had read 'Great spirits have always encountered violent opposition from mediocre minds'. The album contained a mixture of original material with cover versions of Jimi Hendrix's 'If Six Was 9', Dave & Ansil Collins' reggae classic 'Double Barrel' and 'Cold Turkey'. The latter, a reworking of the harrowing Lennon song about heroin addiction, was awarded a triumphalist punchline of 'But I won!' The Hendrix cover found a fan in Levene's old bandmate Jah Wobble, who commented in *Sounds*, 'He's down to earth – he doesn't talk like a pompous arsehole'.

Wobble and Levene had in fact both just worked on the same LP, namely Gary Clail's *End of the Century Party*. Wobble, who had a new album of his own out – the live recording *Without Judgment* – was to become positively ubiquitous in the music scene of the early 1990s. But his return to success had not been without struggle. Clean of booze and drugs from 1986, he had replaced his addictions with a kind of spiritual fulfillment: 'That's when all the dots started to join up. I'd always believed in God, but in a God that inspired fear and who was both distant and disinterested. And that changed into a God of love.'

Typically, Wobble's belief system was anything but simplistic dogma, as he claimed doctrines and practices from a whole range of religions and philosophies.

If Wobble wasn't making his own acclaimed records (of which more shortly), he would be guesting on those made by other people - everyone from Sinead O'Connor and Holger Czukay to The Shamen and The Orb. His list of contacts had always been wide-ranging, partly because of his open-mindedness towards music, but partly because so many musicians, producers and composers had been PiL fans.

In 1994, he recalled in *Melody Maker* that 'The eighties were a shit time for me personally and a shit time in music. Jon Hassell's stuff and David Sylvian's solo albums were just about the only things that turned me on in that entire period.'

The early 1990s, then, were an ideal time, with rock assimilating all sorts of dance, reggae and dub influences, for revisiting PiL's best work. Unfortunately, Virgin Records' bright idea was a curious hotch-potch called *The Greatest Hits...So Far*. A representative compilation, insofar as it featured some of the glorious highs – 'Public Image', 'Death Disco', 'Rise' – but a fair few clunkers too, there was little sign of any rarities or unreleased goodies. Unless you count a clumsy remix of 'This Is Not A Love Song'. Ponderous 12" mixes of late 80s under-achievements padded out the second half of the compilation. Only the final track could genuinely be described as new. 'Don't Ask Me' was a collision of bubblegum pop and environmental politics which scraped into the top thirty, Lydon's highest chart placing in nearly five years. *NME* journalist James Brown was delighted with the single: 'An astounding return to comedic brilliance from the Lord Kitchener of punk'. *Sounds* writer Leo Finlay was simply relieved – 'something resembling top form' – having witnessed a Hammersmith Odeon show so dull the previous year that a fellow journalist had literally snored through it.

The Greatest Hits...So Far was released at the end of October 1990, and immediately raced to number twenty, but according to Lydon, Virgin failed to press enough copies, and within a month, it had dis-appeared from the charts. Again, PiL's frontman became a favourite of supposedly confrontational television programmes – he would appear as a guest on Channel 4's car-crash show *The Word* so often in the next few years that at one point the producers reportedly tried to persuade him to become a presenter.

Meanwhile, in the summer of 1991, a most bizarre reunion was taking place in a North London rehearsal room. Keith Levene and Rat Scabies had decided to form a punk supergroup, The Role Models, aided and abetted by ex-Pistol Glen Matlock. After a few months, Scabies departed and was replaced by none other than Levene's former PiL colleague, Jim Walker. It would have seemed to be the perfect power trio lacking only the right singer to front but, almost right from the off, Walker sensed trouble: 'The first rehearsal was some-where quite plush and Keith had a manager lined-up and everything like that. And Glen and Keith are, you know, great songwriters. You can't take that away from them. So I thought this might just work. Might. But the second session was in some cheap dump with mice and cockroaches and a broken kettle and a blocked toilet and all that. So the management arrangements weren't up to much, which didn't inspire great confidence. And while Keith, and to a lesser extent Glen, still thought it would be easy to score six figure advances and 30 grand videos, I was beginning to have my doubts. Acid house was happening big time and guitar groups were struggling a bit and the Berlin Wall was coming down. Basically, the world was changing and Keith was still locked in 1978, still thinking that record companies would queue up to offer us Abbey Road and world tours and stuff.'

Now called The Mavericks, Levene, Matlock and Walker had an additional dilemma. Walker again: 'They couldn't agree on what kind of singer was wanted – "Should he be like John Rotten? No. Should he be like Midge Ure? No. Should he be like Bono? No". It got exhausting.'

By the third rehearsal, Walker was already looking elsewhere: 'I just thought, "No, it ain't gonna work, we should have done this ten years ago when I first left PiL, it's just too late now." I was gonna stick around to humour them, just on the off chance things went further, but then all the trouble with money and publishing started. It became obvious to me that, no matter what I contributed, every song would become a Levene-Matlock composition. I was still gonna be "just the drummer", I would still have to fight for every point of publishing. It was gonna be hard work, just like Public Image was after the first few months.'

And so, on a few hours' notice, Walker walked out of rehearsals. A matter of weeks later, The Mavericks were no more. 'It wasn't totally their fault,' Walker admits now, 'you see I was then over 30, I'd been drumming for almost quarter of a century and I'd had enough – especially if it involved haggling over every red cent. I was much more intrigued by video anyway by then; that seemed to offer much more excitement, much more of a future. So I split, packed away my drum kit and I've hardly touched it since.'

Early 1992 saw the release of the very last PiL album, *That What Is Not*, recorded in Los Angeles the previous year with Jane's Addiction producer Dave Jerden. Apart from a bit of rather self-conscious swearing, the LP's 'combed pubic hair' sleeve was about the only startling, let alone outrageous, aspect to the record. *Rolling Stone* damned it with very faint praise, calling it 'unduly eclectic... by current art-metal standards it's pretty typical'. Unflattering comparisons were made with Led Zeppelin and the 'old Van Der Graaf Generator band'. Keith Cameron at the *NME* had lost patience – of the single 'Cruel', he wrote, 'hi-tech, lo-bollocks compromise rock'. David Stubbs at *Melody Maker* felt much the same way: 'It's difficult to imagine in what world this record represents a disturbance, or what preconceptions it challenges. Lydon still seems to address us all as if we're Bill Grundy'.

The record has its defenders. Alan Parker, at the time a reporter for music monthly *Spiral Scratch*, saw it as a return to form. 'John Lydon had got it back on track. The recording atmosphere was happy with lots of laughter, and they're all strong tracks on that album – "Luck's Up" is a great one, all about Sid and Keith Levene, I'm told'. A few tracks evoked the past, although not in a particularly welcoming fashion. 'Hope keeps me alive!' Lydon announced on 'Love Hope', which probably represented some kind of progression from the grudging horror of 'I wish I could die/I will survive' from 1978's 'Theme'. More cynically, the robust but somewhat long-winded 'Acid Drops' offered a 'No future' refrain, possibly meaning something, possibly meaning nothing. Elsewhere, 'God' teetered on the burlesque, whilst 'Cruel' was merely a trifling exercise in camp. The big brave PiL experiment had seemingly ended not with a bang, but a whimper.

Augmented by former Smiths drummer Mike Joyce, one of the group's last media engagements was at the BBC. Radio producer Paul Long, who engineered PiL's second and final session for Radio 1's Mark Goodier in February 1992, was far from disappointed. 'I always thought PiL were Lydon's true outlet, rather than the Sex Pistols which I'd always felt were a bit fake. PiL had a good attitude to doing the live sessions, and was really "up for it", although Lydon said that doing the live studio session was a bit like making a record – but not as interesting.'

But Lydon and McGeoch et al could still teach the Beeb's soundmen a thing or two. Continues Long: 'As engineers we learnt a lot that night about how to deal with a full live band with monitor system in the studio, turning it into a kind of club gig. Getting the atmosphere right was as important as the sounds... trying not to be the stuffy old Beeb. Of course, John McGeoch was a hero of mine from Magazine days, a revolutionary player, so it was great for me to meet and work with him. Lydon himself was as nice as pie. I think there was a little bit of Auntie Beeb wondering what he would be like. He was on good form, very funny and wearing an extremely loud suit if I remember rightly. He seemed to enjoy it all, whilst being slightly mystified at the same time...'

In March, Lydon yet again did the 'unexpected' by appearing in his first commercial, for the American beer Schlitz. The rest of 1992 was largely spent touring, including a US jaunt with Mick Jones' BAD II and Blind Melon, a show at Alton Towers theme park in Staffordshire in July where they supported James, and a final British show at the Reading Festival in late August. A short South American tour in September with Russell Webb – who had played alongside McGeoch in The Armoury Show – was not uneventful, although as ever, it was what the audience threw that made the headlines rather than what the band sounded like. In Sao Paulo, spitting crowds led Lydon to curtail the set after fifteen minutes, and two days later in Buenos Aires, a firework narrowly missed Webb and caused the show to be stopped for ten minutes.

The final ever PiL show occurred on Friday 18th September 1992 at The Icon in the American city of Buffalo. A split was not officially announced, but all sorts of information suggested that it was all over. For one thing, Public Image Limited had been dropped by Virgin Records, a casualty of its takeover in March by (ironically) EMI, which prompted them to play the Pistols' 'EMI' as what Alan Parker terms a 'fuck you'. For another, Lydon was ready to start work on an autobiography, and semi-promote a series of Sex Pistols reissues by Virgin that autumn – which did, unlike previous compilations, at least acknowledge implicitly that after Rotten's departure, it was a different group altogether. Finally, at the beginning of 1993, it was announced that Lydon had signed a deal to make a solo album for EastWest Records.

'They were a decent rock band,' comments Alan Parker. 'They should just have recorded another album quickly, within eighteen months or so and that would have been even better. But John's never wanted to front a decent rock band. So he let it all go to shit – again.'

Effectively, PiL was no more. For guitarist John McGeoch, an innovative and influential player over the previous 16 years in almost countless bands, it was an especially difficult period, and his career in music faltered. He qualified as a nurse in 1995, although there were sporadic attempts to restart musical projects, first with Heaven 17's Glenn Gregory and former Spandau Ballet drummer John Keeble, and next with composing music for television. Described by Siouxsie Sioux as 'my favourite guitarist of all-time', McGeoch died in his sleep on 4th March 2004, at the shockingly young age of forty-eight.

13
legacy: then there was one

If you wanna know how badly, or how well, things can go then you should be constantly reviewing the past. John Lydon 1994

We did it to ourselves. Jim Walker 2004

John Lydon was no fan of dance music, or at least the sort that had come to dominate the British scene of the early 1990s. Perhaps showing his age somewhat, he had opined, 'I find the whole *disco* set-up a very great evil,' to Ian Gittins of *Melody Maker* in 1992. 'It's all regurgitated and The Kids slavishly accept it. This generation is the most apathetic and indolent for a long time. They adore stupid dance music which is totally anaesthetised and druggy.'

Lydon made honourable exceptions to this rule, although concrete reasons could be elusive. In June 1992, for instance, he was spotted at The Orb's Brixton Academy gig by *NME* reporter Kris Needs. In December 1992, Leftfield's Neil Barnes told *Melody Maker*: 'It's well known how much he despises dance music but, for some reason, he seems to like us'. For Lydon, the prerequisite to collaboration was artists 'being themselves' and escaping categorisation lest one becomes 'a temporary figure'.

Prior to teaming up in Leftfield, both Barnes and Paul Daley had been inspired by John Lydon in their youth. As we have already discovered, Barnes had actually met the man himself at his house, but had been astonished on hearing *Metal Box* in 1979, later citing it as the record that changed his life. Daley, meanwhile, had established several short-lived bands, each of them 'a very poor imitation of Public Image' – one of them was apparently called Elephant Stampede. Much later, he abandoned synthesisers in favour of percussion and, as Lydon had done, many summers before, worked in playcentres around London.

The Leftfield-Lydon meetings began through mutual friend John Gray, by now a London-based teacher. The first stab at a Leftfield-Lydon track occurred towards the end of 1992, but it 'sounded remarkably similar' to Yothu Yindi's track 'Treaty', so, Paul Daley told *Melody Maker* in December, 'We had to bin that idea'. By May 1993, Barnes and Daley were subjecting Lydon to their current club favourites – from Underworld's expansive remix of Bjork's 'Human Behaviour' to Westbam's 'Hold Me Back' which had sampled PiL's 'Four Enclosed Walls'. That same month, a new song called 'Open Up' was recorded at Rollover Studios in London. Barnes told Kris Needs in November 1993 that Lydon had 'always had a voice that's very exciting. I knew he would come out with something special because he was really nervous. He's a professional. He plays that down in himself but he really works at it.' Needs was bowled over by the new track: 'I first heard "Open Up" under oath of secrecy in Hard Hands' office. It took every ounce of willpower not to bellow its magnificence from the rooftops.'

With its unforgettable mantra 'Burn Hollywood burn', the splendid and strident 'Open Up' was released on the first day of November 1993, and hit airplay problems, regrettably because of forest fires in California. Lydon was contemptuous of the censorship: 'There are governing bodies to decide what should and shouldn't be played. I find that bloody offensive. What are we supposed to do, wait until the December floods, which they always have in California, and re-release it then?' Quite apart from anything, he explained, 'The song to me is about not getting a movie part and burning down the studio in sheer frustration.' But regardless of the unofficial ban, the single peaked at number thirteen, and would remain a highpoint when included on Leftfield's stunning LP *Leftism* in 1995.

The Kris Needs feature for the *NME* also contained some vague revelations about Lydon's solo project, which was getting underway in the home studio he had installed in Los Angeles: 'I've amassed a quantity of instruments and things and I'm gonna make it myself. That's something I haven't done for a long time and I need to.' Lydon was being taught about Eastern European music by Lu Edmonds, and there were suggestions that 'the new material will return to the experimental nature of the early PiL stuff.'

Jah Wobble, still a die-hard Tottenham Hotspurs fan, was now finally enjoying a purple patch of success to match the recent triumphs of his favourite football team. Having scored his first ever solo chart hit in early 1992 with 'Visions of You' – featuring lead vocals by Sinead O'Connor, Wobble found himself featured on two albums on the shortlist for the inaugural Mercury Music Prize. One was his own LP *Rising Over Bedlam*. The other was the winning *Screamadelica* by Primal Scream, whom Wobble described as, 'The only ones that are saying anything to me.' Radio sessions for Andy Kershaw had led to an assortment of television appearances, ranging from a live appearance on *The James Whale Radio Show* in November 1991 to performing 'A13' on the Def II arts programme *Artrageous* on BBC2 in April 1992.

In the years between 1991 and 1995, it seemed as if few records released by anyone mattered unless they featured Wobble's sonorous bass parts, which somehow managed to be doleful and uplifting at the same time. In mid-1992, he featured on The Orb's 'Blue Room' single, his first placing in the top ten since 'Public Image', and the following year was an indispensable presence on Björk and David Arnold's 'Play Dead'. His philosophy towards collaboration was to try not to try: 'I try and keep it free without being too democratic. I like to steer people, and let them find their own thing. It's great, when you're playing, to suddenly not be aware of time, to get into a trance-like state'.

In the early summer of 1994, Wobble finally gained a top twenty album in his own right, with the Invaders of the Heart's *Take Me To God.* 'A vast album,' marvelled Ian Gittins in *Melody Maker*, 'a melange of tropical and oriental soundscapes weighted by Wobble's looming bass and street wisdom.' Certainly, the album demonstrated considerable range, from the almost childlike joy of 'The Sun Does Rise' (featuring lead vocals by The Cranberries' Dolores O'Riordan) to 'I Love Everybody' which lampooned the vacuous side of contemporary club culture. 'I am your left breast, I am Stepney, I am Peru, I am divine, and so are you' intoned Wobble. Some were entertained. Others like Dele Fadele of the *NME* felt it distracted the mood from its seductive context: 'However seriously Jah Wobble takes music he can't resist the temptation to take the piss.' Wobble, for his part, argued that his music had nothing to do with New Age faddishness: 'My music ain't about imitating these funny little people who live thousands of miles away and introducing it as some trendy scene. Spiritual is practical, it's here and now.'

If Wobble wasn't performing on records, he was producing or remixing them. Everyone from a pre-Republica Saffron to Midlands pop trio Dodgy to 4AD's The Wolfgang Press was requesting his services. Slowly, it was becoming clear that the corporate face of the music industry was marking time once again. As he later explained in a 2003 column for *The Independent* newspaper, by 1996, 'It was getting harder not to laugh out loud at the absurdity of it all'. Having delivered Island Records the comparatively accessible *Take Me To God*, the label was not prepared for 1995's *Heaven & Earth*, which contained no likely 'singles' and failed to chart. Realising that, after nearly 15 years of irregularly making records for Island, he was second only to 'Lester the doorman' in terms of receiving a long-service medal, he made three LPs of chart anathema – one inspired by William Blake, a 'Requiem Mass', and an album about Celtic Poets. As Wobble put it, 'The company's response to these records was like mine to a Jehovah's Witness at the front door.'

To Wobble and Island's probably equal relief, he was dropped by the label in 1996 – 'the quickest response I've ever had from a record company over anything', and founded his own label 30 Hertz. If he had already been one of the busiest artists in British music prior to this, the proliferation of Wobble albums over the next decade would make the early 90s seem as though he'd been putting his feet up. To this day, he continues to release at least two albums a year. Even when not making records, he became a book reviewer for *The Independent*, and somehow still found time to undertake and gain a degree course in Humanities at the University of London's Birkbeck College. On completing the course, it was suggested he should continue with a PhD. He was tempted. 'Dr Wobble – I rather like the sound of that,' he told a reporter from *The Daily Telegraph* in 2003.

If Jah Wobble was single-handedly forcing all record stores to build extensions, John Lydon appeared to be busy doing little more than nothing. The publication of his autobiography *Rotten: No Irish, No Blacks, No Dogs* in the spring of 1994, although an inevitably self-serving exercise with a warts-and-all sheen, had been mostly worthwhile. Quite apart from the entertaining anecdotes about early years and the formation, success and collapse of the Sex Pistols, Lydon was generous enough to allow space for opinions from other voices, including members of his family, and old friends like John Gray, Steve Jones and Paul Cook, Chrissie Hynde, Don Letts and even a word or two from Jeannette Lee. Despite the good-natured tone of much of the book, he scorned the process of nostalgia and retrospection. 'There'll be no Sex Pistols reunion. I don't wanna look like some 40-year-old tosser up there, pretending to be a teenager.'

As everyone now knows, of course, there was a Sex Pistols reunion in June 1996, which toured under the name Filthy Lucre, and spawned a live LP of the same name. Lydon had hinted as much in January that year, when he informed reporter Caroline Sullivan, 'It's not nostalgic to think of reforming, because we have no nostalgic memories of the Sex Pistols. The only reason we'd do it would be to antagonise each other. All those old antagonisms would rise to the surface again in seconds, and we all know it. We'd be doing it for all the wrong reasons, which sounds great.'

When the original line-up of the Pistols reconvened for a press conference at the 100 Club on 18th March 1996, Paul Cook was now a drummer for Edwyn Collins. After thirteen years of what *Q* journalist David Cavanagh described as 'underachievement personified', Steve Jones had formed a group with Duran Duran's John Taylor and Duff McKagan of Guns 'N Roses. The name of the new group was The Neurotic Boy Outsiders. As for Matlock, he had a solo record about to be released on Alan McGee's label Creation, entitled *Who's He Think He Is When He's At Home?*

Having now publicly reclaimed his stage name from the clutches of McLaren and Glitterbest for Lydon's memoirs was one thing, but the effects of actually reforming the original Pistols line-up would be far-reaching. Siouxsie and the Banshees announced they were splitting, apparently disgusted by the comeback tour. The most extreme effect, depressingly, came on September 8th, when the body of Sid Vicious's mother Anne Beverly was discovered at her home in Derbyshire, having taken her own life. Beverley had previously described the reunion plans as 'sad and pathetic', firm in the belief that Sid would have 'been rolling in his grave'. Although as David Cavanagh observed, Sid had in fact been cremated.

For Keith Levene, outrage was his first response to Filthy Lucre: 'Although John's broken all the punk rules, that was the one thing I thought he'd never do. The one golden rule of punk was that the Pistols would never, could never, return. Not ever. And then they did. And, of course, after a few days I thought, "So what?" Suddenly it seemed alright.'

Relations between Rotten, Matlock, Cook and Jones seemed buoyant enough, although as ever, with the selective memory that allows such pronouncements, the frontman would declare to the *NME*'s Gavin Martin: 'Nobody ever said a fucking good word to us in our entire life about anything. Ever. We've never got idiot things like respect'. Martin's view, understandably, was that 'It's hard not to see Lydon/Rotten as a desperate man, besieged, fighting to reclaim his heritage...'

On Sunday 23rd June 1996, the Sex Pistols topped a day-long event at Finsbury Park in North London. Populating the support slots on the bill, save for rockers The Wildhearts, was a predominance either of revived punk icons – Stiff Little Fingers, Buzzcocks, Iggy Pop – or the latest second-division representatives of the fleeting Britpop movement – 3 Colours Red, Fluffy, 60ft Dolls and Skunk Anansie. The headlining band was introduced by footballers Gareth Southgate and Stuart Pearce. 'Finsbury Park's never looked so fucking good!' beamed Lydon before parodying himself with the brief improvised singalong 'Fat, Forty and Back!' Wisely, the ensuing set refused to entertain anything as ridiculous as new material.

Predictably, the tour was sniped at by the national press – which at least marked them as consistent in its views. For the likes of the *NME*, perhaps the only reaction could be one of irony. Simon Williams marked the performance as 'very silly, extremely entertaining' and warned the youth that 'this man appears to be wearing gold lamé trousers.' Sprinkled amongst some 40,000 spectators were such celebs as Oasis star Liam Gallagher, supermodel Kate Moss and Hollywood actor Johnny Depp.

PiL's photographer friend Dennis Morris caught the reunion tour at the Zenith in Paris on July 4th: 'It was the first time I'd ever really seen 'em. For once I wasn't working, taking pictures. They were good, of course. I mean, I always knew they could play, it was always just a myth that they couldn't. They weren't allowed to play a lot of the time, that was the real problem the first time round. People say you don't get second chances in life but it's not true – you do get a second chance but you can leave it too late or mismanage it or whatever. You only live twice. I felt the Pistols maybe left it too late but I still enjoyed it, so what the hell...'

On July 17th, swiftly replacing a cancelled gig scheduled for Belfast, the Pistols staged an extra gig at the Shepherd's Bush Empire, where they squeezed four encores before a stunned crowd which included Creation boss Alan McGee and Oasis songwriter Noel Gallagher. McGee was so astonished and moved by the performance that, three days later, he paid for a full-page advertisement in the *NME*, in which he explained his failure to see the group in its original incarnation (they had never played his native Scotland) or in its revived form at Finsbury Park ('I had heard they were like "cabaret"...'). The McGee tribute ended with the declaration, 'The Sex Pistols changed my life in 1977 and 1996. This band are our alternative royal family. God Save The Sex Pistols.'

A more ambivalent response to the Pistols circa 1996 comes from PiL's longest-serving drummer Martin Atkins, who saw another of the shows. 'Some of the songs started to fall apart 'cos they weren't very well rehearsed. There's just a set way Sex Pistols' songs go.' Interestingly, Atkins wonders if this was the ideal opportunity to reform Lydon's other band: 'I felt like he was launching into an ad-lib, like the cycle had begun again and he was ready for a band to start jamming behind him – and have there be no such thing as a mistake. I think everybody would love to see a PiL show, and I think that John is almost ready.'

Tour dates rolled onwards, six months of traversing Europe, then America, next to Australia, New Zealand and the Far East. The final leg of the world tour took place in South America, ending in Santiago on 7th December, where the sold-out set ended in tear-gas. Some of the old animosities had re-emerged, but contrary to expectations that Lydon would clash with Glen Matlock, it was the guitarist and drummer who had been the irritants: 'They're stuck in this 1976 vibe. It's very peculiar.' Of Matlock, he said, 'I got on alright with him because we were just honest with each other'.

Lydon had originally needed to tour, as he had re-signed a 'horrendously underpriced' deal with Virgin in order to complete that solo LP. The two million dollar tour had been originally under-taken in order to pay off some of his growing debts. But, within hours of signing the contract, his wife Nora inherited several million dollars with the death of her publishing magnate father back in Germany. The tour was no longer necessary, financially, not as far as Johnny was concerned.

Four months after its release in Japan, Lydon's solo LP made the most timid of entrances into the British marketplace in July 1997. Entitled *Psycho's Path*, it selected a wide range of targets which, had it been a debut recording, might have seemed provocative. The celebration of serial killers as icons, for instance (on the title track), or organised religion ('Dog') or censorship ('Armies'). For anyone familiar with Lydon's back catalogue, however, it was treading a lot of the same ground. The one real surprise came with 'Take Me', a demonstration of vulnerability and a need to be loved. Writing in *Q*, reviewer Lucy O'Brien remarked that the remixes of tracks by The Chemical Brothers, Moby and Leftfield 'provide the perfect foil for [Lydon's] juddering, incantatory voice. As with PiL, Lydon still needs the alchemy of seasoned collaborators.'

Virgin essentially buried the album, with almost no promotion whatsoever, and delaying a single, 'Sun', until after the album's release. Not even remixes by Leftfield could help the single into the top forty. The *NME*, which in 1979 had made its review of *Metal Box* a cover story, did not even review *Psycho's Path*.

The music press was by now almost completely in thrall to the triumphalism of Oasis, a group who had echoed the spirit of the Sex Pistols on their debut LP, but by 1997, had almost completely neutered such an influence from their actual records. All that remained was, seemingly, the hollow boorishness of interviews. When asked about Liam Gallagher, Lydon was the model of disdain: 'He sees himself as the reincarnation of John Lennon and Johnny Rotten. I'd like to remind Liam that, unlike John Lennon and Johnny Rotten, he's not written a single song. There lies the difference. And I'm sure this'll make him even more angry if you print it. We do like winding each other up.'

With his brother Martin in the backing band on synthesiser, Lydon drew up a tour of solo dates across the USA, Canada and Japan during August and September 1997. Thirty-three shows were planned. Only six shows would take place. And worse still, drummer Robert Williams claimed that he had been unfairly dismissed from Lydon's band, and had been headbutted in a Japanese restaurant by Lydon on 30th July. Both plaintiff and defendant agreed to have the case decided on the American TV court programme *Judge Judy*, hosted by real-life judge Judy Sheindlin. Taped on 20th October, the programme was broadcast on 24th November. Williams' claims seemed plausible enough at first but he had weakened his own case by admitting that he hadn't gone to a doctor until some eight days after the alleged attack. Lydon easily won the case, after Lydon's manager and road manager – both of whom had been present in the sushi restaurant – confirmed that no violence had taken place.

In March 1999, Virgin finally unveiled *Plastic Box*, a four-CD PiL compilation set. Although Lydon contributed 28 enthusiastic pages of jottings to its accompanying booklet, recalling his desire for 'new musical adventures', he maintained that the set 'was Virgin's idea, nothing to do with me'. Martin Atkins claims now that he had called the record company offering some long-awaited unreleased material. 'I said to them, "Listen guys, I've got great unreleased stuff from the *Flowers Of Romance* [sessions], I've got John singing over the top of The Beatles, I've got stuff that's never been heard, I've got stuff that's amazing. And I'd be happy to talk to you and John about coming to some arrangement where we could make this an unbelievable album for the fans." And they were like, "How dare you interrupt our schedule with this trivia!" John's management said exactly the same kind of thing. They also tried it on, "That tape is our property, Mister Atkins" ...So I just said, "No, it isn't, I've had it for over 20 years, if you wanna go through every single master tape and outtake and find it, then go and do that".'

Lydon's adaptation of 'Twist and Shout' remains in the vaults to this day, as does 'You Stupid Person', the original recording of 'The Cowboy Song', 'Vampire' from the *Flowers Of Romance* sessions, and several *Renovations* re-recordings from 1987. The main attractions in *Plastic Box*'s contents were the two Radio 1 sessions from 1979 and 1992, never before commercially released, and some 'Death Disco' mixes making their debut on CD. B-sides like 'Question Mark' from 1984 and rare tracks like 1980's 'Pied Piper' may have been helpful to completists but had little value in terms of listenability. While the set as a whole was a useful career package, the vast majority of tracks were easily available on existing albums, and so it fell frustratingly short of being a truly worthwhile purchase.

At the time of writing, there have been no further PiL reissues. The cupboard of outtakes may be far from bare, but the fanbase's appetite continues to be whetted.

14
careerings

The Pistols' second successful get-together was staged in 2002, the year of Queen Elizabeth II's Golden Jubilee. A reissued 'God Save The Queen' – banned during 1977's Silver Jubilee – hit the top twenty for a second time, with its promotional video finally getting a play on *Top of The Pops*, only a quarter of a century too late. Leftfield contributed a remix of the song to some of the formats, even though Virgin's bright idea for them to remix 'Pretty Vacant' in 1993 had caused Lydon to spit, 'A pathetic idea. With an idea like that, you should shoot yourself in the morning.'

On Saturday 27th July, the Pistols at the Palace appeared at the National Sports Centre in Crystal Palace, South London. When a journalist asked why the band weren't doing a full UK tour Lydon replied, ''Cos I'm not interested in a full tour. It's my Jubilee. God Save the Queen, thank you very much. Twenty-five years on and you silly bastards still ain't fucking learnt, have you?' Later he referred back to the PiL-era police activity that had driven him away from London: 'For so many years I got endless police raids and none of you fuckers were backing me up at all! And there were several set-ups going on there. Victimization seemed to be a natural, par for the course, thing, Rotten-style, and you lot never said a word, did you? You went along with your middle class shite, as per usual.'

As with past confrontations with the press, Lydon foresaw – and spiked – any possibly awkward questions before they could even be asked. 'Would you like to talk about the money? Are you Pistols going to make a lot of money out of this?' 'Fucking right we are! This is about being working class... This is our Britain and we've kind of lost that idea, alright...? It's a much worse place now than it was in 1977. Blair has fucked up royally... And when I start to see dark doubts cast out there about the Union Jack and should we get rid of it? I just think, "Oh for fuck's sake! What are you gonna hold up? A plate glass? Or a window? And for what? Whatcha got? What have you got as respect for yourselves, as British folk? Fuck all". Well, you got me. Here I am. Come and see. It's only £32.50!'

With support from, amongst others, The Libertines and ...And You Will Know Us By The Trail Of Dead, the Crystal Palace show started with a cover version of Hawkwind's 'Silver Machine' – a Pistols' first. There were other surprises – warm words for Matlock from Lydon, a cover of The Creation's 'Through My Eyes' and a set that lasted almost 90 minutes. The *NME* responded with a rave review, although the jeers from the nationals was more predictable.

John Lydon had otherwise been quietly living in Los Angeles, occasionally appearing on TV chat shows with the likes of Jonathan Ross. He had even fronted a short-lived show for VH-1, *Rotten TV*. Then on 26th January 2004, he became a contestant on the third series of ITV's celebrity challenge reality show *I'm A Celebrity Get Me Out of Here!* Also appearing in the hope of either raising money for charity or, at the very least, raising awareness in their careers, were former BBC News royal correspondent Jennie Bond, George Best's wife Alex, former pop singers Peter Andre and (formerly of Atomic Kitten) Kerry McFadden, topless model Jordan, footballer Neil Ruddock, disc-jockey Mike Read, former athlete Diane Modahl and Lord Brocket.

Lydon hoped to win £100,000 for the charity of his choice, a child-related one, and was the favourite of the bookies to be the outright winner of the contest. He kicked a camera or two, got pecked at by ostriches while showered in birdseed, had a tea-party organised for his 48th birthday ('Day 6') and it seemed as if every e-mail from the public was describing him as 'legendary'.

But he was rapidly growing bored, and after viewers voted to keep him on the island on Tuesday 3rd February ('Day 9'), he called them 'fucking cunts' on post-watershed, but still peak-time, television. Out of an audience of over ten million, a far greater number than the original unwitting viewers who had witnessed the Pistols on *Today* 25 years earlier, only 98 complaints were received. The controversial can only be truly controversial when no-one is expecting it. No-one, not even the Sex Pistols themselves, could have predicted the direction of the Grundy interview with any real certainty. Contrastingly, with John

Lydon's presence on live television while under physical and psychological pressures in an intensely uncomfortable climate, it was only a matter of time before he let some obscenity slip. Everyone knew this, from producers Granada, to the press, to the viewers, to Lydon himself – and ITV escaped serious censure. Furthermore, proving that you could only be taken off the air in the context of reality television if you bored the viewing public, it was Lydon who orchestrated his own departure. At 3am British time on Thursday 5th February, he walked off the show – although not before he had had various squabbles with 'silicon-chested, blown-up balloon' Jordan, plus some rather more enlightening conversation with Jennie Bond.

Back in the UK, Lydon was a returning guest on BBC1's *Friday Night With Jonathan Ross*, as Pistols and PiL back-catalogue sales reputedly rose by some 20 per cent in HMV stores. The mass of the Great British Public finally discovered that punk's Mister Evil isn't really that evil but is, in fact, a man of some wit and charisma - when he wants to be. Of course, to many an old punk, Lydon's appearance on *I'm A Celebrity* would have been the final nail in his coffin as far as any real credibility went. *Metal Box* must have seemed a long, long time in the past.

Whatever, Johnny seemed keen to continue his TV career. When Channel Five approached him over fronting a television series based around tropical wildlife he gladly accepted their offer. The resulting *Lydon Goes Ape* aired in November 2004, and cable channel Discovery invited him to front *Megabugs!*, a series of documentaries about killer insects. Such commitments led to the cancellation of several Pistols' gigs in the US and Japan.

Meanwhile, pop star Justin Timberlake has been mooted by Lydon himself as the ideal lead for a big-screen version of *No Irish, No Blacks, No Dogs*. Producer Penelope Spheeris, previously responsible for punk movies like *Suburbia* and comedies like *Wayne's World*, is at the helm for the adaptation. Lydon told *Record Collector* in 2005 that Mike Leigh's way of working with a cast might be the optimum route: 'It's hardcore acting in the proper truest way, where the vanity is gone and everyone is oblivious to the cameras.'

Lydon continues to live in California with Nora, dividing their time between one home overlooking Venice Beach, and a second one thirty miles north in Malibu. They sail their yacht Fantasia, while Lydon enjoys surfing, skiing and skateboarding. He has become a doting grandfather, as Nora's daughter Ariane now has two children of her own. As regards forays into music, Lydon has claimed to be far too much 'into the internet and technology. I don't think any of us ever need to use traditional instruments again. I don't even like the sound of 'em.'

Thus, a PiL reunion, while technically possible, remains unlikely. Jim Walker, only half-jokingly, says he would only agree to a PiL reunion tour if it were to take place in Baghdad, Iraq, 'over three nights. It would be for the troops – first night for American troops, second night for the Brits and then the third night would be mixed, Brits and Yanks, just so they could slug it out between them in the audience. Can you imagine the coverage you'd get? It'd make a Pistols reunion look like just another Saturday night pub gig.'

Most of PiL's central participants seem united in two ways: satisfaction at the quality of their very best work, and a reluctance to repeat their pasts. For Lydon, PiL has apparently never really stopped, thus making any get-together irrelevant. The PiL founders' motivations are now, Lydon told *Mojo* in late 2003, 'so set in such different directions it would be fake to even try it...'

'I bear no grudges over PiL,' maintains Jah Wobble. '[Lydon] made mistakes but we all make fucking mistakes, you know. His were pretty gargantuan, but were not hanging offences. I suspect he suffered from those mistakes more than anyone else; that's normally how it works. I made a few mistakes myself over the years, because yes I too, believe it or not, am mortal. Most of those mistakes occurred when I was bang on the bottle, especially towards the end of my drinking when I really was a mess. I allowed one or two good people to be driven out of my bands, and I gave publishing away to people who didn't deserve it and so on and so forth. I didn't like the price my conscience made me pay for those errors of judgment. All of which eventually taught me to run a tight ship - pay those who should be paid, you know, and keep the hangers-on out.

'There isn't any one person out of that band [Public Image] who I hate. Don't think that I'm an angel, there are one or two people that I've met over the years in this business that I still dislike immensely, however I met them well after PiL. I was even talking to Keith Levene until about ten years ago - he wanted to form a band. I said "I'm not forming a band... besides, I thought you was in LA?"

'He says, "Well, yeah, yeah I was but my house fell in the sea."

'And I thought "How careless, what bad luck!" Anyway, I said no to the band but like an idiot I then said "Tell you what, I'm doing well with this studio of mine, why don't you drop down and have some studio time?" And we booked him in for the next morning but, of course, he didn't turn up. Next thing I hear he's apparently gone down Warner-Chappell, the song publishers, the same morning saying he's co-written Jah Wobble's new single and he wants money.

'As if they're not gonna cotton on and check with me. And that was it, I'd finally had it with him - "Goodbye, Keith." Enough's enough. [So] he's the only one I wouldn't really wanna talk to much - and that cut-off only came some 14 years after I'd left the band...'

Keith Levene continues to be 'seriously into video technology. I love the way the cameras have gotten so small that you can film anywhere and just slap it up on your computer, edit it, finish it and get it sent anywhere. It's just so convenient. And you can do it with a broad brush, fast, or slowly with every single hair showing, real detail – whatever you want to do.'

Original PiL drummer Jim Walker currently lives in North London and shoots adverts, videos and documentaries. At the time of writing Walker is starting to make his first full-length feature film. For him, the disappointments of what PiL became are largely tied up with financial disagreements. 'PiL was basically this really great band when there was just the four of us, and we had some really great people. But once it became Rotten with a bag of money and Levene trying to get money, it all became about who can suck up to Rotten the most and I just can't do that personally. I cannot bend over for people, I'd rather not be part of it. I've never been much of a careerist, to my great chagrin, but that's just the way it is. You are what you are.'

He now sees bands like Soundgarden as mastering the experiments that PiL patented: 'In my era, we were trying to do stuff but it was very stilted; 20 years later, they've now perfected odd-time music, they've figured out how to make it rocky and off-time so it works.'

Jah Wobble retains plenty of passion for Public Image Limited's finest work, sometimes favouring their more unlikely output: 'I actually like "Fodderstompf" because of the bee-line. You even hear it now and you think "that's some fucking bee-line". "Low Life", so satisfying to play. Off the second album, "Poptones", without a doubt – people like The Edge from U2 obviously got a lot from that.' Of the PiL circle, he has mixed feelings: 'As a band, it was strong all around: Keith was a bit of a bad spirit, but a great guitarist. Jim Walker was a solid drummer, everyone knew that, a real rock drummer but he actually had a good bass drum – and he kinda handled pick-up and push notes and twelve notes, kind of. Almost a funky kinda feel. Dennis Morris was a good photographer, good ideas man.'

If Wobble found the presence in PiL of Jeannette Lee somewhat disconcerting at the time, 'Funnily enough, now, whenever I see her I get on with her. She's actually one of the few sensible people from that time. You can actually have a conversation with her. [She]'s moved on and done well.' Extremely well, in fact. On 28th November 2002, fifteen years into a successful business partnership with Rough Trade's Geoff Travis, Jeannette Lee was awarded the Lifetime Achievement gong at the Silver Clef Women of the Year Awards, an annual event designed to pay tribute to women in the music industry. Consistently publicity-shy, her triumph was a tribute to her many years of commitment towards new musical talent. Between them, Travis and Lee have helped dozens of artists and bands achieve success, including The Strokes, The Jesus & Mary Chain, The Libertines, Belle & Sebastian and Pulp. Indeed, it was Pulp lead singer Jarvis Cocker who presented Lee with her award. She continues to decline almost all opportunities to discuss her association with PiL. People still send her PiL-related emails, 'interviews with Keith Levene or whatever,' she says, 'and I always delete them without reading them...'

Jah Wobble now lives in Cheshire with his wife Zi Lan Liao and their two children and continues to record and perform. Perhaps the most surprising of his many associations came in 2002 when he contributed a remix to a number one single by *Neighbours* actor-turned-singer Holly Valance. The best starting point for anyone interested in Wobble's capacious back catalogue is 2004's self-compiled *I Could Have Been A Contender* which spans three discs and numerous choice cuts from Wobble's sometimes brilliant career. He explained: 'Getting licenses went smoother than expected which is a sign of the times. Three or four years ago, it would have been harder to get the tracks from different labels, but now the music industry is in such a state they're grateful for whatever they can get.'

Wobble was also to work briefly with Martin Atkins in 2000 under the name Damage Manual, releasing material on Atkins' Invisible label. Despite some good feedback it became, at least with Wobble, a one-off. 'Martin's an amazing drummer but I really don't think he's that strong as a producer – at least not with the things I wanna do.' Atkins himself recently toured the US with a Wobble-less Damage Manual before releasing some intriguing new Keith Levene tracks – entitled 'Murder Global: Killer In The Crowd' – which received some positive reviews but little in the way of airplay.

Of his time in PiL, Atkins is slightly bewildered: 'I dunno if you could recreate that situation now: "Hey! It's Johnny Rotten from the Sex Pistols!" There was a unique point in time to do what we did. It seems like it was yesterday, it sometimes seems now like it never happened. It's interesting because there was an Emperor's New Clothes element that I felt sometimes we took advantage of. It was about the band. And when guys from, say, Massive Attack talk about like, "Early PiL," they say, "not Johnny Rotten, we like PiL."'

'The point isn't that there were only a few albums that were great,' comments Don Letts, 'the point is that there were moments of genius on every record and the miracle is that John managed to harness all these wild horses together.'

'There was an unbelievable spark there, something very primal like a huge malcontentment,' says Wobble. 'My overriding memory, actually, of the best album, *Metal Box*, is of John's words. They were just so strong, just fitted with the music so well.'

But those very words were sung in a voice that was always strongest and clearest when it was backed by the likes of Wobble, Walker, Levene, Atkins et al. Most of whom still harbour some affection and/or respect for a man who, like most big names in rock, has become increasingly isolated from his roots – and from many of his oldest friends, seemingly spending more time with bodyguards than anyone else...

On the other hand, the PiL boys didn't just yearn for a bloody good laugh. Although some became betrayed by their egotism, others by enemies and drugs, all of them entered the world of Public Image Limited for one overriding reason: despite all the compromises and squabbles and lies, they really did do it in order to find a legitimate path to self-expression.

They'd only 'wanted to be loved', they'd sneered on *First Edition*'s 'Fodderstompf' in 1978. And yet, oddly enough, they were and they are. They still are...

'A lot of shit happened with that band,' says Jah Wobble. 'A lot of it bad, a lot of it very dark, but the ultimate question is – like with any piece of music, any art – is there quality there? Was it worth it? And I think, with those first few releases, the answer's "Yes".'

postscript

September 9, 2004, Cargo nightclub, east London. It is a balmy hot night, under the arches in trendy Shoreditch. As the climate change killer called Hurricane Ivan starts to gather murderous force south of the Caribbean, Jah Wobble returns to the East End – a London he no longer lives in. Partly to plug his Trojan boxed set anthology *I Could Have Been A Contender*, partly for the hell of it.

A be-hatted Wobble is joined onstage by Liz Carter, a female folk singer. After her turn and some strong indie guitar from Chris Cookson, Wobble contributes some astounding bass workouts. Coincidentally, the solid percussive backing is provided by Mark Sanders, the very drummer who was turned down in the PiL auditions of Spring '78 that had yielded Jim Walker.

Harry Beckett's blaring trumpet works wonders with pipes from Jean-Pierre Rosie and Clive Bell.

Next up are Molam Lao, a trio of singers from Laos in South East Asia. Then hooded rapper Spikey T leaps up and starts bouncing words around. By now, everyone is dancing, and even the overworked barmaids start bobbing their heads.

The addition of the keyboards represent the final ingredient in this musical stew, which for the final ten minutes of the set, blossoms into a truly intoxicating racket, a joyously messy concoction. In a way it was – it is – what PiL were all about. Something strong and different. Genuine world music, a real blend of all sorts from all around the planet. And it works magnificently. The hysterical crowd, which includes John Gray, journalist Simon Mattock and Dennis Morris, urges the group back for an encore.

It's well past one in the morning before the club's security guards manage to edge the last fans away from the stage and out through the glass doors. Outside it's no longer so hot now that a fine drizzle has started to fall.

The group's after-gig party turns out to be at a venue miles away. No transport had been laid on...

personnel

Gregg 'J.P.' Arreguin:
rhythm guitar
October - December 1991

Martin Atkins: drums
October 1979 - June 1980
October 1980
May 1982 - February 1985

Ginger Baker: drums
September - November 1985

Gary Barnacle: saxophone
January - April 1984

Louie Bernardi: bass
May 1983 - April 1984

Curt 'Kirbee B' Bisquera:
drums, percussion
October - December 1991

Jebin Bruni: keyboards
September 1984 - January 1985

Karl Burns: drums
September 1979

Ed Caraballo: video
May 1981

Ted Chau: keyboards
January - November 1989
January - September 1992

Richard Cottle: keyboards
January - April 1984

Dave Crowe: 'company secretary'
November 1979 - June 1980

Alan Dias: bass
March 1986 - July 1992

Richard Dudanski: drums
April - September 1979

Lu Edmonds: keyboards, guitar
March 1986 - September 1988

Joseph Guida: guitar
May - December 1983

Bret Helm: bass
September 1984 - January 1985

Dave Humphrey: drums
February - March 1979

Pete Jones: bass
August 1982 - April 1983

Mike Joyce: drums
December 1991 - September 1992

Bill Laswell: bass/producer
September - November 1985

Jeannette Lee: video
November 1979 - August 1982

Keith Levene: guitar
April 1978 - May 1983

Ken Lockie: keyboards
May - September 1982

John Lydon: vocals
April 1978 - September 1992

John McGeoch: guitar
March 1986 - September 1992

Steve New: guitar
July - October 1980

Ryuichi Sakamoto: keyboards
September - November 1985

Mark Schulz: guitar
September 1984 - January 1985

Shankar: strings
September - November 1985

Bonnie Sheridan & Julie Christensen: backing vocals
October - December 1991

Bruce Smith: drums
March 1986 - January 1990

Arthur Stead: keyboards
September - December 1983

Tower of Power: horn section
October - December 1991

Sam Ulano: drums
May 1981

Steve Vai: guitar
September - November 1985

Jim Walker: drums
May 1978 - January 1979

Russell Webb: bass
July - September 1992

Jah Wobble: bass
April 1978 – July 1980

Jimmie Wood: harmonica
October - December 1991

Simon Woore: guitar
January - April 1984

Tom Zvoncheck: keyboards
May - September 1983

discographies

PiL Singles

Public Image
Released: 13.10.1978
Peak Position: #9
7" Single: Virgin VS 228
b/w The Cowboy Song

Death Disco
Released: 29.06.1979
Peak Position: #20
7" Single: Virgin VS 274
b/w And No Birds Do Sing
12" Single: Virgin VS 274-12
Death Disco (1/2 Mix)/
Megamix (Fodderstompf)

Memories
Released: 12.10.1979
Peak Position: #60
7" Single: Virgin VS 299
b/w Another
12" Single: Virgin VS 299-12
Memories (Mix)/Another

Flowers Of Romance
Released: 27.03.1981
Peak Position: #24

7" Single: Virgin VS 397
b/w Home Is Where The Heart Is
12" Single: Virgin VS 397-12
Flowers of Romance
(Mix) Flowers of Romance
(Instrumental)/Home Is Where
The Heart Is

This Is Not A Love Song
Released: 05.09.1983
Peak Position: #5
7" Single: Virgin VS 529
b/w Public Image
12" Single: Virgin VS 529-12
This Is Not A Love Song/Blue
Water/This Is Not A Love Song
(12" Mix)/Public Image
3" CD Single (08.1988): Virgin
VSCDT 14
This Is Not A Love Song/Blue
Water/This Is Not A Love Song
(Remixed Version)/Public Image

Bad Life
Released: 08.05.1984
Peak Position: #71
7" Single: Virgin VS 675
b/w Question Mark

12" Single: Virgin VS 675-12
Bad Life/Question Mark

Rise
Released: 20.01.1986
Peak Position: #11
7" Single ['Single']: Virgin VS 841
b/w Rise (Instrumental)
12" Single ['12" Single']: Virgin
VS 841-12
Rise/Rise (Instrumental)

Home
Released: 21.04.1986
Peak Position: #75
7" Single: Virgin VS 855
b/w Round
12" Single: Virgin VS 855-12
Home/Round/Home (7" Edit)

Seattle
Released: 10.08.1987
Peak Position: #47
7" Single: Virgin VS 988
b/w Selfish Rubbish
Cassette Single: Virgin VSC 988-12
Seattle/The Suit (87 Remix)/
Selfish Rubbish
12" Single: Virgin VS 988-12
Seattle/The Suit (87 Remix)/
Selfish Rubbish

The Body
Released: 26.10.1987
7" Single: Virgin VS 1010
b/w Angry
12" Single: Virgin VST 1010
The Body/Religion (87 Remix)/
Angry
12" Single Remix: Virgin VSR 1010

The Body (UK Remix)/The
Body (US Remix)/Angry

Disappointed
Released: 24.04.1989
Peak Position: #38
7" Single: Virgin VS 1181
7" Limited Gatefold Sleeve:
Virgin VSG 1181
b/w Same Old Story
12" Single: Virgin VST 1181
Disappointed (12" Version)/
Disappointed/Same Old Story
CD Single: Virgin VSCD 1181
Disappointed (12" Version)/
Disappointed/Same Old Story

Warrior
Released: 17.07.1989
7" Single: Virgin VS 1195
7" Limited Gatefold Sleeve:
Virgin VSG 1195
b/w U.S.L.S. 1
12" Single: Virgin VST 1195
Warrior (Extended
Mix)/U.S.L.S. 1/Warrior
(Instrumental)
12" Remix: Virgin VSTX 1195
Warrior (Extended Mix)/Warrior
(Instrumental)
CD Single: Virgin VSCD1195
Warrior (Edit)/U.S.L.S. 1/
Warrior (Extended Mix)

Don't Ask Me
Released: 08.10.1990
Peak Position: #22
7" Single: Virgin VS 1231
b/w Rules and Regulations
12" Single: Virgin VST 1231

Don't Ask Me/Rules and
Regulations/Warrior
Cassette Single: Virgin VSC 1231
Don't Ask Me/Rules and
Regulations
CD Single: Virgin VSCDT 1231
Don't Ask Me/Rules and
Regulations/Warrior

Cruel
Released: 10.02.1992
Peak Position: #49
7" Single: Virgin VS 1390
b/w Love Hope
10" Single: Virgin VSA 1390
Cruel/Love Hope/Happy (Live)
Cassette Single: Virgin VSC 1390
Cruel/Love Hope
CD Single: Virgin VSCDG 1390
Cruel/Love Hope/Rise (Live)/
Home (Live)

PiL Albums

Public Image: First Edition
Released: 08.12.1978
Peak Position: #22
LP: Virgin V 2114
Cassette: Virgin TCV2114
CD Reissue (04.1986): Virgin
CDV 2114
Theme/Religion I/Religion II/
Annalisa/Public Image/Low
Life/Attack/Fodderstompf

Metal Box
Released: 23.11.1979
Peak Position: #18
Limited edition three 12" singles

in tin: Virgin METAL 1
CD Reissue (29.05.1990):
Virgin MTLCD 1
Albatross/Memories/Swan
Lake/Poptones/Careering/No
Birds Do Sing/Graveyard/The
Suit/Bad Baby/Socialist/Chant/
Radio 4

Second Edition
Released: 22.02.1980
Peak Position: #46
Double LP: Virgin VD 2512
Cassette: Virgin MBCAS 1
CD Reissue (06.1986): Virgin
CDVD 2512
Albatross/Memories/Swan Lake/
Poptones/Careering/No Birds
Do Sing/Graveyard/The Suit/
Bad Baby/Socialist/Radio 4

Paris Au Printemps (Paris In The Spring)
Released: 14.11.1980
Peak Position: #61
LP: Virgin V 2183
Cassette: Virgin TCV 2183
CD Reissue (17.04.1990):
Virgin CDV 2183
Theme/Chant/Careering/Bad
Baby/Low Life/Attack/Poptones

Flowers Of Romance
Released: 10.04.1981
Peak Position: #11
LP: Virgin V 2189
Cassette: Virgin TCV 2189
Four Enclosed Walls/Track 8/
Phenagen/Flowers of Romance/
Under The House/Hymie's

Him/Banging The Door/Go
Back/Francis Massacre
CD Reissue (17.04.1990):
Virgin CDV 2189
+ 3 bonus tracks: Flowers of
Romance (Instrumental)/Home
Is Where The Heart Is/Another

Live In Tokyo
Released: 26.09.1983
Peak Position: #28
LP: Virgin VGD 3508
Cassette: Virgin VGDC 3508
CD (Reissued 06.1986): Virgin
VGCD 3508
Annalisa/Religion/Low Life/
Solitaire/Flowers of Romance/
This Is Not A Love Song/Death
Disco/Bad Life/Banging The
Door/Under The House

**This Is What You Want, This Is
What You Get**
Released: 09.07.1984
Peak Position: #56
LP: Virgin V 2309
Cassette: Virgin TCV 2309
CD: Virgin CDV 2309
Bad Life/This Is Not A Love
Song/Solitaire/Tie Me To The
Length Of That/The Pardon/
Where Are You?/1981/The
Order of Death

Album
Released: 03.02.1986
Peak Position: #14
LP ['Album']: Virgin V 2366
Cassette ['Cassette']: Virgin
TCV 2366

CD ['Compact Disc']: Virgin
CDV 2366
F.F.F./Rise/Fishing/Round/Bags/
Home/Ease

Happy?
Released: 14.09.1987
Peak Position: #40
LP: Virgin V 2455
Cassette: Virgin TCV 2455
CD: Virgin CDV 2455
Seattle/Rules and Regulations/
The Body/Save Me/Hard Times/
Open and Revolving/Angry/
Fat Chance Hotel

9
Released: 30.05.1989
Peak Position: #36
LP: Virgin V 2588
Cassette: Virgin TCV 2588
CD: Virgin CDV 2588
Happy/Disappointed/Warrior/
U.S.L.S. 1/Sand Castles In The
Snow/Worry/Brave New World/
Like That/Same Old Story/
Armada

The Greatest Hits... So Far
Released: 22.10.1990
Peak Position: #20
Double LP: Virgin V 2644
Cassette: Virgin TCV 2644
CD: Virgin CDV 2644
Public Image/Death Disco/
Memories/Careering/Flowers of
Romance/This Is Not A Love Song/
Rise/Home/Seattle/The Body/Rules
and Regulations/Disappointed/
Warrior/Don't Ask Me

That What Is Not
Released: 24.02.1992
Peak Position: #46
LP: Virgin V 2681
Cassette: Virgin TCV 2681
CD: Virgin CDV 2681
Acid Drops/Luck's Up/Cruel/
God/Covered/Love Hope/
Unfairground/Think Tank/
Emperor/Good Things

Plastic Box
Released: 01.03.1999
4 x CD Box Set:
Virgin PILBOX 1
CD 1: Public Image/The
Cowboy Song/Theme/Religion
I/Religion II/Annalisa/Low
Life/Attack/Poptones (John
Peel Session)/Careering (John
Peel Session)/Chant (John Peel
Session)/Death Disco (12"
Remix)/Half Mix-Mega Mix/No
Birds Do Sing/Memories
CD 2: Another/Albatross/
Socialist/The Suit/Bad Baby/
Radio 4/ Pied Piper/Flowers of
Romance/Four Enclosed Walls/
Phenagen/Track 8/Hymie's
Him/Under The House/Banging
The Door/Go Back/ Francis
Massacre/Home Is Where The
Heart Is
CD 3: This Is Not A Love Song
(LP Remix)/Blue Water/Bad
Life/Question Mark/Solitaire/
Tie Me To The Length Of
That/Where Are You?/The
Pardon/1981/The Order Of
Death/

F.F.F./Rise/Fishing/Round/
Home/Ease
CD 4: Seattle/Angry/The Body
(US 12" Mix)/Selfish Rubbish/
Disappointed/Happy/Warrior
(UK 12" Remix)/U.S.L.S. 1/
Don't Ask Me/Criminal/Luck's
Up/God/Cruel (Mark Goodier
Session)/Acid Drops (Mark
Goodier Session)/Love Hope
(Mark Goodier Session)/Think
Tank (Mark Goodier Session)

PiL Video

Compilation
Released: 12.1986
VHS: Virgin VVC 144
Public Image/Death Disco/This
is Not A Love Song/Bad Life/
Rise/Home

**PiL Exclusive Compilation
Appearances**

Various Artists: **Machines**
Released: 31.10.1980
LP: Virgin V 2177
Features exclusive PiL track
'Pied Piper'

OST: **Point Break**
Released: 09.07.1991
CD: MCA MCD 10202
Features exclusive PiL track
'Criminal'

Various Artists: **The Best of The**

Old Grey Whistle Test
Released: 17.09.2001
DVD: BBC Worldwide
BBCDVD 1073
Features PiL performing
'Careering' on *The Old Grey Whistle Test*

PiL Radio Sessions

John Peel Session
BBC Radio 1
RX: 10.12.1979
TX: 17.12.1979
Poptones/Careering/Chant

Mark Goodier Session
BBC Radio 1
TX: 25.02.1992
 Cruel/Acid Drops/Love Hope/
Think Tank

PiL Selected Bootlegs

Recorded Live In Paris When Nobody Was Looking
1979
LP: VPMF SR 5339
Theme/Low Life/Annalisa/
Public Image/Belsen Was A Gas/
Attack/Problems/Religion
[Recording of 22.12.1978
concert from Le Stadium, Paris.
Omits second encores of 'Public
Image' and 'Annalisa'.]

Extra Issue
1979

LP: Vicious Records V 2612
Theme/Low Life/Belsen Was A
Gas/Annalisa/Public Image/Sod
In Heaven (Religion)/Attack/
Public Image – 'Goodbyeee'
[Recording of Rainbow Theatre
show from 26.12.1978.]

Nubes
1979
LP (US): Impossible Recordworks
IMP 1.20
Theme/Low Life/Belsen Was A
Gas/Annalisa/Public Image/Sod
In Heaven (Religion)/Attack/
Public Image – Encore
[Recording of Rainbow Theatre
show from 26.12.1978.]

No Life Like Low Life
1979
LP (Japan): PI 2612
Theme/Low Life/Belsen Was A
Gas/Annalisa/Public Image/Sod
In Heaven (Religion)/Attack/
Public Image – Encore
[Recording of Rainbow Theatre
show from 26.12.1978.]

Sci-fi
1980
LP (Japan): UD-6531
Chant/Annalisa/Memories/Low
Life/Public Image/Attack/Death
Disco/Another/No Birds... (Do
Sing)
[Recording of Futurama: Sci-Fi
Festival gig, Queen's Hall, Leeds,
08.09.1979.]

Profile
1980
Double LP (Japan): Cat.no. unknown
Fodderstompf/Careering/
Annalisa/Attack/Low Life/
Chant/Death Disco/Poptones/
Religion/Bad Baby/Public
Image/Memories/Home is
Where The Heart Is
[Recording of gig at Olympic
Auditorium, Los Angeles on
04.05.1980. Also issued under
the title 'Olympic Auditorium
LA']

Career With A Future
1980
Double LP (US): Music Publicity Inc.
Fodderstompf/Careering/
Annalisa/Attack/Low Life/
Chant/Death Disco/Poptones/
Religion/Bad Baby/Public Image/
Memories/Home is Where The
Heart Is
[Recording of gig at Olympic
Auditorium, Los Angeles on
04.05.1980.]

The Famous Riot Show
1981
7" Single: Good Shape Records
105
[Edited recording of the
Ritz, New York City show,
15.05.1981. Contains an
introduction by cable TV
presenter Lisa Yapp, plus
performances of 'Four Enclosed
Walls' and 'Go Back']

Force
1983
Triple 12" Single (Japan): XL
2872
Immortal (Blue Water)/Where
Are You/Annalisa/Religion/Bad
Baby/Attack/Careering/Mad
Max (Bad Life)/Chant/Death
Disco/Public Image/Low Life/
Under The House/Poptones/
Careering/Flowers of Romance
[Live performance from gig at
Convention Centre, Pasadena
07.11.1982, plus recordings of
'Poptones' and 'Careering' from
The Old Grey Whistle Test, BBC2,
12.02.1980 and 'Flowers of
Romance' from BBC1's *Top of
the Pops*, 09.04.1981.]

**Live In Pasadena, California
08.11.82**
1983
LP (US): Great Live Concerts
D-548 (6012 4299)
I Wish I Could Die (Theme)/
Where Are You/Religion/
Careering/Swan Lake (Death
Disco)/Mad Max (Bad Life)/
Low Life/Public Image/Under
The House

Metal Box Demos
Date unknown
Compilation LP (Italy): Cat.
No. unknown
Careering (John Peel Session)/
Poptones (John Peel Session)/
Where Are You (Live in
Pasadena, 08.11.1982)/Death

Disco (Live in Pasadena, 08.11.1982)/Bad Life (Live in Pasadena, 08.11.1982)/Chant (John Peel Session)/Poptones (*Old Grey Whistle Test*)/Careering (*Old Grey Whistle Test*)/Under The House (Live in Pasadena, 08.11.1982)
[Also appeared under the title 'Rotten The Money', on an Italian bootleg, cat. no. SPVR 1631]

Where Are We?
1983
LP (US): Gothic Records LP 001
Where Are You/Mad Max (Bad Life)/Under The House/Banging The Door/Chant/Careering/Bad Baby/Death Disco/Annalisa
[Recording of PiL gig at Paramount Theatre, Staten Island, New York on 26.03.1983.]

Loughborough 8.12.83: No More Limits
1984
Picture Disc LP (Italy): Cat. No. unknown
Public Image/Low Life/ Annalisa/Religion/Flowers of Romance/Poptones/Chant/ Anarchy in the UK/This Is Not A Love Song
[Recording of gig at Loughborough University, 08.12.1983.]

This Is Not A PiL Album
Compilation
1984
LP (Australia): Porpak SEX 3525
Blue Water (Live in Pasadena, 08.11.1982)/Where Are You (Live in Pasadena, 08.11.1982)/ Mad Max (Live in Pasadena, 08.11.1982)/Profile (Home Is Where The Heart Is) (Live at Olympic Auditorium, Los Angeles, 04.05.1980)/ Poptones (*Old Grey Whistle Test*, 12.02.1980)/Careering (*Old Grey Whistle Test*, 12.02.1980)/ Belsen Was A Gas (Rainbow Theatre, London, 26.12.1978)/ Problems (Le Stadium, Paris, 22.12.1978)/Another (Queen's Hall, Leeds, 08.09.1978)/Pied Piper

More Bermuda Than Pizza (Velvet Underground Mispressing)
1987
Picture Disc LP (Germany): Cat No. unknown
Kashmir/FFF/Low Life/Fishing/ Poptones/Pretty Vacant/Banging The Door/Four Enclosed Walls/ Flowers of Romance
[An otherwise unavailable recording of the infamous Austrian gig on 12.09.1986 during which John McGeoch was injured by a flying bottle (although this edited recording, thankfully, does not include that incident).]

Holidays In Estonia
1991
CD (Germany): Chapter One
CO 25169
Public Image (ending only)/
FFF/Seattle/Home/Bags/Rise/
Hard Times/Religion/Rules
and Regulations/Angry/Open
and Revolving/Holidays in the
Sun/The Body
[Recording of live show at the
Glasnost Rock Festival, Tallin,
Estonia on 26.08.1988.]

Acid Party
1993
CD (US): Kiss de Luxe KISS 32
This Is Not A Love Song/
Criminal/Rules and Regulations/
Disappointed/Acid Drops/
Covered/Rise
[Recording of gig at U.C. Irvine,
Crawford Hall, California on
26.03.1992.]

Rotten To The Core
1993
CD (Italy): Big Music 054
This Is Not A Love Song/
Criminal/Love Hope/Think
Tank/Rules and Regulations/
Acid Drops/Cruel/Don't Ask
Me/The Body/Disappointed
[Live recording of gig at the
Provinssrock Festival, Finland,
06.06.1992.]

Boxing Day
1996
CD (Japan): Rag Doll Music

RDM 951020
Theme/Low Life/Belsen Was A
Gas/Annalisa/Public Image/Sod
In Heaven (Religion)/Attack/
Public Image – 'Goodbyeee'
[Recording of Rainbow Theatre
show from 26.12.1978.]

Metal Tape
1996
CD (Japan): Element of Crime 021
Fodderstompf/Careering/Chant/
Annalisa/Poptones/Attack/Low
Life/Public Image/Swan Lake
(Death Disco)/Memories
[Live recording of gig at
Agora Ballroom, Atlanta on
24.04.1980.]

**John Lydon: Live In Japan 1997
Complete!**
2000
CD (Japan): Cat. No. unknown
Sun/Armies/Another Way/Take
Me/Psychopath/Tie Me To The
Length Of That/Rise/Dog/
Public Image/Careering/Under
The House/Stump/Grave Ride/A
No And A Yes/Dis-Ho
[Live recording at Club Citta,
Kawasaki, Japan, 25.09.1997.]

PiL Solo Projects / Collaborations

Sex Pistols: **Anarchy In The UK**
[Johnny Rotten, Glen Matlock,
Steve Jones, Paul Cook]
Released: 26.11.1976
Peak Position: #38

7" Single: EMI 2566
b/w I Wanna Be Me

Sex Pistols: **God Save The Queen**
Scheduled Release: 03.1977
Withdrawn
7" Single: A&M AMS 7284
b/w No Feelings

Sex Pistols: **God Save The Queen**
Released: 27.05.1977
Peak Position: #2
7" Single: Virgin VS 181
b/w Did You No Wrong

Sex Pistols: **Pretty Vacant**
Released: 01.07.1977
Peak Position: #6
7" Single: Virgin VS 184
b/w No Fun

Sex Pistols: **Holidays In The Sun**
Released: 14.10.1977
Peak Position: #8
7" Single: Virgin VS 191
b/w Satellite

Sex Pistols: **Never Mind The
Bollocks, Here's The Sex Pistols**
Released: 04.11.1977
Peak Position: #1
LP: Virgin V 2086
Cassette: Virgin TCV 2086
CD Release: Virgin CDV 2086
Holidays In The Sun/Bodies/No
Feelings/Liar/God Save The
Queen/Problems/Seventeen/
Anarchy in the UK/Submission/
Pretty Vacant/New York/EMI
Unlimited Edition

Jah Wobble & Wayne Dobson:
**Dreadlock Don't Deal In
Wedlock**
Released: 13.10.1978
12" Single: Virgin VOLE 9
Dreadlock Don't Deal In
Wedlock/Pthilius Pubis

The Steel Leg: **The Steel Leg Vs.
The Electric Dread EP**
[Jah Wobble, Don Letts, Keith
Levene, Vince Bracken]
Released: 01.1979
7" Single: Virgin VS 239
Steel Leg/Stratetime and the
Wideman/Haile Unlikely by the
Electric Dread/Unlikely Pub
12" Single: Virgin VS 239-12
Steel Leg/Stratetime and the
Wideman/Haile Unlikely by the
Electric Dread/Unlikely Pub

Sex Pistols: **The Great
Rock'n'Roll Swindle**
Released: 02.03.1979
Peak Position: #7
Double LP: Virgin VD 2410
Cassette: Virgin TCVD 2410
CD Release: Virgin CDV 2410
[Rotten features on the
following: Johnny B. Goode-
Road Runner/Anarchy In The
UK/Don't Give Me No Lip
Child/I'm Not Your Stepping
Stone/I Wanna Be Me]

Jah Wobble: **Dan McArthur**
Released: 29.06.1979
7" Single: Virgin VS 275
b/w Dan McArthur II

12" Single: Virgin VS 275-12
Dan McArthur (Disco Dancer)/
Dan McArthur II

Cowboys International:
Original Sin
Released: 05.10.1979
LP: Virgin V 2316
[Levene plays on 'Wish']

Brian Brain: **They've Got Me In**
The Bottle
[Martin Atkins, Pete Jones]
Released: 21.03.1980
7" Single: Secret Records
SHH101
b/w I Get Pain (1+2)

Jah Wobble: **Betrayal**
Released: 18.04.1980
7" Single: Virgin VS 337
12" Single: Virgin VS 337-12
b/w Battle of Britain by Mr. X

Jah Wobble: **The Legend Lives**
On: Jah Wobble In 'Betrayal'
Released: 08.05.1980
LP: Virgin V 2158
CD Reissue (07.1990): Virgin
CDV 2158
Betrayal/Beat the Drum for Me/
Blueberry Hill/Not Another/
Tales from Outer Space/Today
is the First Day of the...? /Dan
McArthur/Pineapple
[CD reissue contains seven
extra tracks: Blueberry Hill
(Computer Version)/I Need You
by My Side/Message from Pluto/
Sea Side Special/Something

Profound/Dreadlock Don't Deal
in Wedlock/Battle of Britain]

Brian Brain: **Another Million**
Miles
Released: 04.07.1980
7" Single: Secret Records
SHH105
b/w Personality Counts

Jah Wobble: **V.I.E.P.**
Released: 25.07.1980
Mini-LP: Virgin VS 361-12
Blueberry Hill/Blueberry Hill
(Computer Version)/I Need
You By My Side (Message
from Pluto)/Seaside Special/
Something Profound/Blood
Repression

Brian Brain: **Unexpected Noises**
Released: 01.08.1980
LP: Secret Records BRAIN 1
Another Million Miles/Our
Man in Hong Kong/They've
Got Me In The Bottle/The Hots
for You/The Asthma Game/
Brainstorm/Unexpected Noises/I
Get Pain/Dirty Dealing in the
Lone Star State/Turn it Into
Noise/I'm Suffocating/Jet Boats
in the Ganges

Brian Brain: **Culture (EP)**
Released: 21.11.1980
12" Single: Secret Records 12
SHH109
Fun People/Working in a
Farmyard in a White Suit/At
Home He's a Tourist/Careering

Jah Wobble & Holger Czukay:
Full Circle
Released: 1981
LP: Spoon Records
CD Reissue (11.05.1992):
Virgin CDOVD 437
How Much Are They?/Where's
The Money?/Full Circle R.P.S.
(No. 7)/Mystery R.P.S. (No. 8)/
Trench Warfare/Twilight World

Positive Noise: **Heart Of
Darkness**
Released: 15.05.1981
LP: Statik STATLP 1
[Levene plays on 'Darkness
Visible']

Holger Czukay, Jah Wobble &
Jaki Liebezeit: **How Much Are
They?**
Released: 06.1981
7" Single: Island 105117
b/w Twilight World
12" Single: Island 12"WIP 6701
How Much Are They?/Where's
The Money?/Trench Warfare/
Twilight World

Vivien Goldman: **Launderette**
Released: 03.07.1981
7" Single: Window WIND 1
b/w Private Armies
[Produced by Goldman, Lydon
and Levene. Levene plays on
both sides of the single.]

The Human Condition: **The
Human Condition**
[Jah Wobble, Dave Animal,

Jim Walker]
Released: 09.1981
Cassette: THC
Apocalypse Parts 1 & 2/City of
Gold/Neon/Sleazy/Reality/
Tension/Oil Pump/Frantic/
Human Condition/Red Indian/
Neon
[Recorded live at Collegiate,
London, 13.09.1981]

Deadly Headly: **35 Years From
Alpha**
Released: 11.1981
LP: On-U Sound ONU-LP 14
[Levene plays guitar on
'Without A Love Like Yours']

Singers & Players featuring Bim
Sherman: **War Of Words**
Released: 11.1981
LP: On-U Sound ONU-LP 5
[Levene performs on 'Devious
Woman', and also – uncredited
– on 'Quante Jubila', 'Sit and
Wonder', 'Fit to Survive' and
'Reaching the Bad Man']

Brian Brain: **Jive Jive**
Released: 15.01.1982
7" Single: Secret Records SHH
119
b/w Hello to the Working
Classes (Live)

Holger Czukay: **On The Way To
The Peak Of Normal**
Released: 22.01.1982
LP: EMI EMC 3394
[Wobble features on 'Hiss N

Listen'. The LP is reissued on
CD – SPOONCD 36 – in
January 1998]

Creation Rebel / New Age
Steppers: **Threat To Creation**
Released: 25.01.1982
LP: On-U Sound/Cherry Red
BRED 21
[Levene performs on 'Last
Sane Dream', and appears
– uncredited – on the title
track.]

Jah Wobble & Mark Lusardi:
Fading
Released: 19.03.1982
12" Single: Jah Wobble JAH 1
Fading/Nocturnal

The Human Condition: **Live In
Europe, November 1981**
[Jah Wobble, Dave Animal, Jim
Walker]
Released: 04.1982
Cassette: THC 1
Waves/The End/The Human
Condition/Soundcheck/
Condemned

Jah Wobble & Animal: **Long
Long Way**
Released: 01.10.1982
12" Single: Jah Wobble JAH 2
Long Long Way/Romany Trail/
Berlin

Brian Brain: **Funky Zoo**
Released: 08.10.1982
7" Single: Secret Records SHH 142

b/w flies Flies
12" Single: Secret Records
12SHH 142
Funky Zoo/Funky Zoo (Dub)/
Flies

Bartok: **Insanity**
Released: 11.1982
12" Single: On Records ON-1
[Wobble appears on the A-side.]

Jah Wobble & Ben Mandleson:
Body Music Mokili
Released: 12.1982
12" Single: Island 12 WIP 6822
Body Music (Hot)/Motema
(Cool)/Body Music
(Soundtrack)

Invaders Of The Heart: **Invaders
Of The Heart**
[Jah Wobble, Dave Maltby,
Oliver Marland, Neville Murray,
Lee Partis]
Released: 22.04.1983
12" Single: Lago Records LAGO 4
Invaders of the Heart (Mix
1)/Invaders of the Heart (Mix
2)/Invaders of the Heart (Mix 3:
Exotic Decadent Disco Mix)

Jah Wobble, The Edge & Holger
Czukay: **Snake Charmer**
Released: 10.1983
Mini-LP: Island IMA 1
Snake Charmer/Hold On To
Your Dreams/It Was A Camel/
Sleazy/Snake Charmer (Reprise)

Jah Wobble, The Edge & Holger Czukay: **Snake Charmer**
Released: 28.10.1983
12" Single: Island WOB 1
Snake Charmer/Hold On To Your Dreams

Keith Levene: **Commercial Zone**
Released: 11.1983
LP: PiL Records Inc. XYZ 007
Love Song/Mad Max (Bad Life)/
Bad Night/Solitaire/The Slab
(The Order of Death)/Lou Reed
Part 1/Lou Reed Part 2 (Where
Are You)/Blue Water/Miller
Hi-Life
[Reissued in August 1984, with
a different sequence of tracks, a
retitling of 'Solitaire' (as 'Young
Brits') and an edited version of
'Bad Night'.]

Joolz: **Denise**
Released: 11.1983
12" Single: Abstract Sounds
12ABS 018
Denise/The Latest Craze/War of
Attrition
[Produced and co-written by Wobble]

Joolz: **The Kiss**
Released: 07.1984
12" Single: Abstract Sounds
12ABS 025
The Kiss/The Kiss (Dance Mix)/
Paved with Gold
[Produced and co-written by Wobble]

Winston Tong: **Theoretically Chinese**

Released: 08.1984
12" Single (Import): Crepuscle
12 TWI310
[Wobble performs on the A-side.]

Jah Wobble, Ollie Marland &
Polly Eltes: **Voodoo / East**
Released: 15.10.1984
12" Single: Lago Records LAGO 5
Voodoo / East

Timezone: **World Destruction**
[John Lydon & Afrika
Bambaataa]
Released: 31.12.1984
Peak Position: #44
7" Single: Virgin VS 743
b/w World Destruction
(Instrumental Mix)
12" Single: VS 743-12
World Destruction (Industrial
Remix)/World Destruction (12"
Instrumental Blast)
Cassette Single: TVS 743-12
World Destruction (12"
Mix)/World Destruction (12"
Instrumental Blast)/World
Destruction
(7" Mix)/World Destruction
(Instrumental Mix)

Brian Brain: **Fun With Music**
Released: 1985
12" Single: Plaid Records
PLAID 001
Fun With Music (Part 1)/Big
Drugs/Happy?/USA

Jah Wobble & Ollie Marland
featuring Shara Nelson: **Love**

Mystery
Released: 22.04.1985
7" Single: Island IS 288
12" Single: Island 12 IS 288
Love Mystery/Love Mystery
(Instrumental)

Jah Wobble & Ollie Marland:
Neon Moon
Released: 13.05.1985
LP: Island ILPS 9828
Cassette: Island ICT 9828
Love Mystery/Love Mystery
(Instrumental)/Running Away/
Neon Moon/Life On The Line/
Life On The Line (Dub)/The
Beast Inside/Despike

Dub Syndicate: **Tunes From The
Missing Channel**
Released: 17.06.1985
LP: On-U Sound ONLP 38
CD: On-U Sound OUCD 38
[Wobble performs and co-writes
'Overboard']

Winston Tong: **Theoretically
Chinese**
Released: 10.1985
LP: Crepuscle TWI 549
[Wobble performs on the title
track.]

Jah Wobble: **Blow Out**
Released: 02.12.1985
12" Single: Lago Records LAGO 6
Blow Out/Blow Out
(Instrumental)

The Golden Palominos: **Visions**

Of Excess
Released: 12.1985
LP: Celluloid CEL 6118
CD Reissue: Charly CPCD
8151
[Lydon contributes guest vocals
to 'The Animal Speaks']

Brian Brain: **Fun With Music
(Remix) (EP)**
Released: 1986
12" Single: Twin Tone TTW 8671
Fun With Music (Muscle
Mix)/Fun With Music (Bonus
Beats)/Fun With Music (Back
Words)/Fun With Music
(Minneapolis Mix)/Fun With
Music (Cathedral Mix)/Fun
With Music (Acapella)

Jah Wobble & Brett Wickens:
Between Two Frequencies
Released: 28.04.1986
12" Single: General Kinetics G
2001/Between Two Frequencies/
The Harbour/6020

African Head Charge: **Off The
Beaten Track**
Released: 08.1986
LP: On-U Sound ON-U LP 40
CD reissue: On-U Sound ON-
U CD 40
[Wobble features on 'Some
Bizarre']

Jah Wobble & Ollie Marland:
Trade Winds
Released: 10.1986
LP: Lago Records LAGO 7

Trade Winds/Hard Luck Story/The Desert Song/Seven Dials/Night People/The Calling/Medley

Brian Brain: **Time Flies When You're Having Toast**
Released: 1987
LP: Plaid Records PLAID PB002
Who Hung The Monkey?/Nature/Positive Thinking/Watching TV (With My Baby)/Australian Style/Style/Sex For The Sake Of Sex/Big Drugs/Don't Tell Me About Your World/Happy?

Brian Brain: **Who Hung The Monkey?**
Released: 1987
12" Single: Moving Target MT505
Who Hung The Monkey?/Who Hung The Monkey? (Bedtime For Bonzo)

Holger Czukay: **Rome Remains Rome**
Released: 12.01.1987
Cassette: Virgin TCV 2408
CD: Virgin CDV 2408
[Wobble co-writes and performs on 'Blessed Easter' and 'Sudtenland'.]

Jah Wobble: **Psalms**
Released: 09.1987
LP: Island WOB 7
Sakharov/Island Paradise/Enough/No Second Chances/

Dark Horse/To Erase/Alcohol/Jihad/NO Message/Sales Target/The Hymns

Jah Wobble: **Island Paradise**
Released: 28.09.1987
12" Single: Island WOB 8
Island Paradise (Club Mix)/Alcohol/Jihad/Island Paradise (White Mix)

Keith Levene: **2011: Back Too Black (EP)**
Released: 11.1987
12" Single: Iridescence 154
Black Too Black/2011/Cops I/Cedd Moses (Not Walsh)/Cops II/Heavy 4 Hire/Cops III/John Williams

Keith Levene: **Looking For Something (EP)**
Released: 05.1988
12" Single: Taang Ting T19
I'm Looking For Something/Cops Too/Taang Ting!/If Six Was Nine

Sex Pistols: **Anarchy In The UK**
Reissued 08.1988
3" CD Single: Virgin VSCDT 3
Anarchy in the UK/No Fun/EMI (Unlimited Edition) (Live in Trondheim)

Keith Levene: **If Six Was 9**
Released: 09.1988
CD Single (USA): Rykodisc RCD3-1004
If Six Was 9/Back Too Black/

Fast Brass Slam (Version II)

Timezone: **World Destruction**
Reissued: 05.12.1988
3" CD Single: Virgin VSCDT 29
World Destruction (Extended
12" Remix)/World Destruction
(12" Instrumental Blast)/World
Destruction (7" Version)/World
Destruction (7" B-Side)

Sex Pistols: **God Save The Queen**
Reissued: 05.12.1988
3" CD Single: Virgin VSCDT 37
God Save The Queen/Did You
No Wrong/Don't Give Me No
Lip Child

Brian Brain: **Brian Brain (EP)**
Released: 1989
12" Single: Black Man, White
World/Heard It Through The
Grapevine/Fun People/Flies

Happy Valley: **Love Is (Not
Enough)**
[Jah Wobble & David Jaymes]
Released: 1989
12" Single: Vinyl Cuts
Productions VC 120001
Love Is (Not Enough) (Dance
Version)/Love Is (Not Enough)
(7" Version)/Over You

Pulse 8: **Radio Morocco**
[Jah Wobble & Justin Adams]
Released: 06.1989
12" Single: Nation Records NR
0002T
Radio Morocco (Adrian

Sherwood Mix)/Radio Morocco
(Youth Dub Mix)/Radio
Morocco (Double Dee Techno
Mix)

Keith Levene: **Violent Opposition**
Released: 22.09.1989
LP: Taang Ting T-33
CD: Rykodisc RCD 10049
I'm Looking for Something/
Taang! Ting (Version 1)/If
Six Was 9/Cops Too/Double
Barrel/Fast Brass Slam (Version
1)/Liquidator/Fast Cars/Back
Too Black/2011/Heavy 4 Hire/
Cold Turkey

Glass: **It's Amazing**
Released: 16.10.1989
7" Single: RCA PB 43251
Cassette Single: RCA PK 43251
12" Single: RCA PT 43252
CD Single: RCA PD 43252
[Wobble produces the B-side,
'Real Love']

The Barmy Army: **The English
Disease**
Released: 10.1989
LP: On-U Sound ON-U LP 48
CD: On-U Sound ON-U CD 48
[Wobble performs on two
tracks: 'Civil Liberty' and
'Psycho & The Wombles Of
Division 1']

Gary Clail/On-U Sound System:
End Of The Century Party
Released: 11.1989
LP: On-U Sound ON-U LP 49

CD: On-U Sound ON-U CD 9
[Wobble features on and co-
writes 'Beef']

Invaders of the Heart featuring
Zahreme: **The Unspoken Word**
Released: 06.11.1989
12" Single: Nation Records NR
0003T
The Unspoken Word/The
Unspoken Word (Instrumental)

Invaders of the Heart: **Without
Judgment**
Released: 04.12.1989
LP: KK Records KK 039
Bungalow Park/What the
Problem Is/Anything Can
Happen/A13/Drowned and
Saved/So Many Years/Message
from our Sponsor/Coypu/Good
Ghosts/Saracen/Eternal Vendor/
Invisible Cities/Inferno/
Location/Uncommercial Road/
Will the Circle Be Unbroken?

Dub Syndicate: **Strike The Balance**
Released: 02.1990
LP: On-U Sound ONU-LP 47
[Levene is credited with 'sound
sampling' and 'pre-production'
on the whole LP]

Sinead O'Connor: **I Do Not
Want What I Haven't Got**
Released: 12.03.1990
Peak Position: #1
LP: Ensign CHEN 14
Cassette: Ensign ZCHEN 14
CD: Ensign CCD 1759

DCC (released 1993): Ensign
DCCCHEN 14
MD (released 1993): Ensign
MDCHEN 14
[Wobble performs on 'The Last
Day of Our Acquaintance']

Ginger Baker: **Middle Passage**
Released: 21.06.1990
LP: Mango/Island AXLPS 3001
Cassette: Mango/Island AXCT
3001
CD: Mango/Island AXCD 3001
[Wobble plays bass on all album
tracks: Mektoub/Under Black
Skies/Time Be Time/Alamout/
Basil/South to the Dust]

Gary Clail / On-U Sound
System featuring Bim Sherman:
Beef
Released: 02.07.1990
Peak Position: #64
7" Single: Perfecto/BMG PB 43843
12" Single: Perfecto/BMG PT 43844
12" Remix: Perfecto/BMG PT 43846
CD Single: Perfecto/BMG PD
43844
[Wobble and Levene co-write
and appear on all mixes.]

Jah Wobble's Invaders Of The
Heart: **Bomba**
Released: 08.10.1990
7" Single: Boys Own/London BOI 2
b/w Bomba (Miles Away Mix)
Cassette Single: Boys Own/
London BOICS 2
Bomba (Nonsonicus Maximus
Mix) (7-Inch)/Bomba (Miles

Away Mix)
12" Single: Boys Own/London
BOIX 2
Bomba (Nonsonicus Maximus
Mix)/Bomba (Miles Away Mix)/
Bomba (Live)
CD Single: Boys Own/London
BOICD 2
Bomba (Nonsonicus Maximus
Mix)/Bomba (Miles Away Mix)/
Bomba (Live)

The Shamen: **En-tact**
Released: 22.10.1990
Peak Position: #31
Double LP: One Little Indian
TPLP 22 SP
Cassette: One Little Indian
TPLP 22 C
CD: One Little Indian TPLP
22 CD
Re-issued (with different mixes
of all tracks): 25.11.1991
LP: One Little Indian TPLP 22 US
Cassette: One Little Indian
TPLP 22 CUS
CD: One Little Indian TPLP 22
CDUS
[Wobble features on 'Evil Is Even'.]

Edie Brickell & The New
Bohemians: **Ghost Of A Dog**
Released: 05.11.1990
LP: Geffen/WEA WX 386
Cassette: Geffen/WEA WX 386C
CD: Geffen/WEA 924-304-2
[Lydon contributes backing
vocals to 'Strings of Love']

Killing Joke: **Extremities, Dirt
& Various Repressed Emotions**
Released: 05.11.1990
Double LP: Aggressive Rock/
Noise International AG 0541
CD: AGR 0542
Money is Not Our God/Age
of Greed/Beautiful Dead/
Extremities/Intravenous/Inside
the Termite Mound/Solitude/
North of the Border/Slipstream/
Kaliyuga Struggle
[Atkins performs and co-writes
all tracks]

Gary Clail / On-U Sound
System: **Emotional Hooligan**
Released: 22.04.1991
Peak Position: #35
LP: Perfecto/BMG PL 74965
Cassette: Perfecto/BMG PK
74965
CD: Perfecto/BMG PD 74965
[Levene and Wobble co-write
and appear on 'Beef']

The Orb: **Perpetual Dawn**
Released: 27.05.1991*
Peak Position: #61*
7" Single: Wau!/Big Life BLR 46
Cassette Single: Wau!/Big Life
BLRC 46
12" Single: Wau!/Big Life BLRT 46
CD Single: Wau!/Big Life
BLRCD 46
[Wobble features on two mixes.
'Perpetual Dawn (Solar Flare
Extended Mix)' features on the
12" and CD single. 'Perpetual
Dawn (Solar Youth Mix)'

appears on the 7", cassette and CD single]
[*The single was re-released, in all formats, on 24.01.1994, and this time peaked as high as #18]

The Orb: **Towers Of Dub / Perpetual Dawn (Orb In Dub)**
Released: 27.05.1991
12" Remix: Wau!/Big Life BLRR 46
[Wobble performs on 'Perpetual Dawn (Ultrabase II)']

Primal Scream: **Higher Than The Sun (Remix)**
Released: 10.06.1991
Peak Position: #40
12" Remix: Creation CRE 096 X
[Jah Wobble features on 'Higher Than The Sun (A Dub Symphony in Two Parts)']

Primal Scream: **Screamadelica**
Released: 23.09.1991
Peak Position: #8
Double LP: Creation CRELP 076
Cassette: Creation CCRE 076
CD: Creation CRECD 076
DCC (released 1993): Creation CREDCC 076
MD (released 1993): Creation CREMD 076
[Jah Wobble features on 'Higher Than The Sun (A Dub Symphony in Two Parts)']

Jah Wobble's Invaders Of The Heart: **Rising Above Bedlam**
Released: 30.09.1991
LP: Oval/Warner Music OVLP 601
Cassette: Oval/Warner Music OVMC 601
CD: Oval/Warner Music 9031754702
Visions of You/Relight the Flame/Bomba/Ungodly Kingdom/Rising Above Bedlam/Erzulie/Everyman's an Island/Soledad/Sweet Divinity/Wonderful World

Invaders of the Heart: **Erzulie**
Released: 04.11.1991
7" Single: Oval OVAL 102
b/w Remind Me to Be Nice to Myself
12" Single: Oval OVAL 102 T
Erzulie (Extended Dependent Mix)/Erzulie (Radio Edit)/Remind Me to Be Nice to Myself
CD Single: Oval 102 CD
Erzulie (Radio Edit)/Erzulie (Extended Dependent Mix)/Remind Me to Be Nice to Myself

Pigface: **Welcome To Mexico... asshole**
Released: 25.11.1991
Double LP: Devotion DVN 003
Double Cassette: Devotion TDVN 003
CD: Devotion CDVN 003
The Love Serenade (I Hate You?)/Blood & Sand/Peaking Too Early (William)/Little Sisters/Twice Removed/Beneath My Feet/Point Blank/Stowaway/Suck/Weightless/T.F.W.O./Lash-Herb-Taxi/Tapeworm/The Breakfast Conspiracy

[Atkins writes all songs except for 'The Love Serenade (I Hate You?)', 'Stowaway' and 'T.F.W.O.']

Chris Connelly: **Come Down Here**
Released: 1992
12" Single: Devotion 12DVN 108
CD Single: Devotion CDVN 108
Come Down Here/Souvenir
From A Dream
[Atkins performs on both tracks]

Jah Wobble's Invaders of
the Heart (featuring Sinead
O'Connor): **Visions Of You**
Released: 20.01.1992
Peak Position: #35
7" Single: Oval 103
Visions of You (Radio Edit)/
Visions of You (Ade Phases the
Parameters of Sound)
Cassette Single: Oval 103 C
Visions of You (Radio Edit)/
Visions of You (Ade Phases the
Parameters of Sound)
12" Single: Oval 103 T
Visions of You (The Welsh Mix)/
Visions of You (Ade Phases the
Parameters of Sound)/Visions of
You (The Secret Love Child of
Hank and Johnny Mix)/Visions
of You (Pick n Mix 1)/Visions of
You (Pick n Mix 2)
CD Single: Oval 103 CD
Visions Of You (Radio Edit)/
Visions of You (Ade Phases the
Parameters of Sound)/Visions of
You (The Secret Love Child of
Hank and Johnny Mix)/Visions
of You (Pick n Mix 1)/Visions of
You (Pick n Mix 2)

Dub Syndicate: **Stoned Immaculate**
Released: 24.02.1992
LP: On-U Sound ONU-LP 56
CD: On-U Sound ONU-CD 15
[Wobble plays keyboards on
'Wadada (Means Love)']

Jah Wobble's Invaders of the
Heart: **The Love Forever (EP)**
Scheduled Release: 06.1992
Cancelled
12" Single: Oval 105 T
Love Forever/Do You Live What
You Sing?/Saeta/Love Life

Invaders of the Heart:
The Ungodly Kingdom
Released: 06.1992
7" Single: Oval 107
b/w Saeta (Andy Kershaw
Sessson Version)/Josey Walsh/
Love Life
12" Single: Oval 107 T
The Ungodly Kingdom
(Transformed Mix)/Saeta (Andy
Kershaw Session Version)/Josey
Walsh/Love Life
CD Single: Oval 107 CD
Ungodly Kingdom
(Transformed Mix)/Saeta (Andy
Kershaw Session Version)/Josey
Walsh/Love Life

The Orb: **Blue Room**
Released: 08.06.1992
Peak Position: #8
12" Single: Big Life BLRT 75
Blue Room (Part One)/Blue

Room (Part Two)
Cassette Single: Big Life BLRC 75
Blue Room (Part One)/Blue
Room (Part Two)
CD Single: Big Life BLRDA 75
Blue Room [39'58" version]
CD Single: Big Life BLRDB 75
Blue Room (Radio 7)/Blue
Room (Excerpt 605)/Towers of
Dub (Mad Professor Remix)
[Wobble co-writes and appears
on all mixes of 'Blue Room']

Chris Connelly: **Phenobarb
Bambalam**
Released: 07.1992
LP: Devotion DVN 013
Cassette: Devotion TDVN 013
CD: Devotion CDDVN 013
The Whistle Blower/July/
Souvenir from A Dream/Come
Down Here/Too Good To Be
True/Heartburn/No Lesser of
Two Evils/Ignition Times Four/
Dirtbox Tennessee
(CD contains extra track: Heartburn
(Twister Mix))
[Atkins performs on all tracks, and
co-writes 'The Whistle Blower', 'July',
'Heartburn' and 'Dirtbox Tennessee']

The Orb: **U.F. ORB**
Released: 06.07.1992
Peak Position: #1
Double LP: Big Life BLRLP 18
Cassette: Big Life BLRMC 18
CD: Big Life BLRCD 18
[Wobble co-writes and performs
on 'Blue Room']

Nine Inch Nails: **Broken (EP)**
Released: 21.09.1992
Mini-LP: Island ILPM 8004
Cassette: Island ICM 8004
CD: Island IMCD 8004
[Pigface, featuring Atkins, co-
write and collaborate with Nine
Inch Nails on the track 'Suck'.]

Sex Pistols: **Anarchy In The UK**
Reissued: 21.09.1992
Peak Position: #33
7" Single: VS 1431
b/w I Wanna Be Me (Alternate Take)
Cassette Single: VSC 1431
Anarchy In The UK//I Wanna
Be Me (Alternate Take)
CD Single: VSCDT 1431
Anarchy In The UK/Anarchy
In The UK (Alternate Take)/I
Wanna Be Me (Alternate Take)
CD Single: VSCDX 1431
Anarchy in the UK/Anarchy
In The UK (Alternate Take)/I
Wanna Be Me (Alternate Take)

Sex Pistols: **Kiss This**
Compilation
Released: 05.10.1992
Peak Position: #10
Double LP: Virgin V 2702
Cassette: Virgin TCV 2702
CD: Virgin CDV 2702
[Lydon appears on all but two
tracks: Anarchy In The UK/God
Save The Queen/Pretty Vacant/
Holidays In The Sun/I Wanna
Be Me/Did You No Wrong/
No Fun/Satellite/Don't Give
Me No Lip Child/I'm Not

Your Stepping Stone/Bodies/
No Feelings/Liar/Problems/
Seventeen/Submission/New
York/EMI (Unlimited Edition)]
Limited Edition Double CD:
Virgin CDVX 2702
[As above, but with the
following second disc of rarities,
all recorded live in Trondheim,
Sweden on 21.07.1977: Anarchy
In The UK/I Wanna Be Me/
Seventeen/New York/EMI
(Unlimited Edition)/No Fun/No
Feelings/ Problems/God Save
The Queen

Pigface: **Fook**
Released: 26.10.1992
LP: Devotion DVN 018
Cassette: Devotion TDVN 018
CD: Devotion CDVN 018
Alles Ist Mine/Ten Ground
and Down/Seven Words/
Insemination/Hips, Tits, Lips,
Power!/Satellite (Needle in the
Groove)/I'm Still Alive/Auto
Hag/Go!/I Can Do No Wrong
[Atkins co-writes and performs
on all tracks]

Sex Pistols: **Pretty Vacant**
Reissued: 23.11.1992
Peak Position: #56
7" Single: Virgin VS 1448
b/w No Feelings
12" Single: Virgin VST 1448
Pretty Vacant/No Feelings
(Demo Version)/Satellite (Demo
Version)/Submission (Demo
Version #1)

CD Single: Virgin VSCD 1448
Pretty Vacant/Seventeen (Demo
Version)/Submission (Demo Version
#2)/Watcha Gonna Do About It
CD Single: Virgin VSCDG 1448
Pretty Vacant/No Feelings
(Demo Version)/Unlimited
Supply (Demo Version)/Satellite
(Demo Version)

(c) [Leslie Winer]: **Witch Witch
Witch**
Released: 1993
CD: Transglobal GLOBAL 1CD
He Was/Flove/N1 Ear/The
Boy Who Used 2 Whistle/John
Says/5/1nce Upon a Time/Skin/
Dream 1
[Wobble plays bass parts on all tracks]

Saffron: **World Of You**
Released: 19.04.1993
7" Single: WEA SAFF 10
Cassette Single: WEA SAFF 10 C
12" Single: WEA SAFF 10 T
CD Single: WEA SAFF 10 CD
[Wobble co-writes and produces
the A-side.]

Nicky Skopeltis: **Ekstasis**
Released: 19.04.1993
Cassette: Axiom 514-518-4
CD: Axiom 514-518-2
[Wobble co-writes and performs
on 'Tarab', 'Sanctuary', 'Heresy',
'Jubilee' and 'Witness']

Holger Czukay: **Moving Pictures**
Released: 19.04.1993
LP: Mute STUMM 125

CD: Mute CDSTUMM 125
[Wobble plays bass on 'All Night Long']

Peace Together: **Be Still**
Released: 17.05.1993
7" Single: Island PCE 71
12" Single: Island PCE 121
Cassette Single: Island PCEMC 1
CD Single: Island PCECD 1
[Featuring Sinead O'Connor
and Peter Gabriel. Wobble
performs on several mixes of
the A-side, including remixes
by Sabres of Paradise and Robin
Guthrie]

Various Artists: **Peace Together**
Compilation
Released: 19.07.1993
LP: Island ILPS 8018
Cassette: Island ICT 8018
CD: Island CID 8018
[Wobble appears on 'Be Still' by
Peace Together]

Oui 3: **Oui Love You**
Released: 26.07.1993
Peak Position: #39
LP: MCA 10833
Cassette: MCC 10833
CD: MCD 10833
[Wobble appears on the title track.]

Joolz: **Recorded 1983-85**
Compilation
Released: Late 1993
CD: Get Back/Abstract Sounds
GBR 4
[Wobble co-writes and performs
on several songs: 'War of

Attrition', 'Denise', 'Latest Craze',
'The Kiss', 'The Kiss (Dub Mix)'
and 'Paved with Gold'.]

Jam Nation: **Way Down Below
Buffalo Hell**
Released: 13.09.1993
CD: Real World CDRW 36
[Wobble appears on 'La Visite
est Terminee']

One Dove: **Morning Dove White**
Released: 13.09.1993
Peak Position: #30
Double LP: Boys Own/London
828-352-1
Cassette: Boys Own/London
828-352-4
CD: Boys Own/London 828-352-2
[Wobble appears on 'There Goes
The Cure']

Loca!/Invaders of the Heart:
Timbal / The Unspoken Word
Released: 11.10.1993
12" Single: Nation NR 024 T
Loca!: Timbal/Invaders of the
Heart featuring Zahrema: The
Unspoken Word

Björk/David Arnold: **Play Dead**
Released: 11.10.1993
Peak Position: #12
7" Single: Island IS 573
b/w Play Dead (Tim Simenon
Orchestral Mix)
Cassette Single: Island CIS 573
Play Dead (Tim Simenon
7" Remix)/Play Dead (Tim
Simenon Orchestral Mix)

12" Single: Island 12IS 573
Play Dead (Tim Simenon
12" Remix)/Play Dead (Tim
Simenon Orchestral Mix)/Play
Dead (Tim Simenon 7" Remix)/
Play Dead (Tim Simenon
Instrumental)
CD Single: Island CID 573
Play Dead (Tim Simenon
7" Remix)/Play Dead (Tim
Simenon Orchestral Mix)/
Play Dead (Tim Simenon
12" Remix)/Play Dead (Tim
Simenon Instrumental)/Play
Dead: End Titles
[Wobble co-writes the A-side
with Björk and Arnold and also
performs on the track]

OST: **The Young Americans**
Released: 11.10.1993
LP: Island ILPS 8019
Cassette: Island ICT 8019
CD: Island CID 8019
[Wobble co-writes and features on
'Play Dead' by Björk/David Arnold]

Leftfield Lydon: **Open Up**
Released: 01.11.1993
Peak Position: #13
7" Single: Hard Hands
HAND009
b/w Open Up (extended)
12" Single: Hard Hands
HAND009T
Open Up (Full Vocal Mix)/
Open Up (Dervish Overdrive)
12" Remix: Hard Hands
HAND009R
Open Up (I Hate Pink Floyd

Mix by Sabres of Paradise)/
Open Up (Open Dub by Sabres
of Paradise)/Open Up (Dust
Brothers Remix)
Cassette Single: Hard Hands
HAND009MC
Open Up (Radio Edit)/Open
Up (Full Vocal Mix) /Open Up
(Dervish Overdrive)
CD Single: Hard Hands
HAND009CD
Open Up (Radio Edit)/Open
Up (Full Vocal Mix)/Open Up
(Dervish Overdrive)

Pigface: **Truth Will Out /
Washing Machine Mouth**
Released: 01.11.1993
Double CD: Devotion CDDVN 025
CD 1: Can You Feel Pain?/War
Ich Nicht/Point Blank/I Can Do
No Wrong/Weightless/White
Trash Reggae-Pigface in Your
Face/Alles Ist Mine/Hips, Tits,
Lips, Power!/Seven Words/
Henry/Jingle Bells/Suck
CD 2: Flowers Are Evil/Cutting
Face/Medley: Red Around
The Eye-The Calm Before the
Storm-The Return of Wet Brain
2000/Cutting Face (Gas Mask
Mix)/Satellite (Needle in the
Groove)/Prepare to Die – Go!
Go! Go!The Last Word

Various Artists: **Deep Cuts**
Compilation
Released: 01.11.1993
Double LP: Sabres of Paradise
SOP 001 LP

CD: Sabres of Paradise SOP 001 CD [Wobble features on and co-writes 'Ooh Baby' by Secret Knowledge]

OST: **In The Name Of The Father**
Released: 24.01.1994
Cassette: Island ICM 8026
CD: Island CID 8026
[Wobble features on 'Billy Boola' by Gavin Friday & Bono, and 'You Made Me The Thief Of Your Heart' by Sinead O'Connor]

Bill Laswell, Jah Wobble & Divination: **Ambient Dub Volume 2: Dead Slow**
Released: 28.01.1994
CD: Subharmonic SD 7003
Dead Slow/Baraka/Silent Fields/ Evil Eye/Dream Light/Journeys

Sinead O'Connor: **You Made Me The Thief Of Your Heart**
Released: 07.02.1994
Peak Position: #42
7" Single: Island IS 588
Cassette Single: Island 8583464
12" Single: Island 12IS 588
CD Single: Island CID 588
[Wobble performs on all versions of the A-side.]

Natacha Atlas: **Dub Yalil**
Released: 28.02.1994
CD Single: Nation/Beggars Banquet NR 28 CD
[Wobble features on 'Stotinki']

Jah Wobble's Invaders of the Heart: **Becoming More Like God**
Released: 18.04.1994
Peak Position: #36
7" Single: Island IS 571
Becoming More Like God (Radio Edit)/Wine, Women & Song
Cassette Single: Island CIS 571
Becoming More Like God (Radio Edit)/Wine, Women & Song
12" Single: Island 12 IS 571
Becoming More Like God/ Wine, Women & Song/ Becoming More Like God (Secret Knowledge To Hell And Back Mix)
CD Single: Island CID 571
Becoming More Like God (Radio Edit)/Wine, Women & Song/Football/Becoming More Like God (Secret Knowledge To Hell And Back Mix)

Baaba Maal: **Firin' In Fouta**
Released: 12.05.1994
Double LP: Mango/Island MLPSD 1109
Cassette: Mango/Island ICT 1109
CD: Mango/Island CIDM 1109
[Wobble appears on 'Njilou']

Jah Wobble's Invaders of the Heart: **Take Me To God**
Released: 16.05.1994
Peak Position: #13
Double LP: Island ILPSD 8017
Cassette: Island ICT 8017
CD: Island CID 8017
God in the Beginning/Becoming More Like God/Whisky Priests/

I'm An Algerian/Amor/Amor
(Dub)/Take Me To God/The
Sun Does Rise/When the Storm
Comes/I Love Everybody/Yoga
of the Nightclub/I Am The
Music/Bonds of Love/Angels/No
Change is Sexy/Raga/Forever

Jah Wobble's Invaders of the
Heart: **The Sun Does Rise**
Released: 13.06.1994
Peak Position: #41
7" Single: Island IS 587
b/w Yalil Ya Aini/Raga
Cassette Single: Island CIS 587
The Sun Does Rise (Radio Edit)/
Yalil Ya Aini/Raga
12" Single: Island 12 IS 587
The Sun Does Rise (Radio Edit)/
Yalil Ya Aini/Raga/Om Namah
Shiva (Transformation of the
Heart Mix)
CD Single: Island CID 587
The Sun Does Rise (Radio Edit)/
Yalil Ya Aini/ Om Namah Shiva
(Transformation of the Heart
Mix)/Raga
CD Single: Island CIDX 587:
The Sun Does Rise (Radio Edit)/
Snake Charmer (Reprise)/A13/
So Many Years

Ian McNabb: **Go Into The Light**
Released: 05.09.1994
Peak Position: #66
7" Single: This Way Up/
PolyGram WAY 3699
12" Single: This Way Up/
PolyGram WAY 3622
CD Single: This Way Up/

PolyGram 8561032
[Features 'Celestial Dub Mix' by
Wobble of 'Go Into The Light']

Jah Wobble: **Amor**
Released: 03.10.1994
Cassette Single: Island CIS 602
Amor (Radio Edit)/Amor (Dub)
12" Single: Island 12 IS 602
Amor (The More Rockas Mix)/
Amor (Kingston Lic)
CD Single: Island CID 602
Amor (Radio Edit)/Amor
(The More Rockas Mix)/Amor
(Kingston Lic)/Amor (Dub)
CD Single: Island CIDX 602
Amor (Evol Dub)/Sahara/Amor (Dub)
CD Single: Island CIDT 602
Amor (Radio Edit)/Amor (Dub)

Apollo 440: **Liquid Cool**
Released: 24.10.1994
Peak Position: #35
12" Single: Stealth Sonic
Recordings/Sony Music SSXT 3
CD Single: Stealth Sonic
Recordings/Sony Music SSXCD 3
[Features 'Jah Wobble Remix' of
A-side]

Dodgy: **So Let Me Go Far**
Released: 26.12.1994
Peak Position: #30
Cassette Single: Bostin/A&M
5809054
12" Yellow Vinyl: Bostin/A&M
5809051
CD Single: Bostin/A&M
5809032
[Wobble contributes a remix

of the A-side called 'So Let Me Wobble Jah' to all formats]

The Wolfgang Press: **Going South**
Released: 09.01.1995
CD Single: 4AD BAD 5001CD
[Features 'Wobble Mix' of 'Chains']

Leftfield: **Leftism**
Released: 30.01.1995
Peak Position: #3
Double LP: Hard Hands HANDLP 2D
Cassette: Hard Hands HANDMC 2
CD: Hard Hands HANDCD 2
[Lydon appears on 'Open Up']

Bomb The Bass: **Clear**
Released: 03.04.1995
Peak Position: #22
LP: Stoned Heights/Island BRLP 611
Cassette: Stoned Heights/Island BRCA 611
CD: Stoned Heights/Island BRCD 611
[Jah Wobble features on '5ml Barrel']

The Philistines: **Hard Work**
Released: 06.1995
CD: Peppermint PRCD 001
[Levene co-writes three songs: 'Problem', 'Get Real' and 'Modern Metal']

David Holmes: **This Film's Crap, Let's Slash The Seats**
Released: 26.06.1995
Peak Position: #51
Double LP: Go! Discs 828 631-1

Cassette: Go! Discs 828 631-4
CD: Go! Discs 828 631-2
[Wobble co-writes and performs on 'Got Fucked Along The Way']

Shara Nelson: **Friendly Fire**
Released: 25.09.1995
Peak Position: #44
LP: Cooltempo CTLP 48
Cassette: Cooltempo CTTC 48
CD: Cooltempo CTCD 48
[Jah Wobble co-writes and performs on 'After You']

Ramshackle: **Isn't This The Life**
Released: 10.1995
10" Single: Big Life BLRT 119
Isn't This The Life (Main Mix)/
Isn't This The Life (Deptford Dub)
CD Single: Big Life BLRD 119
Isn't This The Life (Radio Edit)/
Isn't This The Life (Main Mix)/
Isn't This The Life (Deptford Dub)
[Wobble appears on all mixes]

Brian Eno & Jah Wobble:
Spinner
Released: 02.10.1995
Peak Position: #71
LP: All Saints AS 23
Cassette: All Saints ASC 23
CD: All Saints ASCD 23
Where We Lived/Like Organza/
Steam/Garden Recalled/Marine Radio/Unusual Balance/Space Diary 1/Spinner/Transmitter and Trumpet/Left Where It Fell/Hidden on Spinner

Jah Wobble: **Heaven And Earth**
Released: 13.11.1995
Double LP: Island ILPSD 8044
Cassette: Island ICT 8044
CD: Island CID 8044
Heaven & Earth/A Love Song/
Dying Over Europe/Divine
Mother/Gone to Croatan/Hit
Me/On Namah Shiva

Ramshackle: **Depthology**
Released: 27.11.1995
Cassette: Big Life BLRMC 30
CD: Big Life BLRCD 30
[Wobble performs on 'Isn't This
The Life']

Abel Ali Slimani: **Mraya**
Released: 01.1996
CD: Real World CDRW 55
Laziza/Habibti/Zeyna/Mraya/
Yasmin/Alger/Hadi/Ana
Guellile/Ana Guellile (Dub)
[Wobble co-writes and performs
on all tracks]

Gavin Friday: **You, Me And
World War III**
Released: 29.01.1996
12" Single: Island 12IS 621
CD Single: Island CID 621
[Wobble performs on 'Movie
Mix' of 'Billy Boola' by Gavin
Friday & Bono]

Definition of Sound: **Child**
Released: 12.02.1996
Peak Position: #48
Cassette Single: Fontana 8526284
CD Single: Fontana DOSCD 3

[Jah Wobble Remix of A-side]

Bel Canto: **Magic Box**
Released: 26.02.1996
Cassette: Lava/Warner Music
7567926994
CD: Lava/Warner Music
7567926992
[Wobble produces two tracks:
'Kiss Of Spring' and 'Paradise']

Sex Pistols: **Pretty Vacant (Live)**
Released: 15.07.1996
Peak Position: #18
7" Single: Virgin VUS 113
Pretty Vacant (Live)/Bodies (Live)
CD Single: Virgin VUSCD 113
Pretty Vacant (Live)/Bodies
(Live)/No Fun (Live)/Problems
(Session Version)

Sex Pistols: **Filthy Lucre Live**
Released: 29.07.1996
Peak Position: #26
LP: Virgin VUSLP 116
Cassette: Virgin VUSMC 116
CD: Virgin VUSCD 116
Bodies/Seventeen/New York/
No Feelings/Did You No
Wrong/God Save The Queen/
Liar/Satellite/I'm Not Your
Steppin' Stone/Holidays In The
Sun/Submission/Pretty Vacant/
E.M.I./Anarchy In The UK/
Problems

Jah Wobble: **The Inspiration Of
William Blake**
Released: 23.09.1996
LP: All Saints AS 29

Cassette: All Saints ASC 29
CD: All Saints ASCD 29
Songs of Innocence/Lonely London/Bananas/Tyger Tyger/ Holy Thursday/Breathing Out the World/Swallow in the World/The Kings of Asia/ Swallow in the World (Reprise)/ Bob and Harry/The Angel/ Gateway/Auguries of Innocence

Sinead O'Connor: **Gospel Oak (EP)**
Released: 05.05.1997
Peak Position: #28
12" Single: Chrysalis 12CHS 5051
Cassette Single: Chrysalis TCCHS 5051
CD Single: Chrysalis CDCHS 5051
[Wobble appears on 'Petit Poulet']

Can: **Sacrilege**
Remix Compilation
Released: 12.05.1997
Triple LP: Spoon/Mute SPOON 3940
Double CD: Spoon/Mute SPOONCD 3940
[Wobble features on 'Secret Knowledge Mix' of 'Oh Yeah']

Jah Wobble's Invaders of the Heart: **The Celtic Poets**
Released: 09.06.1997
CD: 30 Hertz 30HZCD 1
The Dunes/A Man I Knew/ Market Rasen/London Rain/ Star of the East/Third Heaven/ Bagpipe Music/Saturn/Gone in the Wind/Thames

John Lydon: **Psycho's Path**
Released: 14.07.1997
Cassette: Virgin America VUSMC 130
CD: Virgin America CDVUS 130
Grave Ride/Dog/Psychopath/ Sun/Another Way/Dis-Ho/Take Me/A No And A Yes/Stump/Armies

John Lydon: **Sun**
Released: 21.07.1997
Peak Position: #42
Cassette Single: Virgin America VUSC 122
Sun (Leftfield Remix)/ Psychopath (Leftfield Remix #3)
12" Single: Virgin America VUST 122
Sun (Leftfield Remix)/Grave Ride (Moby Remix)/Psychopath (Leftfield Dub Remix)/ Psychopath (Leftfield Remix #3)
CD Single: Virgin America VUSCD 122
Sun (Leftfield Remix)/Sun (Lydon Remix)/Psychopath (Leftfield Dub Remix)/ Psychopath (Leftfield Remix #3)

Jah Wobble: **Requiem**
Released: 11.08.1997
CD: 30 Hertz 30HZCD 2
Requiem 1/Requiem 2/Requiem 3/The Father/Mother

Sly & Robbie/Simply Red: **Night Nurse**
Released: 08.09.1997
Peak Position: #13
12" Single: EastWest

3984207480
Cassette Single: EastWest EW 129 C
CD Single: EW 129 CD1
CD Single: 3984204902
[All formats contain 'Jah Wobble
Radio Mix' of 'Night Nurse'.
Cassette single and CD1 also
contain a 'Jah Wobble 12" Mix']

Material: **Seven Souls**
Reissue with Extra Tracks
Released: 15.09.1997
CD: Mercury 534-905-2
[Wobble appears on 'The
Western Lands (A Dangerous
Road Mix)']

Jah Wobble: **The Light Programme**
Released: 20.10.1997
CD: 30 Hertz 30HZCD 3
Veneer/One in 7/Might/
Appearance and Thing In-Itself/
Nice Cop = Nasty Cop/Magical
Thought/Maieusis/15 Dohs/
Tranquiliser

Sly & Robbie: **Friends**
Released: 29.09.1997
Cassette: EastWest 3984206004
CD: EastWest 3984206002
[Features 'Jah Wobble Radio
Mix' of 'Night Nurse']

Jah Wobble: **Magical Thought**
Released: 10.11.1997
CD Single: 30 Hertz 30HZCD 4
Magical Thought/Magical
Thought (Radio Edit)/15
Dohs/30 Hertz

Holger Czukay: **On The Way To
The Peak Of Normal**
Compilation
Released: 19.01.1998
CD: Spoon/Mute SPOONCD 36
[Wobble performs on 'Ode
to Perfume' and 'Witches'
Multiplication Table' – both
released 1981]

Jah Wobble: **I Offer You Everything**
Released: 29.06.1998
CD Single: 30 Hertz 30HZCD 6
I Offer You Everything/Il
Jevedro Il Oblanco/Train

Jah Wobble: **Mount Zion**
Released: 27.07.1998
CD Single: 30 Hertz 30HZCD 7
Mount Zion (Radio Edit)/
Mount Zion (Dance Mix)/
Mount Zion (Live Version Edit)

Jah Wobble: **Umbra Sumus**
Released: 24.08.1998
CD: 30 Hertz 30HZCD 5
Il Jevedro Il Oblanco/Mehmeda
Majka Bubage/Paternal
Kindness/Moon Slowbeat Part
1/Moon Slowbeat Part 2/Just
a Prayer/St. Mary Le Bow/I
Offer You Everything/Organ
Meditation/Compound/ Chela/
Umbra Sumus Part 1/Umbra
Sumus Part 2/Four Basses, An
Organ, Jaki & A Train/Mount
Zion/Limehouse Cut

Sacred System & Bill Laswell:
Nagual Site

Released: 25.08.1998
CD: Wicklow/BMG
09026632632
[Wobble co-composes 'Driftwork'
and performs on it too]

Suggs: **The Three Pyramids Club**
Released: 07.09.1998
Cassette: Warner Music
3984238154
CD: Warner Music 3984238152
[Wobble performs on 'Sing']

Jah Wobble & Zi Lan Liao: **The
Five Tone Dragon**
Released: 28.09.1998
CD: 30 Hertz 30HZCD 8
Five Tone Dragon/The River

Jah Wobble: **Deep Space**
Released: 05.04.1999
CD: 30 Hertz 30HZCD 9
The Immanent/The
Transcendent/Disks, Winds and
Veiling Curtains/Funeral March/
Girl Amazed at the Perfection of
a Rose Fails to Meditate Upon
Chaos/Debussy Turning to his
Friend Said, 'Let's Go, He's
Starting to Develop'

Holger Czukay: **Good Morning
Story**
Released: 04.10.1999
CD: Tone Casualties TCCD 9944
[Wobble performs on 'Invisible Man']

Jah Wobble: **30 Hertz**
Released: 04.2000
Double CD: Eagle Rock

Entertainment EDMCD 107
The Dunes/Requiem 2/Night/I
Offer You Everything/The
Immanent/Ethos/Five-Tone
Dragon/Lam Tang Way/30 Hertz

Jah Wobble's Invaders of the Heart:
**Full Moon Over The Shopping
Mall**
Released: 04.04.2000
CD: 30 Hertz 30HZCD 10
Full Moon Over the Shopping
Mall/Ethos/Waxing Moon/
Waning Moon/Acting the Goat/
I'll Be Sad to See You Go

The Damage Manual: **1**
Released: 24.04.2000
CD: Invisible INV143
Sunset Gun/Damage Addict/
Scissor Quickstep/Blame and
Demand/Leave the Ground/
Bagman Damage/ M60 Dub

Sinead O'Connor: **Faith And
Courage**
Released: 12.06.2000
Peak Position: #61
Cassette: Atlantic 7567833374
CD: Atlantic 7567833372
[Jah Wobble features on 'Jealous',
'Daddy I'm Fine' and 'Til I
Whisper U Something']

Jah Wobble: **Molam Dub**
Released: 10.07.2000
CD: 30 Hertz 30HZCD 12
Lam Saravane/Lam Tang
Way/Lam Tang Way (Female
Vocal)/Lame Bane Xoc/Lam

Siphandone/Saravane/Lam
PhouthayLam Saravane (Dub)/
Lam Long/Lam Tang Way
(Dub)/Lam Phouthay (Dance
Mix)/Hill Music

The Wave Room: **Love Medicine**
Released: 31.07.2000
CD: Bella Union BELLACD 20
[Wobble appears on 'Houdini']

Jah Wobble: **Beach Fervour Spare**
Released: 11.09.2000
CD: 30 Hertz 30HZCD 11
Suddenly Fell into the Underworld/
Beach Fervour Spare/Kinky Mantra/
As Night Falls (Part 1)/As Night
Falls (Part 2)/As Night Falls (Part
3)/Trance

The Damage Manual:
The Damage Manual
[Jah Wobble, Martin Atkins,
Geordie Walker, Chris Connelly]
Released: 11.09.2000
CD: Dreamcatcher CRIDE 31
King Mob/Age of Urges/Top
Ten Severed/The Peepshow
Ghosts/Sunset Gun (303
Edit)/Stateless/Expand/Denial/
Broadcasting/Sunset Gun/Blame
and Demand/Damage Addict/
Stateless (Remix)

Sinead O'Connor: **Jealous**
Released: 25.09.2000
Cassette Single: Atlantic WEA 318 C
CD Single: Atlantic WEA 318 CD
[Jah Wobble features on A-side]

Various Artists: **Last Night A DJ
Saved My Life**
Compilation
Released: 27.11.2000
Double LP: Nuphonic NUX 156
CD: Nuphonic NUX 156 CD
[Features 'Francois Kervorkian
Snake Dub' version of Wobble's
'Snake Charmer']

Jah Wobble & Evan Parker:
Passage To Hades
Released: 12.02.2001
CD: 30 Hertz 30HZCD 14
Passage to Hades/Giving Up the
Ghost/Full On/Finally Crack It

Temple of Sound & Rizwan-
Muazzam Qawwali: **People's
Colony No. 1**
Released: 05.03.2001
CD: Real World CDRW 94
[Wobble appears on 'Beloved']

Jah Wobble: **Largely Live In
Hartlepool And Manchester**
Released: 11.06.2001
Double CD: 30 Hertz 30HZCD 15
Manchester/They Were Planning
Murder/As Thick as Thieves/
Rimshot/Forgetting Myself/
Hartlepool/Liquid/Space/Sides
of Tall Buildings/Slow

Robert Miles: **Paths**
Released: 16.07.2001
Peak Position: #74
CD Single: Salt SALT 002 CD
[Features 'Jah Wobble Remix' of
A-side]

Jah Wobble: **The Early Years**
Compilation
Released: 24.09.2001
Double CD: 30 Hertz 30HZCD 16
The Invaders of the Heart (Mix
1)/The Invaders of the Heart
(Mix 2)/The Invaders of the
Heart (Decadent Disco Mix 3)/
Voodoo/East/Blowout/Blowout
(Alternate Version)/Tradewinds/
Fading/Nocturnal/City/Fading/
Long Long Way/Sense of
History/Hill in Korea/Journey
to Death/The Invaders of the
Heart/Sunshine/Concentration
Camp/Desert Song/Heart of the
Jungle/Long Long Way/Romany
Trial/Berlin

Jah Wobble & Bill Laswell:
**Radio Axiom: A Dub
Transmission**
Released: 24.09.2001
CD: Axiom Records PALMCD
2073
Subcode/Alsema Dub/Virus
B/Orion/6th Chamber/Alam
Dub/Second Sight

Mari Boine: **Remixed**
Released: 10.11.2001
CD: Emarcy/Universal 0147602
[Features 'Jah Wobble Mix II' of
'Cuovgi Liekkas']

Jah Wobble: **Shout At The Devil**
Released: 16.12.2001
CD: 30 Hertz 30HZCD 17
Hayat/Mountains of the Moon/
Cleopatra King Size/Zaardub/

Shout at the Devil/Once Upon
A Time in the East/Maghreb
Rockers/La Citadelle/Symphony
of Palms/Mistralazul 2

Holly Valance: **Kiss Kiss**
Released: 29.04.2002
Peak Position: #1
CD Single: London/Warner
Music LONCD 464
CD Single: London/Warner
Music LONCDX 464
[Features Jah Wobble Remix of
'Kiss Kiss']

Sex Pistols: **God Save The Queen**
Reissued: 27.05.2002
Peak Position: #15
7" Single: Virgin VS 1832
b/w God Save The Queen (7"
Extended Mix)
12" Single: Virgin VST 1832
God Save The Queen/God Save
The Queen (7" Extended Mix)/
God Save The Queen (Dance Mix)
CD Single: Virgin VSCD 1832
God Save The Queen/God Save
The Queen (Dance Mix)/God
Save The Queen (7" Extended
Mix)

Murder Global (aka Keith Levene):
Killer In The Crowd (EP)
Released: 06.2002
CD Single: Acid/Underground
Inc UIN 1084
Killer in the Crowd/Aztek
Legend/Aztek DUBD/Object
B/Sound Stage One

Sex Pistols: **Jubilee**
Compilation
Released: 03.06.2002
Peak Position: #29
CD: Virgin CDV 2961
[Lydon appears on five tracks:
God Save The Queen/Anarchy
In The UK/Pretty Vacant/
Holidays In The Sun/EMI
(Unlimited Edition)]

Jah Wobble & Bill Laswell:
Radio Axiom Remixed
Released: 10.06.2002
12" Single: Palm Pictures PP
127063
Alsema Dub (Carl Craig Remix)/
Alsema Dub/Orion (4 Hero
Dollis Dub Mix)/Virus B

Holly Valance: **Down Boy**
Released: 30.09.2002
Peak Position: #2
CD Single: London/Warner
Music LOCDP 469
[Features Jah Wobble Remix of
'Kiss Kiss']

Jah Wobble: **Fly**
Released: 27.01.2003
CD: 30 Hertz 30HZCD 19
Fly 1/Fly 2/Fly 3/Fly 4/Fly 5/Fly
6/Fly 7/Fly 8/Fly 9/Fly 10/Fly 11

Pigface: **Easy Listening... For
Difficult Fuckheads**
Released: 28.01.2003
CD: Invisible UIN 1037
[Levene features on 'Closer to
Heaven']

Afro-Celts: **Seed**
Released: 24.03.2003
CD: Real World CDRW 111
[Wobble features on the track
'All Remains']

Natacha Atlas: **Something
Dangerous**
Released: 19.05.2003
CD: Mantra Recordings
MNTCD 1035
[Wobble features on 'This Realm']

Yulduz: **Bilmadim**
Released: 31.08.2003
CD: 30 Hertz 30HZCD 23
Ony Kutib (Wait for the Moon)/
Etishganlar Raksy (Dance for
Happy People)/Bilmadim (I
Don't Know)/Donna/Ketmagyl
(Don't Go Away)/Kiss
Me/Druge (Friend)/Sugur
(Thank God)/Oasis/Orol
Dengyz Usmanova (Orol
Sea)/Lola (Flower)/Ketmagyl
Dub/Bilmadim Dub/Kiss Me
(Bill Laswell Remix)/Kiss Me
(Philippe Verga Remix)

Jah Wobble's Invaders of the Heart:
English Roots Music
Released: 20.10.2003
CD: 30 Hertz 30HZCD 21
Cannily Cannily/Banks of the
Sweet Primrose/Unquite Grave/
Blacksmith Dub/Strange Duet/
They Came With A Swagger/
Press Ganged/Sovay/Bykerhill/
Trance of the Willow/Cannily
Cannily Reprise

Various Artists: **Death Disco: Songs From Under The Dancefloor**
Compilation
Released: 25.02.2004
CD: Virgin/EMI 5937862
[Contains not only PiL's 'Death Disco' but also 'Haile Unlikely' by Steel Leg Vs. The Electric Dread.]

Jah Wobble: **I Could've Been A Contender**
Compilation
Released: 23.08.2004
Triple CD Set: Trojan/Sanctuary TJETD 191
PiL: Public Image/Fly 2/
Ketmagyl (Don't Go Away)/
Visions of You/Mehmeda Majka Bubage/Becoming More Like God/Mistralazul 2/I Offer You Everything/Shout at the Devil/Blacksmith/Blacksmith Dub/Elevator Music #3/Josey Walsh/Tyger Tyger/Requiem 3/PiL: Poptones/Betrayal Dub/How Much Are They?/The Invaders of the Heart (Mix #2)/
PiL: Swanlake/Snakecharmer/
Songs of Innocence/Fly 1/
Funeral March/Lam Tang Way/The Dunes/So Many Years/Lam Saravane/A Man I Knew/Elevator Music #1/Gone to Croatan/Brian Eno & Jah Wobble: Spinner/A13/Passage to Hades/Jah Wobble's Solaris: The Mystery of Twilight Part 2/Brian Eno & Jah Wobble: Left Where It Fell/The River Suite

Jah Wobble with Bill Laswell: **Version 2 Version**
Released: 25.10.2004
CD: ROIR Records RUSCD 8288
Dystopia/Simulacra/Space-Time Paradox/Babylon Site/Night City/ System Malfunction

Jaki Liebzeit, Philip Jeck & Jah Wobble: **Live In Leuven**
Released: 08.11.2004
CD: 30 Hertz 30HZCD 24
One/Two/Three/Four

Jah Wobble: **Mu**
Released: 12.09.2005
CD: Trojan/Sanctuary TJZCD 290
Viking Funeral/Universal Dub/Samsara/Kojak Dub/Mu/ Buddha of Compassion/New Mexico Dub/Love Comes, Love Goes/Softwear/Into the Light

Jah Wobble's Solaris: **Solaris Live In Concert**
Released: 03.10.2005
CD: 30 Hertz 30HZCD 18
Mystery of Twilight/Mystery of Twilight 2/Seven Dials/Around the Lake

Pigface: **Pigface Vs. The World**
Compilation
Released: 10.2005
4 CD Set: Eastworld/Plastic Head EWO 010 CD
CD 1: Point Blank/Auto Hag/Suck/ Alles Ist Mine/The Bushmaster/ Tapeworm/Divebomber/Go!/Little Sisters/War Ich Nicht Immer Ein

Guter Junge?/I Can Do No Wrong/
Hips, Tits, Lips, Power!/
Insemination/Satellite (Needle in
the Groove)
CD 2: Fuck It Up/Ten Grand and
Down/Asphole/Seven Words/
Hagseed (Slagseed Slagadelic
Mix)/Empathy/I Can Do No
Wrong/Magazine/Think/Sick
Asp F**k/Satellite/Your Own
You Own/Steamroller/Burundi/
Chickasaurus
CD 3: Nutopia/Closer to Heaven/
Methylated/Bring Unto Me/The
Horse You Rode In On/1st Taken
3rd Found/King of Negativity/
Metal Tangerine/Everything/Kiss
King/Insect-Suspect/Sweetmeat/
You Know You Know You Know/
Gospel of Thomas Dub
CD 4: Martin Atkins Interview/
Dog/Steamroller (Remix)/Psychic
Phonecall/Ogre Interview/Insects/
Insect-Suspect/Insemination/En
Esch Interview/Love Interest:
Bedazzled/Little Sisters (Remix)/
Divebomber/Mickey/William
Tucker Interview

John Lydon: **The Best Of
British £1 Notes**
Compilation
Released: 03.10.2005
CD: Virgin LYDON 1
Sex Pistols: Anarchy In The
UK/PiL: Public Image/PiL: This Is
Not A Love Song/Leftfield Lydon:
Open Up/PiL: Rise/PiL: Don't
Ask Me/PiL: Seattle/Sex Pistols:
Holidays In The Sun/PiL: Death

Disco/ PiL: Flowers of Romance/
Timezone: World Destruction/PiL:
Warrior/PiL: Disappointed/John
Lydon: Sun/PiL: Bad Life/PiL:
Home/PiL; The Body/PiL: Cruel/
Sex Pistols: God Save The Queen/
John Lydon: The Rabbit Song
Special Edition Double CD: Virgin
LYDOND 1
[As above, plus a second disc of
remixes and extra tracks: PiL:
Death Disco (12" Mix)/PiL:
Poptones/PiL: Careering/PiL:
Religion/PiL: Banging The
Door/PiL: The Pardon/PiL: Rise
(12" Mix)/PiL: Disappointed (12"
Mix)/PiL: Warrior (12" Mix)/PiL:
Acid Drops/Leftfield Lydon: Open
Up (Full Vocal Mix)/Sex Pistols:
God Save The Queen (Dance
Mix)]
DVD: Virgin LYDONVD 1
[Features promo videos for the
following: Sex Pistols: Anarchy in
the UK/Sex Pistols: God Save the
Queen/PiL: Public Image/PiL:
Death Disco/PiL: This is Not
A Love Song/PiL: Bad Life/
Timezone: World Destruction/PiL:
Rise/PiL: Home/PiL: Seattle/PiL:
The Body (Uncensored Version)/
PiL: Warrior/PiL: Disappointed/
PiL: Don't Ask Me/PiL: Cruel/PiL:
Covered/Leftfield Lydon: Open
Up/John Lydon: Sun]
[Also contains live footage of: Sex
Pistols: 'Pretty Vacant (Finsbury
Park 1996)', 'Bodies (Phoenix
Festival 1996)' and 'Silver Machine
(Crystal Palace 2002)'

bibliography

Heylin, Clinton, *Babylon's Burning*, Viking, 2007
Heylin, Clinton, *Public Image Limited – Rise/Fall*, Omnibus Press, 1989
Letts, Don, *Culture Clash: Dread Meets Punk Rockers*, SAF, 2007
Lydon, John with Zimmerman, Keith & Kent, *Rotten: No Blacks, No Irish, No Dogs*, Hodder & Stoughton, 1994
Myers, Ben, *John Lydon, Pistol, PiL, Anti-Celebrity*, IMP, 2004
Parker, Alan, *The Clash: Rat Patrol from Fort Bragg*, Abstract, 2003
Parker, Alan, *Vicious: Too Fast To Live*, Creation Books, 2004
Paytress, Mark, *Vicious*, Sanctuary, 2004
Reynolds, Simon, *Rip It Up and Start Again*, Faber & Faber, 2005
Savage, Jon, *England's Dreaming: The Sex Pistols & Punk Rock*, Faber & Faber, 1991
Various (Editor: Peachy, Mal) *Classic Albums*, Harpercollins, 1999

Websites

www.fodderstompf.com
Staggering, encyclopaedic and enthusiastic site about everything PiL.
Includes exclusive interviews with relevant collaborators.

www.rocksbackpages.com
An excellent, ballooning archive of music press articles.

www.johnlydon.com
Official website for PiL's main man.

www.30hertzrecords.com
Website for Jah Wobble's record label.

www.murderglobal.com
Official website for Keith Levene.

www.dennismorris.com
Official website for photographer extraordinaire.

www.myspace.com/martinatkins
Former PiL drummer online.

www.pete-jones-uk.co.uk
Website for former PiL bass player.

Articles

'Punks' by Mick Brown, *Rolling Stone*, 27.01.1977
'Johnny Cool At The Control: John Lydon in Jamaica' by Vivien Goldman, *Sounds*, 04.03.1978
'Man A Warrior' by Vivien Goldman, *Sounds*, 11.03.1978
[Virgin Records classified ad for PiL drummer], *Melody Maker*, 06.05.1978
'Johnny Rotten Doesn't Live Here Anymore' by Neil Spencer, *New Musical Express*, 27.05.1978
'Public Image: John Rotten and the Windsor Uplift' by Caroline Coon, *Sounds*, 22.07.1978
'Would You Pay This Man Money for Writing The Singles?' by John Lydon, *New Musical Express*, 22.07.1978
'Love Thy Neighbour' by Andy Courtney, *Sounds*, 07.10.1978
'Rotten Show' by Andrew Nickolds, *Melody Maker*, 14.10.1978
'The Danceable Solution' by Chris Brazier, *Melody Maker*, 28.10.1978
'Johnny's Immaculate Conception' by Chris Salewicz, *New Musical Express*, 23.12.1978
'The Image Has Cracked' by Ross Crighton, *Sounds*, 06.01.1979
'Johnny Goes A-Courting' by Steve Clarke, *New Musical Express*, 17.02.1979
'The Odd Combo' by Danny Baker, *New Musical Express*, 16.06.1979
'And Another Teen Icon Bites The Dust', Jaws, *Sounds*, 07.07.1979

'Upstart Upsets Rotten On TV Show' by Danny Baker, *New Musical Express*, 21.07.1979
'Set The Controls For The Squalor Of Leeds' by Andy Gill, *New Musical Express*, 15.09.1979
[Metal Box 'lyrics' advertisement], *New Musical Express*, 24.11.1979
'A Wobble Way of Knowledge' by Angus MacKinnon, *New Musical Express*, 09.02.1980
'PiL in Hollywood' by Sylvie Simmons, *Sounds*, 24.05.1980
'No More Gigs As PiL Sack Drummer', *Sounds*, 28.06.1980
'Public Image: Corporation Executive Report to Shareholders' by Chris Bohn, *New Musical Express*, 05.07.1980
'Wobble Walks Out On PiL', *Sounds*, 16.08.1980
'Wild Man of Punk Goes Free', *New Musical Express*, 13.12.1980
'Company Lore And Public Disorder' by Gavin Martin, *New Musical Express*, 14.03.1981
'Baker for PiL', *New Musical Express*, 04.04.1981
'Riot at the Ritz' by Richard Grabel, *New Musical Express*, 23.05.1981
'PiL Get a Ritzy Bottling' by David Fricke, *Melody Maker*, 23.05.1981
'An Englishman's Home Is His Hassle' by Neil Spencer, *New Musical Express*, 07.08.1982
'Invader Of The Lost Art' by Richard Cook, *New Musical Express*, 20.11.1982
'This Is Not A Rotten Interview' by Lynden Barber, *Melody Maker*, 05.11.1983
'The Keith Levene Guide To Being Rotten' by Julie Panebianco, *New Musical Express*, 12.11.1983
'Situation Vacant' by Patrick Zerbib, *The Face*, 12.1983
'Commercial Potential' by Andy Hurt, *Sounds*, 01.09.1984
'The Primal Yawn' by Adam Sweeting, *Melody Maker*, 08.02.1986
'The Punk: Ten Years After (Part 1)' by Jack Barron, *Sounds*, 08.02.1986
'This Is What You Get' by Paul Morley, *New Musical Express*, 08.02.1986
'John Lydon: The Private Eye' by Jack Barron, *Sounds*, 15.02.1986
'I'm My Favourite Charity' by Andy Strickland, *Record Mirror*, 15.02.1986
'Dick' by Peattie/Warren, *Melody Maker*, 01.03.1986
'Happy Talk' by Mat Smith, *Melody Maker*, 08.08.1987
'I Cry Alone' by Jack Barron, *New Musical Express*, 10.10.1987
'Rock Around The Bloc' by Steve Sutherland, *Melody Maker*,

17.09.1988; 24.09.1988

'Is That A Pistol In Your Pocket (Or Are You Just Pleased To See Me?)' by Neil Perry, *Sounds*, 22.04.1989

'Cloud Nine' by Chris Roberts, *Melody Maker*, 20.05.1989

'Levene Dangerously' by Jane Garcia, *New Musical Express*, 16.12.1989

'Public Interest Unlimited' by John Robb, *Melody Maker*, 16.12.1989

'I Came, I Warsaw, I'm Bonkers!' by Steven Wells, *New Musical Express*, 27.10.1990

'If You're Looking For Wobble (You've Come To The Right Place)' by Mandi James, *New Musical Express*, 01.02.1992

'Cruel As F***' by Ian Gittins, *Melody Maker*, 07.03.1992

'Release The Pressure' by Push, *Melody Maker*, 05.12.1992

'Dance's Inferno' by Kris Needs, *New Musical Express*, 27.11.1993

'Massagin' A Wobble' by Ted Kessler, *New Musical Express*, 16.04.1994

'Rebellious Jukebox: Jah Wobble', *Melody Maker*, 16.04.1994

'Burn Bassbins Burn', author unknown, *Mixmag*, 02.1995

'Gauche Busters!' by The Stud Brothers, *Melody Maker*, 18.03.1995

'Happy Birthday Mr. Rotten' by Caroline Sullivan, *Milwaukee Sentinel Journal*, 28.01.1996

'The Oldest Swindlers In Town' by David Cavanagh, *Q*, 06.1996

'Gauche In The Machine!' by Roger Morton, *New Musical Express*, 04.05.1996

'I Want You All To Lick My Arse' by Gavin Martin, *New Musical Express*, 15.06.1996

'Sham 96!' by Simon Williams, *New Musical Express*, 29.06.1996

'CRE 1976: A Creation Records Statement' by Alan McGee, *New Musical Express*, 27.07.1996

'One Man And His Gob' by Roger Morton, *New Musical Express*, 12.07.1997

'Me & My God: The Sisters of Mercy, Johnny Rotten & Me' by Jah Wobble, to John Morrish, *The Sunday Telegraph*, 10.01.1999

'More Bass! More Power! More Rumbling Noises!' by Ian Harrison, *Mixmag*, 09.1999

'Honouring Music's Top Women' by Paul Williams and Joanna Jones, *Music Week*, 07.12.2002

'Wobble Keeps It Steady' by Richard Wolfson, *The Daily Telegraph*, 09.01.2003

'The Story of the Song: Public Image' by Robert Webb, *The Independent*, 12.12.2003

'Ain't It Fun...' by Keith Cameron, *Mojo*, 01.2004

'My Father Had A Heart Attack And Died After My Secret Marriage To Johnny Rotten' by Nick Pryer and Peter Sheridan, *The Mail on Sunday*, 01.02.2004

'Wobble's Bass Odyssey' by Andrew Cowen, *The Birmingham Post*, 12.08.2004

'The Ten Best Dub Tracks' by Jah Wobble, *The Independent*, 13.08.2004

'This Cultural Life: Jah Wobble', *The Independent on Sunday*, 22.08.2004

'The Ace of Bass' by Alastair McKay, *The Independent*, 09.09.2005

'These Are Not Love Songs' by Joel McIver, *Record Collector*, 11.2005

Record Reviews

'Anarchy in the UK', Alan Lewis, *Sounds*, 27.11.1976

'Anarchy in the UK', Cliff White, *New Musical Express*, 04.12.1976

'Public Image', Julie Burchill, *New Musical Express*, 14.10.1978

First Edition, Pete Silverton, *Sounds*, 09.12.1978

First Edition, Nick Kent, *New Musical Express*, 09.12.1978

First Edition, Simon Frith, *Melody Maker*, 09.12.1978

'Death Disco', Ian Birch, *Melody Maker*, 30.06.1979

'Death Disco', Roy Carr, *New Musical Express*, 30.06.1979

'Memories', Danny Baker, *New Musical Express*, 06.10.1979

'Memories', Garry Bushell, *Sounds*, 06.10.1979

Metal Box, Angus MacKinnon, *New Musical Express*, 24.11.1979

Metal Box, Dave McCullough, *Sounds*, 24.11.1979

Machines, Ian Penman, *New Musical Express*, 01.11.1980

Paris au Printemps, Vivien Goldman, *New Musical Express*, 15.11.1980

Paris au Printemps, Lynden Barber, *Melody Maker*, 15.11.1980

Paris au Printemps, Dave McCullough, *Sounds*, 15.11.1980

'Flowers of Romance', Paul du Noyer, *New Musical Express*, 28.03.1981

Flowers of Romance, Ian Penman, *New Musical Express*, 04.04.1981

Flowers of Romance, Lynden Barber, *Melody Maker*, 04.04.1981

'Bad Life', Adam Sweeting, *Melody Maker*, 12.05.1984

This Is What You Want, This Is What You Get, Lynden Barber, *Melody Maker*, 07.07.1984

'World Destruction', Danny Kelly, *New Musical Express*, 12.01.1985
'Rise', 'Mr. Spencer', *Sounds*, 25.01.1986
'Rise', Adam Sweeting, *Melody Maker*, 25.01.1986
'Rise', Simon Witter, *New Musical Express*, 25.01.1986
Album, Gavin Martin, *New Musical Express*, 08.02.1986
Album, The Stud Brothers, *Melody Maker*, 08.02.1986
Album, Neil Perry, *Sounds*, 08.02.1986
'Seattle', Mat Snow, *Sounds*, 15.08.1987
Happy?, Biba Kopf, *New Musical Express*, 19.09.1987
Happy?, 'Ron Rom', *Sounds*, 19.09.1987
Happy?, Simon Reynolds, *Melody Maker*, 19.09.1987
9, Keith Cameron, *Sounds*, 20.05.1989
9, Steve Sutherland, *Melody Maker*, 27.05.1989
9, Jack Barron, *New Musical Express*, 03.06.1989
'Don't Ask Me', Leo Finlay, *Sounds*, 13.10.1990
'Don't Ask Me', James Brown, *New Musical Express*, 13.10.1990
'Cruel', David Stubbs, *Melody Maker*, 15.02.1992
'Cruel', Keith Cameron, *New Musical Express*, 15.02.1992
That What Is Not, Neil Perry, *Melody Maker*, 22.02.1992
Take Me To God, Ian Gittins, *Melody Maker*, 21.05.1994
Take Me To God, Dele Fadele, *New Musical Express*, 21.05.1994
Psycho's Path, Lucy O'Brien, *Q*, 08.1997
Umbra Sumus, Richard Cook, *New Statesman*, 24.05.1999

acknowledgements

Additional research by Justin Lewis

With many thanks to:
Sean Body, Graeme Milton, Fodderstomp (fodderstompf.com), Pat Gilbert, Alan Parker, the late Dave Goodman, Dennis Morris, Alan McGee, Tony Wilson, Clive Stewart... and all those who were Public Image Limited.

Added input from:
Simon (Suburban Kid) Mattock – who would like to dedicate this work to the wonderful Clare – and James, Billy Joe and Lola Mae plus to all the freaks and misfits called my friends (you know who you are), especially Gary Dansco, Tommy, Mickey P and Simon @ trakmarx. com. Finally I would like to thank Joe Strummer for his inspiration and for keeping it real, without whom...

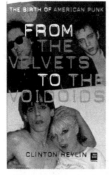

From The Velvets To The Voidoids

by Clinton Heylin
Paperback ISBN 1-905139-04-7
288pp 234 X 156mm 16pp b/w photos
UK £14.99

Exhaustively researched and packed with insights to give a detailed and all-encompassing perspective of American punk rock's 60s roots through to the arrival of new wave - this is the definitive story. Long overdue, fully revised and updated edition of the definitive account of the rise of US punk and the 'new wave' movement, led by acts such as Richard Hell, Television, The Ramones, Blondie and Talking Heads. This was originally published by Penguin in the early 90s. Clinton Heylin is the acclaimed author of a number of books including highly regarded biographies of Bob Dylan, Van Morrison and Orson Welles. *No other book or account succeeded so well in accurately bringing the period to life.* **Richard Hell**

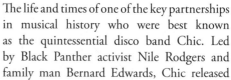

Everybody Dance: Chic And The Politics Of Disco

by Daryl Easlea
Paperback ISBN1-900924-56-0
288pp 234 X 156mm b/w ill. throughout
UK £14.00 US $19.95

The life and times of one of the key partnerships in musical history who were best known as the quintessential disco band Chic. Led by Black Panther activist Nile Rodgers and family man Bernard Edwards, Chic released and produced a string of era-defining records: 'Le Freak', 'Good Times', 'We Are Family', 'Lost In Music'. When disco collapsed, so did Chic's popularity. However, Rodgers and Edwards individually produced some of the great pop dance records of the 80s, working with Bowie, Robert Palmer, Madonna and ABC among many others until Edwards's tragic death in 1996. There are drugs, bankruptcy, uptight artists, fights, and Muppets but, most importantly an in-depth appraisal of a group whose legacy remains hugely underrated.
Daryl Easlea's triumphant Everybody Dance *is the scholarly reappraisal the 'black Roxy Music' deserve.'* **Time Out**